And.

0812

Brickwork

HISTORY, TECHNOLOGY
AND PRACTICE

Volume 1

To my wife Fiona, my son Liam
and my daughter Rósalín,
whose continuing fight against
a life-threatening illness
has been an inspiration to
battle on regardless

Brickwork

HISTORY, TECHNOLOGY
AND PRACTICE

Volume 1

Gerard Lynch

DONHEAD

First published in the United Kingdom
in 1994 by
Donhead Publishing Ltd
28 Southdean Gardens
Wimbledon
London SW19 6NU
Tel: 081-789 0138

ISBN 1 873394 02 0, Volume 1
ISBN 1 873394 07 1, Volume 2

A CIP catalogue record for this book is available from
the British Library

Typeset by Carnegie Publishing, Preston
Printed in Great Britain at The Alden Press,
Osney Mead, Oxford

Contents

Foreword

Brickwork in Britain is as commonplace as green grass and blue skies. The extensive choice of colour and texture available, the versatility and economy of application, and confidence in its durable nature, have all led to the widespread acceptance of brickwork during the many centuries of its use. The history of the development of brick-making and of brickwork in architecture is a rich and varied one, but paradoxically, despite its undeniable popularity, brick is often taken for granted and not considered remarkable. There are, however, champions of both the material and the craft skills that have created the wide range of functional and attractive buildings which form the backdrop of our everyday life.

Devotees of a particular subject are often motivated by their enthusiasm to write a book, but such intentions are frequently abandoned because the aspiring author is unable to establish either a significant personal viewpoint or a hitherto unexplored perspective. Neither of these inhibitions threatened this book. As a highly skilled craftsman, bricklayer and specialist consultant with particular experience in the restoration of historic buildings, the author, Gerard Lynch, has an intimate appreciation of brickwork. Generally, the available books on brickwork history have been written by architects or architectural historians and so they tend to concentrate on the parallels with the established pattern of the history of architecture. However, Gerard Lynch brings to his treatise the insights and understanding of an experienced craftsman, a viewpoint that often gives a new slant to the appreciation of an otherwise familiar subject matter.

From this particular standpoint the reader is introduced to all the pertinent facts that are relevant to a full understanding of bricks, brickwork and the craft of bricklaying. However, although the first volume contains an extensive commentary on the development of brick construction, the complete work should not be regarded as an historical treatise. It primary intention is to be a comprehensive textbook covering the manufacture and application of brick masonry materials and the technology and craft aspects of their use in the construction of contemporary brickwork.

As well as being an active craftsman the author has considerable experience in teaching and was formerly Head of Trowel Trades at the Bedford College of Higher Education. His commentary on the establishment of craft training and recognition from the medieval period to the present day and on details of materials and techniques used in brick masonry building methods long since abandoned make fascinating reading, but more germane to the purpose of this book is his appreciation of the skills and knowledge required of the present day craftsman. Each topic is explored in detail and technical guidance given regarding its significance to the craft process and to the performance of the completed structure.

Interest in historic building techniques grew throughout the 1980s, often from somewhat nostalgic attitudes and initially it tended to be superficial, but the study of the technologies of the past has become more scholarly. This book includes valuable guidance on techniques which may have been obsolete for many years but still offer desirable characteristics of appearance or performance.

The work will consist of six volumes which, when complete, will form a comprehensive reference to modern brickwork practice in its various applications. It deals with new construction following contemporary specification and also repair and restoration work in connection with traditional or historic structures where the application of special materials and craft techniques may be more sympathetic.

This series will be of primary interest and importance to established craftsmen and craft trainees, but it will also give valuable insight into the potential of brickwork and the bricklayers craft to architects, engineers, other building professionals and anyone involved with or interested in the building construction process.

Michael Hammett, Dip arch, ARIBA
Architect – Brick Development Association
Honorary Secretary – British Brick Society

Preface

In cities, towns and villages and throughout the countryside of England stand houses, factories, bridges and a wealth of other buildings and structures that are a priceless legacy from times gone by, many indeed, that have withstood the ravages of wars and the elements for centuries: all monuments to expertise and skill of architects and craftsmen who had a particular regard for bricks and brickwork. They portray designs and craftsmanship that reflect a degree of quality and dedication which became the victims of a post-war innovation that has done little to preserve their charm and elegance. This work is intended to ensure, as far as possible, that this legacy shall continue to enjoy its well-earned and rightful place in the affections of the nation.

For almost fifty years the brick has been under constant threat from a variety of innovations in building materials, but its popularity has not been dented. Brick is well established as an important indigenous building material, where for centuries its properties of strength and durability, versatility of construction, combined with its warm and attractive appearance, have made it a first choice for the many varied applications of domestic and industrial building and works of civil engineering.

Changes in fashion and architectural practices, often associated with a desire for speed and economy, have meant that potential bricklayers/craftsmen have been forced to make do with crash courses and other limited tuition. This, coupled with a severe building slump in the 1990s has almost been a disaster for all building trades. It could be argued that a man's pride in his work is proportional to his knowledge of how to do it: only when he knows what to do and how to do it can he look at what he has done with a sense of pride. He should be aware that he has a duty to preserve and transmit those cultures and traditions that have been handed down to him from an age that enjoyed pride and excellence.

Today we stand at a crossroads. If we truly want to see craftsmanship in brick, whether restoring old buildings or constructing new ones, we must provide a much broader base of knowledge in the subject than has been more recently available. The present trends in 'apprenticeship' training indicate that sadly this will not be so, the emphasis being mainly on 'fixing' skills for modern house building; woefully inadequate for the full range of skills necessary for a true craftsman, able to work with confidence in all areas of his craft.

This study is born out of a desire to link past knowledge and practices with present-day skills and materials, so that both can be examined fully and understood. Modern technical books and training programmes for bricklayers and designers rarely elucidate on traditional techniques and this information is being lost from the craft at a time when conservation and restoration needs increasingly demand such knowledge and practical skills.

A craftsman must acquire a deep understanding of the characteristics of the materials that were and are still used so that he can make sound judgements as to the appropriateness of their correct use in a given situation. His craft skills must be based on the best of traditional practices and executed with subtlety of touch. He must gain an understanding of how and why his ancestors worked in the way they did as well as ensuring that his work today is in harmony with current practices and regulations.

This book, however, is not written entirely for the bricklayer and those learning bricklaying. It will also be an essential source of reference on the many aspects of bricklaying and brickwork. I hope it will be invaluable to the architect, the surveyor, and for those who specialize in the restoration and conservation of historic brick buildings, so that work can be specified and executed to the highest standards, using, as far as possible, the correct materials and methods associated with the period of the property. It should also be of great interest to students of those disciplines and to historians and all who have a love of brick.

I hope the reader will find in *Brickwork: History, Technology and Practice* a comprehensive combination, of well-researched information, with analysis of the craft, its materials, tools and practices etc., covered in depth and with clarity so that the subjects are fully understood and can be acted upon in the pursuance of high-quality brickwork.

Acknowledgments

To my wife for typing this work, and for her help and support.

Mr Michael Hammett ARIBA, Senior Architect of the Brick Development Association, who very generously gave a tremendous amount of time to read, comment and advise me on the content of all of this work and who was always readily available to help. Also for the use of photographs.

Mr Gwynfor Williams, Architect, for the many excellent drawings in these books.

I should like to take this opportunity to thank the following who willingly gave helpful comments on the many varied areas of my text:

♦ My friend Mark Simmons, stone mason and tuck pointer.
♦ Iain McCaig, Mike Stock, Juliet West, Steven Parissien and John Thorneycroft of English Heritage.
♦ John Dorrington Ward.
♦ Douglas Johnston, Masons Mortars Ltd.
♦ Laurie Watson, ARIBA.
♦ Brian Oxley.
♦ Richard Filmer and Kenneth Major, Tool and Trade History Society.
♦ Alan Cox, Historian.
♦ Terry Knight Consultancy.
♦ Barry Roe and Reg Murphy, Guild of Bricklayers.
♦ Michael Baker, North Lincolnshire College.
♦ Jess Perrin.
♦ Bill Walsh.
♦ Professor Prentice, Geologist.
♦ George Blake, Blakes Profiles.

- Mr Bates, Totternhoe Lime Company.
- Mr Jeff Parmley.
- Mr J. Peck, Worshipful Company of Tylers and Bricklayers.
- Mr Alain Kahan, Working-Class History Museum, Salford.
- Mr Jamieson, Archivist, British Waterways Museum.
- Mr S. E. Patrick, Executive Director, Hammond Harwood House, Maryland, USA.
- Mr T. Frankland, Salford Local History Museum.
- Catherine Duckworth, Accrington Library.
- Derek Seddon.
- Bedford College Library staff.

To any other individuals that may have been omitted, please accept both my apologies and this general expression of gratitude.

Thanks are also due to the following companies:

- Blue Circle Cement.
- British Cement Association.
- Brick Development Association.
- British Brick Society.
- Joseph Arnold & Sons (Sands for Industry).
- Mortar Producers Association.
- Marley Building Products.
- Tilson Mortar.
- Concrete Brick Association.
- Calcium Silicate Brick Association.
- Butterfly Bricks Ltd.
- Boral Edenhall.
- The Michelmersh Brick Company.
- Marshalls Clay Products.
- London Brick Company.
- Ryarsh Brick Ltd.

I should like to conclude by thanking my publisher Jill Pearce for her support and encouragement over the long period of this book's gestation.

Gwynfor Williams

Gwynfor Williams trained as an architect at the Welsh School of Architecture, Cardiff, and for many years worked for local authorities and private practices in North Wales. After working as a Senior Lecturer in the School of Construction at the North East Wales Institute of Higher Education for 14 years, he joined the Brick Development Association as Educational Architect lecturing to students, architects and contractors on the correct use of brickwork. He is now a freelance consultant back in North Wales. He is married with three grown-up children.

1

Historical Development of the English Brick

Brick has a history of use in buildings extending over 10,000 years. Several advantages of the material were quickly recognized: the raw materials were often close at hand; they were easy and inexpensive to produce in a variety of shapes, sizes and textures, they can be of excellent durability, and have good insulation properties; they are easy to work with and can be combined effectively with other kinds of building materials.

The earliest use of brick so far recorded is in Jericho c.8000 BC. Other very early examples of use may be found in the hot countries of the Indus valleys, between the Tigris and Euphrates, and in Egypt, where alluvial clay was mixed with straw, to reinforce and prevent shrinkage. Their bricks were hand-moulded and placed in the sun to heat and dry, ready for building. Firing of bricks commenced from the third millennium BC, but due to a shortage of timber for fuel these areas reserved fired bricks for weather-resistant outer casings only.

EARLY HISTORY

Although the burnt brick has a great antiquity, it is to the Romans that we look for its introduction and use in England. They had high standards and rules of manufacture, as recorded by Vitruvius, *c.*25 BC. Their bricks, were relatively long and thin. From 1″ (25mm) to 1½″ (37mm) in thickness, they were in fact more akin to tiles; they came in three sizes known by the Greek names *pentadoron* (*doron* means palm, or a hand's breadth), five palms each way for public buildings, *tetradoron*, four palms each way, and *didoron*, 12″ × 6″ wide (304mm long × 152mm), both used in private dwellings. These bricks were collectively termed *tegulae*, Latin for tile.

The Romans employed burnt and sun-dried bricks widely in provincial work, and varied their practice according to the climate of the occupied country, although Vitruvius refers almost exclusively in his architectural treatise to sun-dried bricks. When fired, their bricks were well burnt and very hard. They were laid with mortar courses often as thick as the bricks, mainly as 'bonding' or 'lacing courses' or as facings to walls containing a concrete core. The Romans developed excellent lime mortars incorporating volcanic ash which produced a very hard set, enabling thinner walls to be built and inspiring adventurous techniques in the structural and architectural use of brick reflected in the remains of many Roman buildings.

Following the departure of the Romans from Britain in AD 412 the brickmaking craft declined. During the Saxon period there was a movement towards permanence in the building of ecclesiastical and some public buildings, and builders were quick to remove bricks from dilapidated Roman buildings and re-use them (see figure 1.1), a practice also carried out by early Norman conquerors.

All Saints Church, Brixworth, Northamptonshire, said to date from the seventh century, is an early example of re-use, as is St Albans Abbey tower in St Albans (*Verulamium*). It became apparent to the Saxon builders that the supply of this very handy building material was going to run out and that new bricks would be needed. At St Botolph's Church Priory, Colchester (*Camulodunum*), where an eleventh-century abbey chronicler relates the use of *opere laterito* (brickwork), there is much evidence in the different sizes and conditions of the bricks to indicate that native Saxon bricks were being used in its construction along with salvaged Roman bricks.

The use of bricks did not entirely cease in Europe with the fall of the Roman Empire. Brickwork was employed in the Byzantine Empire, in Moorish work in parts of Italy and Spain, especially Aragon,

Figure 1.1 Re-used Roman bricks used by Anglo-Saxon builders constructing Holy Trinity Church, Colchester (photograph reproduced by courtesy of the Brick Development Association).

Andalusia and Castile. The use of brick was revived in Flanders and the Netherlands by the eleventh century and in the thirteenth century Flemish bricks were being exported to England, confirmed by identification for the construction of Little Wenham Hall in Suffolk, *c.*1275.

Among the earliest known use of post-Roman bricks in England is Little Coggeshall Abbey, Essex *c.*1190, where new bricks were used for strengthening the flint Abbot's lodging. The kiln found in an excavation in 1845 was sadly not preserved; this authenticated the bricks

as new ones. The brick size was similar to the Roman didoron brick –
310mm × 150mm × 51mm. Early medieval 'great bricks' were still
occasionally used, although rarely, after c.1370 where they are seen
at Waltham Abbey Gatehouse, Essex. Generally by the mid-thirteenth
century a size of 216mm × 102mm × 51mm was in use.

It is important to stress that brick size cannot be used as an
historical guide to the date of bricks, as they have often varied even
in recent 'standard' times. Texture is a better guide, with the developments in clay weathering, mixing, moulding and firing.

Early thirteenth-century bricks were made either from estuarine
clay of Jurassic deposits on the banks of rivers, or shallow clay beds,
often termed 'brickearth', a loam clay found especially in the Pleistocene of the Thames Valley and eastern England. From the 1700s this
sedimentary deposit would be mixed with various combustible materials to make stock bricks.

Generally clay was excavated in shallow digs close to or within the
proposed site; without pumps, these could never be deep. Digging was
manual and always seasonal. The clay was dug or 'won' before 1
November, stirred or turned before 1 February and wrought before 1
March. During the winter the dug earth was left to weather and break
down with rain and frost, and was turned over a few times to ensure
full exposure. The weathered or 'tempered' clay was then thrown into
a shallow pit to be trodden by men or oxen, ready for shaping or
moulding; stones or other foreign bodies were removed at this stage.

In the thirteenth century although using a timber mould was
established, some moulding of what were known as 'place bricks' took
place by spreading tempered clay on a flat base of grass or straw, then
cutting it into approximate brick shapes using a spade. Individual
bricks may also have been formed by using wooden bats in a manner
similar to making butter. Certainly by the middle of the fourteenth
century it was normal to use a mould or 'forme'. The bricks were laid
out flat on a bed of straw to dry. They would then be 'fired' or burnt
in a simple kiln (old English *cylene* from the Latin *culina* – a kitchen or
burning place) of the updraught type, or in a temporary kiln known
as a clamp.

A clamp was an outer shell of previously burnt bricks or 'casings'
(called in some areas 'burnovers'). Inside the green (unfired) bricks
were arranged on, and with, layers of fuel (wood faggots, charcoal,
heather or turf). The top was then closed with a layer of burnt bricks.
The clamp, which could contain up to two million bricks, was set alight
from a series of points on the windward side. It was uncontrollable and
allowed to burn itself out, often taking several weeks. This resulted in a
large percentage of 'wasters' or spoilt bricks, used in the twelfth
century as hardcore to fill in foundations and so on.

The under-burnt bricks were referred to as 'semels' or 'samels'. This is a word with a long history in brickmaking, being mentioned in medieval building accounts. It was thought to have originated from the 'salmon'-like colouring of the least burnt bricks, many of which were produced at the cooler extremities of the clamp. It is more likely, however, that 'samel' is a compound of the old English word *sam* from the Latin *semi* meaning half and 'aelden' – 'to burn or fire'. Sometimes also called 'peckings', they were soft and uneven of texture and colour and could not be used for building where durability was required. Lack of control also led to a wide variation in the colour of different 'clamped' bricks although this was often not a problem if the work was to be rendered or colour washed, a common practice in medieval times.*

The Hanseatic League

During the Middle Ages there was a tremendous increase in social and economic intercourse between the eastern counties and ports of England and the Continent. Here the crafts of brickmaking and bricklaying were experiencing a revival of their use in buildings. This was true of Flanders, Holland and North Germany – areas short in stone and which were united in trade and industrial discourse through the founding of the Hanseatic League in 1241.

Through ports at Norwich, Lynn, Boston and Hull, the east of England forged trade links with the League, which were to have a profound and lasting effect on English brickmaking and bricklaying crafts, and promote a major Dutch/Flemish influence on much of its architecture. Considerable quantities of Flemish bricks were shipped into England for important works, such as 202,500 bricks from Ypres in 1278 for the Tower of London. As native brickmaking techniques quickly caught up, however, this trade declined. The town of Kingston-upon-Hull, for example, established a corporation brickyard in 1303.

The size of brick, occasioned by foreign influence and local demand, varied from $8\frac{1}{2}'' \times 4'' \times 2''$ (216mm × 102mm × 51mm) up to 10" × 5" × 2" (254mm × 127mm × 51mm). Long bricks, as in Roman times, were generally intended for mass walling. The size of a brick was dictated by the necessity to make it easy for the bricklayer to handle, who preferred to keep his trowel in his hand during laying. This is especially true of the width of a brick, which is in direct relation to the span of a hand, and has therefore varied the least during seven centuries of domestic use.

*   Terence Paul Smith puts forward this theory in 'A Note on Samel Bricks', British Brick Society *Information*, no. 31, pp. 5–7 (1983).

Figure 1.2 Hampton Court Palace, *c.*1515 (photograph by courtesy of the Brick Development Association).

The word brick is probably derived from the old French *briche* quoted by Godefrey, 1264. This may in turn come from the Teutonic word *brekan*, meaning a 'broken piece' or 'bit' of baked material. It is likely the connection comes from the burnt brick's similarity in shape to a baked loaf and the phrase 'a piece of bread' or 'brique de pain' is still used in dialect. Hence 'brique' the shaped object was in use earlier than 'la brique' the substance. 'Brick' appears to come into recorded English use in the early fifteenth century and was recorded in 1405–6 as 'Brike', at Hornchurch and in 1416 in the accounts at Crockernend as 'de Bricke' and 'de Brykes', and by 1437 and again in 1444 accounts record 'Tegulis vocalis Breke' – 'tiles called brick'.

TUDOR BRICK AND ITS MANUFACTURE

The mid-fifteenth century witnessed the first flowering in the craft of bricklaying. The acceptance by the aristocracy and church of brick as a desirable material to clothe their houses led to its increasing domestic use in middle-class homes. Someries Castle in Luton, *c.*1448, is an excellent example of Tudor bricks and of technical expertise in bricklaying. In 1515 Cardinal Wolsey built the episcopal palace at Hampton Court (see figure 1.2), the largest brick building of its day. The size of brick here was generally $9\frac{1}{2}'' \times 4'' \times 2''$ (242mm × 102mm × 51mm).

Further evidence for the growing demand for brick comes from the establishment in some areas and provincial towns by the late fourteenth century of commercial yards with permanent kilns. A brick maker, often itinerant, would be hired to search for a suitable clay and then paid to excavate, mould, fire and deliver the bricks to the client. The clay was sometimes dug from the site of the proposed building itself, the excavation perhaps used to form a cellar or moat. Nothing, it appears, was added to medieval bricks, although sand has been definitely traced in some exceptions, showing early knowledge of the value of sand to help reduce cracking due to shrinkage.

By the middle of the fifteenth century it was common for the moulder to work at a bench and throw his clay lump a 'clot' (or 'clod', of Teutonic origin, *klutto – klott* meaning lump; also called a 'warp', Old English *wearpen*, to throw or cast) into a now open mould positioned over a flat wooden board called a 'stock', nailed to the bench and sprinkled with water to prevent the clay sticking, in a process known today as 'slop moulding'. (See figure 1.3) The excess clay was smoothed off using a flat wooden stick termed a 'strike'. The mould was then lifted and the brick turned out onto a flat thin board called a pallet to be taken away for drying.

Because hand-made bricks had to be very wet for moulding purposes, they were left to dry to enable them to develop a 'leather' skin for handling and help prevent warping and cracking when fired. This involved laying the bricks out flat to dry so they were strong enough for 'clamping' or stacking on edge in a kiln.

The design of medieval kilns had developed from Roman ones, of a simple up-draught type from which the modern Suffolk kiln has its origins. Up-draught kilns were so called because the fires burned at the 'fire holes' along the two longest opposite sides of the chamber and the hot gases rose through the bricks to exit at the top. These kilns were fired by turf (peat), wood faggots or furze, as coal was at this time very expensive. Early kilns had to be filled, fired, cooled and emptied for each batch of bricks, and were therefore known as 'intermittent kilns'. Colours throughout the medieval and Tudor periods varied with local clay, firing temperature, fuel and position of the brick in the kiln or clamp, from pale pinks and yellows, to the more popular deep reds.

Figure 1.3 A brickmaker dashes his clot of clay into his mould (by Jost Amman, from *The Book of Trades*, late sixteenth century).

Disputes between England and the Hanseatic League caused a slackening off of domestic building and the use of brick. These problems were resolved in 1474, and once again continental craftsmen and ideas returned to these shores.

In the sixteenth century the Tylers and Bricklayers Company controlled the manufacture of tiles and bricks within a fifteen-mile radius
of London, emphasizing its new found importance as a major constructional material in the capital.

In 1571 brick size became regulated by government law or statute,
giving rise to the name 'statute bricks'. The measurements were to be
9″ × 4½″ × 2″ (229mm × 115mm × 51mm). This also prevented
abuse on the sale of bricks by number as opposed to weight. During
this period the art of moulding brick shapes began to flourish. In 1619
the Commissioners for Buildings were instructed by the Privy Council
to summon the brickmasters before them to take measures to reduce
overcharging for bricks; an exploitation resulting from the demand
after the Royal Proclamation of 1605 by James I requiring the use of
brick instead of the usual timber-framed buildings. By 1622, to regulate the brick supply, the Tylers and Bricklayers Company was en-
trusted with overall supervision of the brickmaking industry.

Further rules to control the continuing non-uniformity of sizes of
bricks were introduced by Charles I's Royal Proclamation of 1625 in
which bricks were to be 9″ (229mm) long, 4″ (102mm) in breadth,
and 2¼″ (57mm) in thickness. This order went on to stipulate that
the season for digging clay was to be between the Feasts of St Michael
the Archangel and St Thomas the Apostle (between 29 September,
Michaelmas Day, and 21 December, Ember Day). Another proclamation in 1630 ordered brickmaking to be carried out far enough away

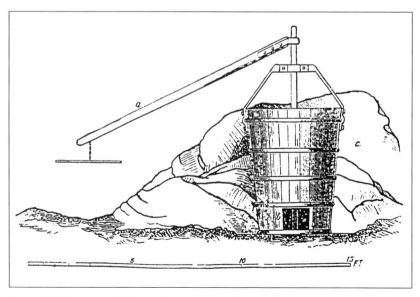

Figure 1.4 Elevation of a horse-drawn pug mill, taken from Dobson's *Treatise on
the Manufacture of Bricks* (1850).

from habitations so as not to cause public nuisance. He also reaffirmed the 1625 statute size of the brick.

SEVENTEENTH- AND EIGHTEENTH-CENTURY DEVELOPMENTS IN BRICK PRODUCTION

The early seventeenth and the eighteenth centuries saw a considerable development in the quality of bricks, largely influenced by Dutch practices. Brickmakers no longer used only the overlaying clay or Pliocene layer, but the older geological clays such as Eocene.

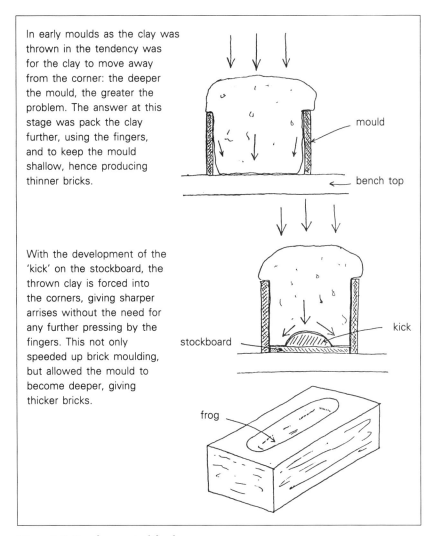

In early moulds as the clay was thrown in the tendency was for the clay to move away from the corner: the deeper the mould, the greater the problem. The answer at this stage was pack the clay further, using the fingers, and to keep the mould shallow, hence producing thinner bricks.

mould

bench top

With the development of the 'kick' on the stockboard, the thrown clay is forced into the corners, giving sharper arrises without the need for any further pressing by the fingers. This not only speeded up brick moulding, but allowed the mould to become deeper, giving thicker bricks.

stockboard

kick

frog

Figure 1.5 Development of the frog.

After the Great Fire of London in 1666, builders were forbidden to build with timber, giving a great impetus to the use of brick. However, to obtain the number of bricks needed, Parliament passed legislation to prevent the restrictive practices of the Tylers and Bricklayers Company and other guilds.

Brick production was often a family affair, all helping in 'winning', weathering, moulding, drying and firing the bricks. Clay winning was hard manual work, although the introduction of the horse-powered pug mill towards the end of the seventeenth century achieved a more workable plastic mass, now often mixed with sand, ashes/breeze, and, if required, lime. The pug mill was a round vertical container with a central shaft and projecting blades. A long beam was attached to a horse, which then walked continuously around the cylinder. (See figure 1.4) The raw materials were fed into the top of the mill to be chopped and beaten until emerging at the bottom as a blended, smooth mass.

New and more refined methods of moulding led to more accurate bricks, special shapes and better textures. 'Sand or pallet moulding' was now more common than 'slop moulding'. In this process the 'puddled' clay was dashed into the wooden mould, which was dusted with sand, preventing the brick from sticking to the mould and stock. However, slop moulding was still used for certain clays which did not suit this new method.

From about 1690, the 'frog' or indentation at the top of the brick appears. This was a clay-saving device, enabling more efficient drying and firing, made the brick lighter, and assisted in giving the mortar a better grip. Its true development was out of necessity in the moulding process. When the moulder dashes a 'warp' of clay onto a flat stock-board the clay does not fully fill the moulding box into the corners. It was found that by placing a raised centre on the stockboard, termed the 'kick', the clay was forced tightly into the corners, ensuring well formed 'arrises' (edges). (See figure 1.5) The origin of the term 'frog' is lost in antiquity, although one idea is its similarity to the cleft in a horse's hoof, a sight familiar in the pug mill area of the brickyard, and itself called the frog. The moulded 'green' bricks might then be dusted with sand for drying or curing, before being taken to be 'hacked'.

Hacking involved 'pitching' or 'setting' the bricks

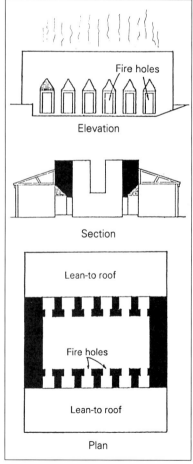

Figure 1.6 The roofless down-draught intermittent 'Scotch' kiln.

into stacked bricks-on-edge rows about two bricks in width and about ½″ (13mm) apart at 90° on the 'hack' or drying platform. Sand-moulded bricks could be hacked immediately after moulding, whereas slop-moulded bricks needed to be laid out flat initially to dry out sufficiently to be able to stand on edge without deforming or marking each other. The long rows were built up slowly, to a height of up to eight courses, where they would be left and given time to harden. When half-dry the rows of bricks would then be 'skintled' (scattered), set slantwise and further apart to complete drying. 'Hacking' took between three and six weeks, in which the brick lost about one quarter of its weight. To protect hacks from intense heat or frost they could be covered with straw, reeds, lee-boards or hack caps.

Firing normally took place from early April, peaked in late August and tailed off from September. Improvements in kilns led to the introduction of the roofless, down-draught 'Scotch kiln', which was intermittent, more controllable and less expensive on fuel (now often coal) than its predecessors. (See figure 1.6) The bricks would be lightly fired for three days to prevent warping, and the heat was increased for two more days. The fire holes, which also acted as vents, were then blocked up and the fire was allowed to burn out. The kiln had to be left to cool down between seven and ten days before removing the bricks.

During the eighteenth century the quality of bricks improved substantially due to the introduction of controllable kilns and the enforcement of government statutes. In 1725 place bricks were to measure 9″ × 4½″ × 2½″ (229mm × 114mm × 64mm) and stock bricks 9″ × 4½″ × 2″ (229mm × 114mm × 51mm). Under-fired bricks were no longer to be sold as cheap place bricks, and brick earth no longer to be mixed with what was known as 'Spanish', ground sea-coal ash (finely sieved with clay mixed to give an integral fuel), a unique feature of the 'London Stock' brickmaking process.

'Spanish' was the name given to soil (domestic refuse from the city containing a large percentage of ash). At a time when 'Sea Coal' was heavily taxed to compensate owners whose sites were lost in the Great Fire, and for financing the cost of public buildings, the use of an integral waste fuel afforded a great saving on raw fuel costs for burning bricks in the clamps around the capital. In 1713, however, due to problems with the quality of the brickwork foundations of St Johns, Smith Square, representation was made by the building's surveyors to the Tylers and Bricklayers Company: 'It is our opinion that no Spanish should be used in the bricks that are made for the brickmaker gets liberty to put in the least quantity of Spanish they will mix what they please and pretend there is no more than allowed by the Commissioners'.

The Tylers and Bricklayers Company explained in a letter to the Commission the problems:

It is with much regret we have for several years past observed the brick made round this city to be very bad and of late worse than ever; and according to the powers granted us by Royal Charter and our ordinances approved by the judges; have yearly appointed searchers . . . to view and destroy such bad materials.

It is our opinion that the badness of bricks proceeds from . . . the practice of using ashes commonly called spanish in making bricks, begun about 40 years since, occasioned by digging up several fields contiguous to the city after the great fire, which fields having been much dunged with ashes it was observed the bricks made with earth in those fields would be sufficiently burned with one half of the coles commonly used since which time, coles being by the high duties on them of more value here, the quantity of spanish is increased, especially since the habit of strewing houses with sand hath prevailed the dust bucket in every house being the common receptacle for sand as well as ashes so that the spanish hath not the force as formerly since the corrupt mixture of it; which excessive quantity so corruptly mixed we take to be a great occasion of the badness of bricks. Another reason is the great quantity of grey stock bricks that are now being made and burn'd in the heart of the clamps where the best place bricks which used to be burn'd within.

This was later found to be inconvenient and in some respects wrong so that in 1729 a ban on selling under-fired stock bricks as place bricks and mixing Spanish with brick earth within a fifteen-mile radius

Figure 1.7 The use of Staffordshire Blue bricks for civil engineering projects (photograph by kind permission of the Brick Development Association).

of London was lifted by George III on condition that the 'fuel' was screened and did not exceed certain laid-down proportions to the making of 100,000 bricks. These bricks had to measure 8″ × 4″ × 2½″ (203mm × 102mm × 64mm). By 1770 that brick measurement was changed to 8½″ × 4″ × 2½″ (216mm × 102mm × 64mm), which was confirmed by a national statute in 1776. The wording gave the reason for nationwide control, 'Inconveniences have arisen to the public by frauds committed in lessening the size of bricks under their usual proportions without diminution of price'. It is at this point when the brick size comes closest to our modern metric brick, 215mm × 102.5mm × 65mm.

Brickmaking was looked on in 1774 as 'very mean employ', and all over Great Britain had lower wages and a worse reputation for violence than other building trades. Brickmaking by hand required very considerable skill and there was a hierarchy of skilled, semi-skilled and unskilled workers. The fully skilled brickmaker was the 'moulder', directly hired by the employer, who paid his assistants himself: off-beaters, temperers, wall-flatters, pug-boys, pushers-out and barrow loaders.

Despite the introduction in 1784 of the Brick Tax, set initially at two shillings and sixpence (12½p) per 1,000 bricks, brick began to be used extensively for small dwellings.

This tax led some brick makers to mould oversize bricks such as the famous 'Wilkes Gobs', from Measham in Leicestershire, measuring 9″ × 4½″ × 4″ (229mm × 114mm × 102mm). To stop these attempts at tax avoidance, the government in 1803 charged a double duty on bricks if they were in excess of 150 cubic inches (2,458cc). The tax was repealed in 1850.

The canal building era, roughly 1750 to 1840, added vast momentum to brick production. When the engineers came upon areas and regions devoid of naturally occurring stone, or the mason's craft not much practised, brick was a ready solution. Developments in excavation equipment and quarrying techniques meant ever-growing sources of deeper geological clay types.

Brickmakers moved ahead of the navvies testing the ground for suitable brick earth and clay deposits and setting up temporary yards and clamps at the site of a proposed bridge, wharf or warehouse. Ordinary-quality bricks would suffice for the latter but for tunnels and aqueducts, bricks of a superior quality were required. These were usually made from blue-grey shale clays (Staffordshire's proving best), and were initially hand-made. Thus began in civil engineering work the use of the now famed Staffordshire Blue engineering brick. (See figure 1.7)

The 3,000 or so miles of canals were of great benefit for the transportation of bricks for domestic building. Following the canals came the railway boom from the 1840s to 1890s. Once more brick was extensively employed for platforms, tunnels and bridges etc., and again itinerant brick makers moulded and fired the clay in semi-permanent brickyards. The Copenhagen Tunnel, north of King's Cross, London (1849/50), was lined with bricks made from clay which the tunnelling navvies had earlier excavated.

Colours of bricks changed with the fashions of the eighteenth century. The aspiring middle classes wanted their houses to resemble the stone Palladian manor houses of the wealthy, and stone-coloured, cream or buff bricks offered the next best thing, reds becoming less well regarded. These sudden changes in colour were only possible due to technological advances. Kilns increasingly fired with the fuel of industrialization – coal – meant that higher temperatures were now possible. These varying temperatures and differing clay types gave a wider range of colours.

Sometimes bricks were a background fabric for stucco; a plaster-like coating usually of sand and Roman cement, incised to give the appearance of stone. Brickmakers responded by supplying mainly inferior bricks. Sadly this habit caused many construction problems when brick facework again became fashionable after the 1840s, and it took a long while for public confidence to be restored.

THE VICTORIAN PERIOD

At the beginning of the nineteenth century the brickmaking process was still primitive. The urban pressure for quickly built homes for factory workers led to a massive demand for bricks. Between 1820 and 1850 over 100 brickmaking machines and new-style, larger kilns were patented to take advantage of this lucrative market. Many new brickyards were located close to the new rail network to gain quick access to growing towns and cities and meet this unprecedented demand.

Mechanization in brick production, with steam engines gradually replacing men or horses, allowed new (harder and less plastic) sources of carbonaceous, shale clay of the North to be exploited from greater depths.

Brick sizes varied little during the nineteenth century, being generally 9″ × 4½″ × 3″ (229mm × 115mm × 76mm). A gauge of 3″ (76mm) became, and remained, popular, although during this period the 'gauge' between the North and South moved noticeably apart. North of a line from the Wash to the Severn, four vertical courses tended to measure 13½″ (342mm), while south of that line 12″ (304mm) was standard.

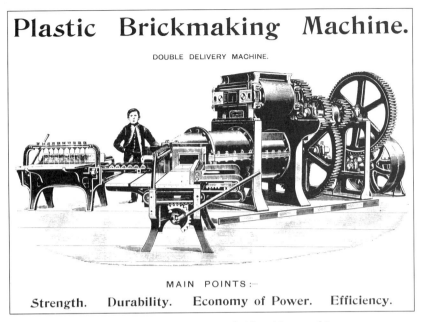

Figure 1.8 A steam-driven Victorian wirecut brickmaking machine.

The Victorians had a love for smooth machine-made bricks and the manufacturers obliged. From 1820 heated drying-sheds reduced the time taken to cure the bricks. By 1860 bricks could be made by the wirecut process, by which a machine extruded a column of clay 900mm long through an aperture the width and length of a brick; this was then pushed sideways through a frame of taut wires which sliced it into about ten bricks to an even gauge. (See figure 1.8) However, they still required a final pressing for accuracy of shape and size.

Renshaw and Atkins, two Manchester brickmakers, were first to set up brickmaking machinery, in 1861. Opposition from societies of hand brickmakers resulted in their engines being blown up and lumps of iron being thrown into the machinery. The Manchester Order of Bricklayers even refused to use machine-made bricks. From spoiling bricks, they turned to burning sheds and then to 'hamstringing horses'. Despite such tactics, machinery spread successfully and was taken up by other employers.

Such were the struggles of a dying industry, that when a Commission visited Manchester in 1867, the brickmakers' organizations were in rapid decline, and vanished a few years later, allowing brickmakers to be subsumed within the flood of general labourers.

The Hoffmann kiln was invented in 1858, which was a significant advance since it replaced the intermittent firing of the kiln with a continuous process, allowing burning to continue without interruption. Openings or 'ports', surrounding the fire chamber, allowed heat

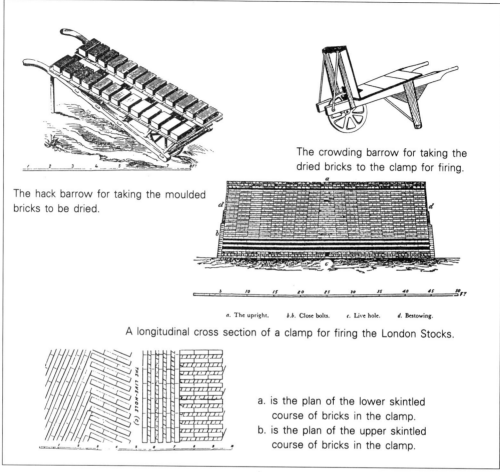

The crowding barrow for taking the dried bricks to the clamp for firing.

The hack barrow for taking the moulded bricks to be dried.

a. The upright.   *b.b.* Close bolts.   *c.* Live hole.   *d.* Bestowing.

A longitudinal cross section of a clamp for firing the London Stocks.

a. is the plan of the lower skintled course of bricks in the clamp.
b. is the plan of the upper skintled course of bricks in the clamp.

Figure 1.9 Manufacturing London Stocks (prints from Dobson's *Treatise on the Manufacture of Bricks and Tiles*, 1850).

to be drawn gradually through the kiln by a draught induced by a tall central chimney, serving to cool the fired bricks and allowing hot air to dry the 'green' bricks.

The London Stock

Despite the unprecedented demands for brick from a fast growing population and rapidly developing industrial towns and urban sprawls, the brick industry was still traditional and labour intensive and seasonal in production. All around London were hundreds of small brickyards excavating surface clay and mixing it with lime and the siftings from ash and rubbish of the city's waste, known as 'soil', to overcome the limitations of the clay and provide an integral fuel for the bricks' vitrification. This was followed by the firing of the not always fully dried bricks in open clamps, as had been done since the late seventeenth century, to produce the famous London Yellow Stocks. (See figure 1.9) The burning lit up the night sky of the capital, and the process brought many complaints and legal actions, mainly over the smell. During the hot, close months of mid-summer (the height of the brick burning season), this could be most nauseating, especially because of the decomposed animal and vegetable matter contained within the ash.

Coal dust was used in some districts instead of ashes and also 'breeze', a casual mixture of cinders, small coal and ashes, its chief use being to provide sufficient heat to ignite the powdered fuel.

These stocks, claimed by many authorities on brick manufacture to be the most durable bricks in the world, and which have played such a significant historical part in the architectural fabric of the capital, are worthy of a deeper study.

By the mid-Victorian period production had spread out of London to Kent, Essex and parts of Berkshire and Buckinghamshire. Brickmaking of stocks had existed in Kent since 1740, where it was chronicled that brickearth mixed with chalk and ashes, ground in horse-powered pug mills, was then fired in clamps. The huge demand for bricks during the early nineteenth century meant that contractors looked to North Kent, around the Swale and the Medway, where there were large sources of easily worked brickearth and the means of transporting the bricks by barge to the city. Deliveries were made to the wharves and drawdocks of, for example, Southwark, the City, Chelsea and Westminster. A web of small waterways – the Wandle, the Lee, Kensington Canal, Regents Canal and Hammersmith Creek among others – was used to carry bricks into London's interior. A cargo of domestic refuse, an important fuel for making London Stock, was carried on the return journey.

One of the most famous of the brickmaking firms was George Smead's (later Smead Dean and Company Ltd of Murston) whose bricks were used on the Hyde Park Exhibition (1851), Kings Cross Station (1850–2), West India Docks (1866), The Law Courts in the Strand (1868–82), Tower Bridge (1886–94) and on parts of the underground railway.

The use of rubbish and ashes from London houses to give the clay an integral fuel continued until 1965, with kilns still in use in the Sittingbourne area of North Kent, when the change to smokeless fuels rendered the supply useless. Today coal dust from coal washeries is an alternative supply.

In *Good and Proper Materials* published by the London Topographical Society in 1989 (p. 4), Alan Cox gives an account of the selection of a new brickfield:

> The discovery of new sources of clay for stocks was always done

Figure 1.10 A family affair: in the moulding shed a young boy places the bricks moulded by his parents on to the 'hacking barrow' for transportation to the hacking ground for drying, *c*.1850 (reproduced by kind permission of Richard Filmer).

on the best scientific lines: a group of men would gather in a likely field and the experienced brickmakers would pop a piece of clay in their mouths; by the taste and feel they could tell whether the clay was suitable or not.

Brickmaking remained a family occupation (see figure 1.10), employing everyone from children of five or six to parents and sometimes even grandparents. The father worked as the moulder and was served by his family, usually in gangs of six. Each had a specific job: mixing, carrying clay, fetching, moulding or hacking. Hours were long, often from five in the morning until seven at night. A gang would expect to produce between 3,000 and 4,000 bricks a day. By this method about 500 million bricks were made annually within a five-mile radius of London Bridge.

The money they worked so hard for was often spent by the parents on liquor from the grog shops which sprang up in almost every brickfield, and the environment was one of foul language and ribald behaviour, with no schooling and little religious observance for the children. Many philanthropists and government ministers, alarmed at this 'national disgrace', lobbied for improvements, so in 1872, when the Factories Act (Brick and Tile Yards) extension was passed regulating child labour and enforcing 'some' daily schooling, it is estimated over 10,000 children were sent, from 'the bricksheds to their homes and school'.

Edward Dobson in his *Treatise on the Manufacture of Bricks and Tiles* of 1850 shows London Stock bricks were graded by some of the following terms:

> Malms. These are the best building bricks, and are only used in the best descriptions of brickwork; their colour is yellow.
>
> Seconds. These are sorted from the best qualities, and are much used for the fronts of buildings of a superior class.
>
> Paviours. These are excellent building bricks, being sound, hard, well shaped, and of good colour. They must not be confounded with paving bricks, having nothing in common with them but their name.
>
> Rough Paviours. These are the roughest pickings from the paviours.
>
> Pickings. These are good bricks, but soft, and inferior to the best paviours.
>
> Washed Stocks. These are the bricks commonly used for ordinary brickwork and are a poor kind of malm brick.
>
> Grey stocks. These are good bricks, but of irregular colour, and are not suited for face work.
>
> Rough Stocks. These are, as their name implies, very rough as regards shape and colour and not suited for good work, although hard and sound.
>
> Grizzles. These are somewhat tender, and only fit for inside work.
>
> Place bricks. These are only fit for common purposes, and should not be used for permanent erections.
>
> Shuffs. These are unsound and full of shakes.
>
> Burrs of Clinkers. These are only used for making artificial rockwork for cascades of gardens, concrete, etc.
>
> Bats. These are broken bricks, and are refuse.

Malm and malmed? The use of the terms 'malm' and 'malmed' in the production of 'London Stocks' can be confusing and is therefore worthy of further study. It is precisely explained by Alan Cox in *Good and Proper Materials*.

> In its pure state it was referred to as 'malm' and 'malms' or malm bricks and considered the best type of London stock brick. The brickearth is high in silica (about 65–75%), low in alumina (8–11%), and with a higher than usual lime content of between 7–9%. Normally the iron oxide in a clay will tend to produce red brick but lime will nullify this and produce a characteristic yellow- or white-coloured brick (this is true of any yellowish or whitish brick whether it be a London stock, a Suffolk white, or a yellow

gault). The lime also diminishes the amount of contraction during the drying of the raw bricks and in addition acts as a flux combining with the silica of the clay to produce a durable, generally well-burnt brick. The colour of stocks could, in fact, vary quite considerably from a deep earthy purplish colour to a bright yellow, but somewhat confusingly they were generally referred to as 'greys' or 'grey stocks'.

The clay was cut by hand using pick and shovel, though a peculiar digging tool like a cross between a spade and a fork evolved for the purpose – it had three prongs with a bar or blade across the bottom. Clay was best dug in the autumn so that it could be left in piles to weather during the winter frosts, being turned over occasionally. Dobson stated that between 1 and 2 cubic yards, according to the nature of the clay, would produce a thousand bricks.

By 1850 supplies of the pure brickearth, the malm, had almost been exhausted and so it was more and more frequently necessary to resort to an artificial mixture by adding chalk and a small amount of natural malm to the clay to improve it, but the elaborate lengths to which the makers of London Stocks went were unique. The chalk had to be brought to the site (Kent was fortunate in this respect since the chalk and clay occurred in close proximity, whereas in London the chalk often had to be brought in by barge), and ground up in a horse-powered chalk mill. This consisted of a circular trough in which the chalk was ground by two heavy wheels with spiked tyres. Water was pumped into the trough and as the chalk was ground into a pulp it was passed by means of a chute into the clay-washing mill. This was similar to the chalk mill but much larger. In its trough the natural malm was mixed with the chalk pulp, then cut and stirred by knives and harrows moved round by two horses. When reduced to the consistency of cream the whole mixture was passed off through a brass grating into the troughs or shoots, (see figure 1.11), and con-ducted to the ordinary clay heaped up to receive it. This was arranged in special pits, known as washbacks, fitted with simple sluices. These were left to settle for a month or more until the mixture was solid enough to bear a man walking on top of it. As it settled excess water would be drained off from time to time via the sluices. 'It was at this stage the adding of "spanish" or "soiling" would take place . . .'

Developments in brick transport

Developments in transport meant the use of brick could extend beyond the locality of the kiln. From the Middle Ages an ox pulling a cart would do well to transport 200 to 300 bricks ten miles in a day. In

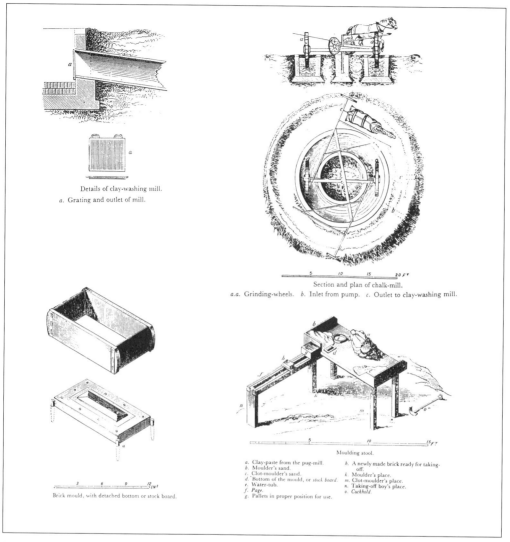

Details of clay-washing mill.
a. Grating and outlet of mill.

Section and plan of chalk-mill.
a.a. Grinding-wheels. *b.* Inlet from pump. *c.* Outlet to clay-washing mill.

Moulding stool.

a. Clay-paste from the pug-mill.
b. Moulder's sand.
c. Clot-moulder's sand.
d. Bottom of the mould, or *stock board.*
e. Water-tub.
f. Page.
g. Pallets in proper position for use.

h. A newly made brick ready for taking-off.
k. Moulder's place.
m. Clot-moulder's place.
n. Taking-off boy's place.
o. Cuckhold.

Brick mould, with detached bottom or stock board.

Figure 1.11 Manufacturing London Stocks. The clay, having been ground in the chalk mill, was passed through a brass grating to the washback to settle and be spanished prior to moulding. Moulding took place at the bench or stool. A close-up of the brick mould with the stock board with the raised 'kick', which creates the frog in the moulded brick is also shown. The stock board was fixed to the wooden bench by the iron spikes at the corners (prints, from Dobson's *Treatise on the Manufacture of Bricks and Tiles*, 1850).

the nineteenth century a horse-drawn cart could only carry about two tons, between 600 to 800 bricks, a similar distance. This could be very expensive as shown by the Bedford estate who for a delivery of just five miles in the first half of the nineteenth century increased the yard price of 1,000 bricks from 34*s.* to 48*s.*

From the earliest times barges travelled the estuaries of East Anglia down the east coast and up the Thames to London. Eastwoods had a fleet of seventy barges by the end of the nineteenth century, known as 'brickies', which remained in use until 1945. On a canal one horse could pull a barge loaded with 25 tons.

It was, however, through the rail network that the use of brick was to spread from being a localized industry to a national one.

The demand for machine-made bricks

By the 1870s the majority of bricks were manufactured by machine, either by the wirecut process or by being 'pressed' into metal moulds, resulting in regularity of colour, texture and size, giving a uniformity to the brickwork which aesthetically could be severe. Early brick machines were based on the 'slop-moulding' principles of the hand-made process. Steam machines of the 1880s produced 1,000 bricks per hour, and from 1850–1900 brick production in England doubled.

Mechanization did not sound the death knell for small hand-made brick yards, however, and during the early 1870s architects such as Basil Champneys and R. Norman Shaw preferred hand-made bricks, even though they were sometimes as much as four times more expensive as machine-made bricks. Despite improvements, transport costs remained high, so local yards were often more economic.

Mechanization also allowed greater development of 'special' bricks, which Victorian architects used to great advantage, such as bullnose, splays, plinths etc. (See figure 1.12) It also allowed for development in the brick itself. Designers, inventors – call them what you will – tried

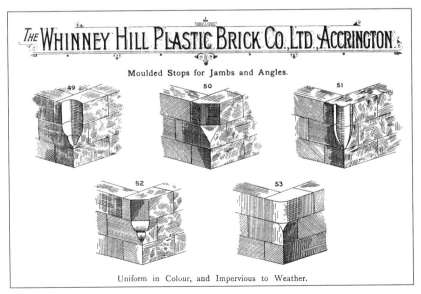

Figure 1.12 A selection of the wide range of Victorian machine-moulded specials available from a manufacturer's catalogue.

to develop a brick system interlocking for added strength or, as the idea of cavity walling was being developed, to tie one leaf to the other. However, all these various patented bricks, despite some use, proved unwieldy, unworkable or unpopular with bricklayers, and fell into disuse.

The Accrington pioneers

During the 1870s in Accrington, Lancashire, it was found to be possible to produce bricks by what became known as the semi-dry process, involving a machine subjecting coal shale dust to tremendous pressure, without further addition of water, into presses, producing the bright red, smooth faced bricks known as 'Accrington Noris' (Nori being iron backwards, a statement of their great strength). The gauge was generally $3\frac{1}{4}''$ (82mm), in line with the northern fashion.

This development had a major effect on brick production within a short time, especially on the Jurassic clay belt from Buckinghamshire to Cambridgeshire known as 'Oxford Clay'. Pressing clay in the 'green' stage so that bricks could be stacked in the kilns able to stand their own weight and doing away with pre-drying, made brickmaking an 'all year round' process – a factory industry. It also made the 'green brick' side of the industry an 8 am to 5 pm job, although the burning sections kept up their traditional practice of starting early and finishing early.

The Fletton industry

Many of the major brick producers existing today came into being at this time, exploiting their own particular clay and producing a brick generally identified as their own. However, the development of the Oxford Clay yards and the Fletton brick deserves deeper study because of its individual nature and its effect on national brick production and use.

For centuries, there had always been small brickyards digging the 'callow', overburden or top brickearth along this belt of shale clay. Unwittingly, however, they were working over a goldmine (early digs of 'Oxford Clay' were nicknamed 'klondyke' and 'kimberley'). Discovered in 1881 at Fletton, near Peterborough, this clay (called Oxford Clay by the geologist Dean Buckland in 1818) had many unique advantages for brickmaking. First was its quality, depth and uniformity of its formations. Second, it was found that its 16–20% natural moisture content meant it simply required heavy grinding to powder then two extreme pressures to form a brick. Third, the green bricks were strong enough to be stacked in the kiln immediately, being dried by the warm draught of the Hoffmann kiln process. Finally, and most

Figure 1.13 'Clay getters' excavating clay in a Bedfordshire pit by hand for the Fletton bricks in the early 1900s.

important of all, a 5% natural fuel content meant the clay itself would burn, reducing fuel cost by two thirds. (See figure 1.13)

These advantages, combined with the developments in the mass production of all the areas of brickmaking, contributed to the Flettons being recognized as commodity bricks, setting the pricing standard for the industry as a whole.

Between 1860 and 1890 vast improvements had been seen on machines processing clays of various characteristics, with pioneering work being carried out in the Accrington area of Lancashire. Mechanization of excavation came later, in 1902, with a 10 hp steam navvy excavator. Early grinding machines or pug mills with stationary steam engines were in use from the 1890s. By the early 1900s a continuous band elevator was taking the 'milled' clay to 'piano wire' screens sieving out unwanted matter.

Pressing bricks was probably the most important area of all and the earliest machines used were between 1889 and 1893. These 'brick-making machines' or presses, gave two short presses of 30-tons pressure each to two or four bricks at a time. These were further developed in 1893 with a second mould box into which each brick was automatically fed for two more pressures. It was this particular

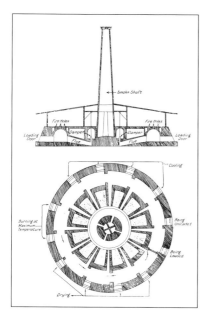

Figure 1.14 Elevation and plan of a circular, continuous 'Hoffmann' kiln.

development that gave the Fletton its undoubted quality, and from which the term 'Phorpres' was coined (discontinued in 1974).

Friedrich Hoffmann, who invented the circular continuous kiln in 1856 (see figure 1.14), had perfected a new model in 1870, rectangular on plan and based on down-draught principles. Sometimes referred to as a transverse arched kiln, it had clear advantages over its predecessor; being of greater size it gave greater output, and better control of firing ensured better quality control. In 1898 at London Brick Company's Fletton yard, Europe's largest Hoffmann kiln was built, with 40 chambers, each with a capacity for 50,000 bricks.

Finally, mechanization of transport through railway access was to be crucial to the development of the Fletton industry. All yards were deliberately located with a frontage to the railway line with one main objective in mind – the huge London market. When in 1898 ten million bricks from the Oxford Clay belt were used in the building of Westminster Cathedral, this was to be the turning point in the fortunes of the Fletton industry.

Initially, Fletton brickmakers were a series of independent competing companies but one company started to emerge as the leader, the London Brick Company. Today it is the only manufacturer of the Fletton brick and provides for about 20% of the clay brick totally manufactured in Great Britain.

At first the Fletton industry only produced a common brick for internal use, footings, side and rear flanks of housing. In 1922 they produced their first facing brick called the 'rustic' realising that machine-made facings were universally accepted. This was a wise move, for whilst commons accounted for 82% of the total production (with the introduction of breeze blocks in the 1940s this fell to 70%) there has since been a vast expansion into facing bricks, shown by the fact that common bricks now only account for 24% of annual brick production which at the time of writing stands at 3,500 million bricks.

THE TWENTIETH-CENTURY BRICK INDUSTRY

In 1866 an American named Van Derburgh patented the first calcium silicate (sand and lime), brick, although the idea did not take off as he did not envisage the use of the autoclave for 'baking'. Further improvements with this type of brick took place in Germany with the development of the autoclave for steam curing at 130–300°C in 1881. In Britain by 1905 there were four factories producing about 16 million calcium silicate bricks *per annum*. From 1905 to 1911 there was a deep recession, made worse by competition from numerous brick producers, who not only drove prices down (sometimes below break-even point), but, in a more positive light, developed multi-coloured (brindled) and mellow toned bricks which broke away from the severity of the Victorian Reds.

High levels of sales were reported during the period 1911–15, although the outbreak of the First World War and the vast mobilization of men meant that many kilns were to close. Unfortunately this was haphazardly done and many rural brickworks never re-opened. During this period the first patents on the now popular tunnel kilns were taken out, a development of the continuous process except the fire remained stationary and the bricks travelled through the kiln. Tunnel kilns were not in common use until the late 1970s.

Recovery came during the period 1919–1923. The construction industry grew rapidly, assisted by large amounts of Government aid intended to help house returning soldiers and to revitalize industry. The brick industry was prosperous during this period, and saw substantial re-investment. Many large firms replaced steam power with electricity, and the introduction of petrol lorries for brick deliveries meant not only the end for the horse and cart but also less reliance on the railways. Also during this perio the Royal Institute of British Architects expressed concern over the continuing difference of the sizes of bricks between the North and South and calling for unity.

A major slump occurred between 1929 and 1933, caused primarily by the world money crisis after the Wall Street Crash in America. By 1933, however, the government resolved to alleviate this problem, providing funds to reduce unemployment via various construction projects. This revitalized the speculative builder and created a good business environment right up to the Second World War. In the 1930s brick production stood at 7,800 million *per annum* in an industry employing 55,000 workers. Of these bricks 97.5% were clay or shale, and of these 85% were common bricks, 12% facing bricks and 3% engineering bricks. By the latter half of the 1930s bricks accounted for 12% of the cost of a house. An average cost of building a house was £334–£409, the bricks being £40–£50. (By 1988 the bricks would cost between 3–4% with laying costs bringing it to 8%).

The Second World War years, 1939–45, once again brought the closure of brickyards, not only for manpower reasons but because the enemy could use the lit kilns as landmarks during the 'black-out' for guidance during bombing raids. Thankfully, the government and the

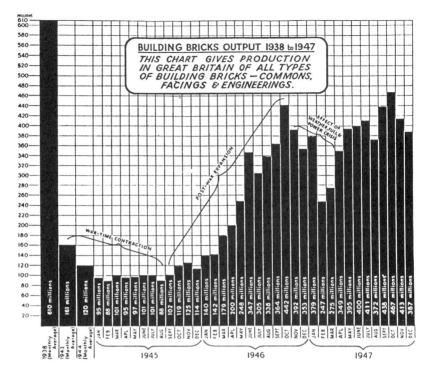

Figure 1.15 Chart illustrating the levels of annual brick production between 1935 and 1947 (reproduced by kind permission of the Brick Development Association).

brick companies had learnt from the First World War and developed a financial scheme to ensure funding for re-opening after the cessation of hostilities. It was at this time the Brick Development Association (BDA) was formed to administer these funds. Its membership included clay and calcium silicate brickmakers, and its objectives were principally research and education in the correct use of brick. Despite this help many small firms were not to re-open. In 1946 it was estimated that there were 1,350 brickworks employing some 40,000 workers. (See figure 1.15)

A boom period came shortly after the war. Post-war rebuilding of the blitzed towns and cities increased sales of bricks from 3,449 million to over 7,000 million. Developments in mechanization during the war led to improvements in the varying processes of brick production, including the introduction of fork lift trucks and bigger, better and more reliable diesel lorries for transportation. These factors helped to keep brick costs down so that between 1918 and 1946 the cost of bricks was to rise by only 75%, compared with 200% for timber; the average for all construction materials was 77%.

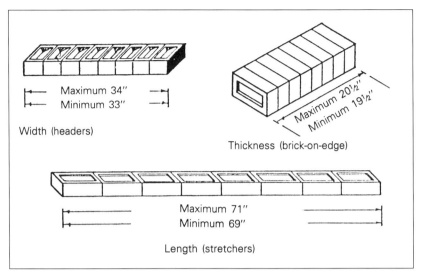

Figure 1.16 The British Standard specification for the dimensions of clay bricks.

By now the Royal Institute of British Architects in conjunction with the Institute of Civil Engineers and the Brickmakers Association had adopted a standard size for pressed or Fletton bricks of 9″ × 4⅜″ × 2¹⁵⁄₁₆″ (229mm × 111mm × 75mm). To allow for slight irregularities the Council of the RIBA recommended the following conditions:

1. Length of brick to be twice the width plus the thickness of one vertical joint.
2. Brickwork should measure four courses of bricks and four joints to a foot (304mm).

Joints ought to be ¼″ (6mm) thick with an extra ¹⁄₁₆″ (2mm), making ⁵⁄₁₆″ (8mm) for the bed joints to cover irregularities, giving a standard length of 9¼″ (234mm) centre to centre of joints. The bricks laid dry should then be measured thus:

1. Eight stretchers laid square end in contact in a straight line to measure 71″ (1805mm).
2. Eight headers laid side by side, frog upwards, in a straight line to measure 34″ (852mm).
3. Eight bricks, the first frog outwards, and then alternatively frog to frog and then back to back, to measure 21½″ (507mm).

A margin of 1″ (25mm) was allowed for the stretchers, and ½″ (13mm) for the headers and brick-on-edge. These measurements applied to both hand- and machine-made walling bricks. (See figure 1.16)

By 1950 the number of separate brickworks had fallen to 1,316, due in the main to take-overs and amalgamations. Yet production capacity was increasing, as did brick deliveries, especially after 1955 when the government lifted war-time restrictions on materials, allowing large developments in private and public sector building.

It was during the 1950s that concrete bricks, a mixture of aggregates and cement, were first introduced into England to help fill the demand for bricks. Early bricks were generally of inferior quality due to manufacturing methods, non-durable colourings and a lack of sufficient testing. This caused concrete bricks to gain a bad image only lost during recent years with vast improvements in all areas of manufacture, including durable colourings, and increased knowledge of its correct use.

The continuing dominance of the clay brick over both the sand-lime and concrete in the UK has its roots in tradition which has played a big part especially through London Bricks 'Flettons' with their naturally occurring fuel included in the clay. This has provided a strong base for clay bricks in the UK not paralleled on the Continent.

From 1964 to 1973 there was a steep fall in demand nationally for brick caused by a slump in private speculative building. This slump saw the demise of many brickyards, especially small yards unable to compete with the more cost-effective big companies. Machine-made bricks were universally popular on housing projects that were remarkable if only for their complete lack of imagination and bland brickwork, mostly of dubious skill.

In 1964 the Brick Development Association (BDA) decided to continue its activities under the direct sponsorship of its member companies. By 1969 a re-organization led to a very important widening of responsibilities to include technical services, education, publicity and, all important, liaison with the construction industry and the Government, and is to be applauded for sterling work in encouraging better use of brick.

By 1967 there were only 581 brickyards, yet due to increasing mechanization and continuing development, production had improved to 1,000 million.

A national unified brick size is achieved

In 1965 the size of a brick became a British Standard BS3921 of $8\frac{5}{8}'' \times 4\frac{1}{8}'' \times 2\frac{5}{8}''$ (219mm × 105mm × 67mm). A first national and unifying standard size, which became metricated in 1969 by BS3921 at 215mm × 102.5mm × 65mm, and this gradually replaced the imperial size brick, though some manufacturers continued to produce imperial bricks particularly for maintenance and repair work. The tolerances on dimensions were to be taken as laid down in BS3921 (1965) and BS3921 (1969).

The use of steel and concrete for structural construction work, and developments in proprietary cladding systems of steel, plastic and glass combined with a poor image of brick from the 'cowboy' building days of the late 1960s, meant brick companies had an uphill battle not only to fight for new markets but to hold on to existing ones.

Many companies realised like any other modern business that they would have to have good technical research and literature not only to support their product but to enhance its correct use. Ibstock was one firm who pioneered this area, offering a complete service to customers' many and diverse needs – design advice, quality assurance, sampling and site services; before and during construction, education, training and research. Technical representatives, well trained in practical and technical aspects of brickwork, added support to these areas. In 1982 Ibstock produced a 'Brickwork Design Magazine' to show designers how, in collaboration with brickmakers, their collective expertise could contribute to the success of a building.

Other firms followed this lead but perhaps the most significant motivator in uniting this movement to better and more imaginative use of brick was the Brick Development Association (BDA). This association comprises nearly forty brickmaking firms which pool their vast area of knowledge, techniques and specialities to promote, encourage and support quality brickwork, through an advisory centre and publication of well-researched technical leaflets, booklets and books. In 1990–1991 this culminated in the publication of an excellent book for all involved in craft education, training and design and use of modern quality brickwork, called *Achieving Successful Brickwork*. The publication is a series of articles written by authorities on various subject areas. It is highly recommended.

In 1993, the British Brick Society celebrated the twenty-first anniversary of its founding. The general objectives of this society are to study bricks used in the British Isles from the Roman times to the present day; Continental bricks and brickwork and their influence on the domestic post-Roman development; to determine, in the absence of written evidence, the origins of bricks by geological, physical and chemical examination; to support the preservation and conservation of bricks and brickwork, clayfields and brickfields and to provide an archive and record system relating to brick. This is available to members and anyone else interested in its study, and is continually being added to by the regular publication of information newsletters.

Brickmaking in an automated 'green age'

It was obvious that the brick industry was going to have to slim itself and invest heavily in automation, pollution control, energy efficiency,

Figure 1.17 Modern brickmaking – a computer-controlled automated process. An overview of the 'Whinney Hill' factory, Accrington, where the famous 'Nori' brick is made, showing the manufacturing and packing lines (photograph reproduced by kind permission of Marshalls Clay Products).

and improve its product range for the highly critical and competitive markets of the 1980s and 1990s.

Automation was rapid, with all areas of production involved, reducing the need for manpower (see figure 1.17), so that by 1988 there were only 205 brickyards, 171 producing clay bricks, 30 concrete bricks and 4 calcium silicate bricks, in an industry employing fewer than 12,000 people. In the 'green age', brick production had to control not only its waste emissions but also its fuel consumption. This is still being achieved by investment in 'scrubbers', as well as changing to new kilns with different fuels giving greater control, and recycling the products of combustion within the process, often under computer control. Strong commitment is also made to controlled land-fill and re-landscaping to improve the use of otherwise waste ground.

During the 1970s much development time was spent to get a more attractive facing brick for a more discerning client and to package it more effectively. Hand-made bricks became, and have remained, very popular, and the big companies did not want to miss out on this lucrative market. Further developing a soft-mud process, pioneered in Holland, manufacturers could imitate hand moulding by machine. Ordinary mass-produced facing bricks were developed in more aesthetically pleasing tones and surface patterns than the majority of bland facings of the 1960s.

The bricks were now delivered by self-stack systems, often in polythene-wrapped packs of about 450 bricks – a far cry from the expensive, time-consuming process of unloading by the recipient firm which used to be necessary.

The BS3921 classification for bricks was revised in 1974 and again in 1985, giving new tolerances on work size limits and a revised durability classification. BS4729, 1971, for special shape bricks was also revised in 1990, as was BS6649 for metric modular bricks, in 1985. All these are covered in detail in Chapter 4 of this volume.

At the time of writing fourteen European member countries have been formalizing the draft CEN proposals for a European standard for clay and calcium silicate units and when these specifications have been adopted, member countries will be required to adopt them instead of their existing national standards.

So we have observed through the centuries the gradual development of the brick, so much associated with Great Britain and its buildings. It is currently enjoying a renaissance in use and in imaginative design, pleasing to all involved in its production and use.

With today's efficient and well-informed companies producing high quality products, the future looks very bright especially with the opening of the European markets. Of course there will be imports; at present they stand at just over 2%, but this has often been due to booms when domestic supplies cannot meet the demand.

The British brick is of good quality, excellent appearance, and is produced in an unrivalled range of colours and textures at an economic price. The trend for yards to close would appear to have reached a turning point and many old yards, especially those producing hand-made bricks for an increasingly conservation-minded consumer and discerning clients, are re-opening and working again. Despite many variations in material, size and manufacture to the standard brick for a multiplicity of reasons, the general shape has and will, I am sure, remain substantially the same in the foreseeable future.

2

Bricklaying – the Evolving Craft

THE MEDIEVAL PERIOD (1200–1485)

The biggest employer for building work between 1200 and 1500 was the Church. As the period progressed, municipal and private work greatly increased, manifesting itself in the erection of town and guild halls, schools such as Eton (begun in 1440) and colleges such as Queens and Jesus at Cambridge. Other secular buildings constructed at this time included hospitals, almshouses and inns. Many used bricks, although these were expensive and were not employed for ordinary buildings. Their use was confined to the east and south-east of England.

Early bricks were irregular in size and shape, not only as a result of poorly controlled burning but also a lack of any national regulation concerning size. In some walling a difference in whole bricks of 2" (51mm) in length is not uncommon, even in one course. Measurements at Herstmonceaux Castle (c.1440) show variations, in what is intended to be about a 2" (51mm) thick brick, from between 1¾" (44mm) to 2⅝" (66mm). A gauge of four courses (both bricks and joints) could therefore vary quite considerably. The bricklayer was compelled to lay thick mortar joints (1″ or 25mm not being un-common), to even out these irregularities. The cross-joints could not always absorb the differing brick lengths so that straight joints occurred occasionally.

Bonding – the structural and aesthetic rationale

The bonding of brick used in the most important buildings generally followed accepted rules. These buildings were constructed by brick-layers such as immigrant Flemish craftsmen fully conversant with craft practices. The majority of bonding, though, was haphazard. It is common to find mainly stretcher courses, with occasional headers to bond back into the inner walling. Sometimes the arrangement at the quoin is technically correct, yet regular bonding is lost along and within the wall. This tells us much about the native builder, who was learning a new craft yet still not fully conversant with its rules and subtleties. Like the mason, he was aware of the need to level, plumb and bond his work, but as with stonework, the bonding arrangement was more flexible and inconsistencies was accepted. This is particu-larly noticeable with the occasional straight joint where a cutting arrangement (to maintain the bond pattern) would have seemed correct to a skilled bricklayer, even of this period. The need fully to interlock these lightweight brick units to maximize their strength was not properly appreciated.

The skills required for building the circular staircase at Rye House gatehouse (c.1443) appear to draw on contemporary stonemasonry practice. Vaulting, corbelling and arch construction all demonstrate how these resourceful craftsmen adapted brick to work previously executed in stone, under the watchful eye of the master mason (*Magister Cementariorum*).

With the advance of knowledge the need for improved bonding, to obtain stability and enhance the brickwork's appearance, was becom-ing better understood. Foreign influences, especially from Holland, Germany and France, helped to determine bonding techniques. Knights returned from France during the Hundred Years War im-pressed with French brick castle construction, and the Gothic brick architecture of Lübeck, Danzig and Ratzburg had a powerful appeal for rich merchant travellers.

Brick patterning and ornamentation

Bricklayers in the late medieval period did attempt simple flat pattern-ing of brickwork, with polychromatic work using overburnt or vitrified bricks laid as headers in simple diaper patterns. These are rudimentary, rarely consistent and erratically positioned – for example, the work at Tattershall Castle (*c.*1434–5), and Herstmonceux (*c.*1440).

The use of purpose-moulded bricks, or burnt bricks shaped by the brick axe, developed from this time. Many fifteenth-century buildings reveal flamboyant and confident use of brick strings, panels and elaborate trefoil and quatrefoil tracery. The majority involved the use of brick, rendered to imitate the stone which it was replacing. Nevertheless, it is brickwork of great skill and energy.

The craft guilds

In the late twelfth century the emergence of boroughs was associated with the establishment of merchant and craft guilds. Towns bought exemption from feudal exactions, and the guild secured the livelihood of member craftsmen by regulating craft practices, training apprentices and controlling the quality of products. Guilds could only be created by a licence from the monarch. Every guild paid a yearly farm (from medieval Latin *firma* – fixed payment – a fixed annual charge in composition for taxes or other monies) to the king's exchequer.

There were two aspects of guild activities: the 'mistery' or 'mystery', and the 'fraternity'. The former regulated and controlled the trade of guild members; the latter constituted the brotherhood, which helped to relieve economic distress among members. This aspect, sanctioned by Church authorities, encouraged a spirit of amity. The fraternity was usually dedicated to a saint, often the patron saint of that craft, and guild members would attend church on the saint's feast day, electing members to positions within the guild each year. Guilds were concerned with maintaining standards of workmanship, materials, training, continuity of work and a strict control of new craftsmen starting up in the area.

Apprenticeships

The earliest records of apprenticeships in the building industry date from the fourteenth century. Each guild had officers called 'searchers' who would oversee the treatment of apprentices ('apprentice' from the old French 'aprentys' or 'aprendre' 'to learn'). Searchers ensured that apprentices were properly housed and fed, not made to work on Sundays, received proper instruction in the craft, and did not divulge the secrets or 'mysteries'. They would also see that the apprentice kept the promises contained in the 'indenture', a binding contract between master and apprentice executed in two or more copies, which were placed together so that their irregularly cut top edges were correspondingly 'indented'. (See figure 2.1)

Until the nineteenth century the apprenticeship period was seven years, a term laid down in an Ordinance of 4 June 1518 which formalized a long-standing practice. The signing of the deed usually took place when the apprentice was thirteen or fourteen years old. The period of time served was linked with the journey from boyhood to manhood. The apprentice gained maturity and experience as well as skill and knowledge. The father or mother (or priest) could sign, though other signatories might include the master-craftsman (the employer) the master of the guild, a lawyer, or sometimes the mayor, representing the freemen. A premium would be paid, not only as a source of money from which the apprentice could be paid over the years of his apprenticeship, at carefully graded rates, but also as a large payment to his master.

Allegiance to the guild, upon recognition of achieving craft qualification, was secondary to civic freedom, or becoming a freeman. Serving one's apprenticeship would lead, on passing the final trade test, to the swearing of allegiance to the mayor and becoming a freeman.

If the newly qualified craftsman wanted to set up on his own account, he had to pay an entry fee (often divided between his guild and the town) and perhaps even host a dinner for his master, master of the guild, and the mayor.

To become a 'journeyman' an apprentice would produce a piece of work which clearly demonstrated his knowledge, skill and ability. This became known as his 'masterpiece'. It would be submitted for assessment to a selected group of masters and if judged to be of suitable quality the craftsman would be granted guild recognition in his new status as a 'free' journeyman, no longer 'bound' to his master. 'Journeyman' is derived from the old French 'journée', meaning a day or a day's travel; hence a journeyman was one who had served his apprenticeship but was qualified to seek work only within a day's journey, and for a day's wage. If he moved to another part of England he would have to prove his ability to the guild in the new area before he would be entitled to pursue his craft.

Until the seventeenth century, work for a single trade was by the 'gross contract', organized and controlled by a master mason assisted by a clerk of works. This system operated by inviting estimates from master craftsmen, either on a schedule of rates or a lump sum basis, to do all or part of a contract. It worked well while the construction of buildings remained relatively simple, involving only a few crafts, and while the cost of work could be based on the experience of similar past work.

The need for craftsmen employed on large building tasks often led the Crown to exercise its powers of 'impressment'. In 1483, for

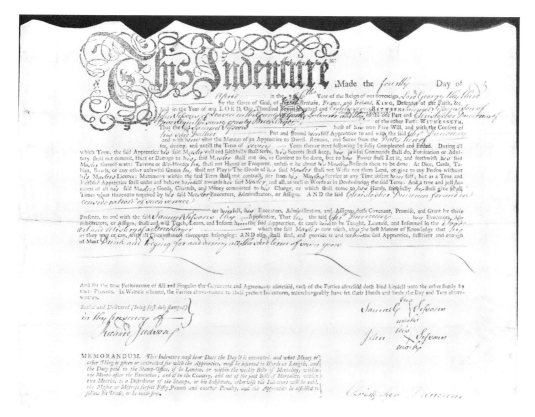

Figure 2.1 An indenture. On this eighteenth-century apprenticeship indenture the 'deckling' or indenting can be clearly seen. The apprentice and his father have only been able to make their marks. It is interesting to note when studying these deeds that until the early nineteenth century the apprentice is recorded as learning the 'art and mystery of a Bricklayer'. From then on it is usually written 'manual trade of a Bricklayer' (DDX 24/281, reproduced by kind permission of the County Archivist, Humberside County Archive Office, Beverley).

example, King Richard III issued a warrant to 'take' bricklayers and labourers:

> for us certaine brikwarke at our towne of Carlisle and other places. We desiring the hasty perfourmyng of the same have yeuen unto our said seruaunt power, licence and auctorite by these our lettres, to take as many artificers expert in breke leying and labourers to serue them for our wages as vnto hym shal be thought necessaire and expedient for the speedy avauncement of our said werkes.

Hours of work were very long, especially in the summer time: from 4 am until 7 pm (that is, seventy hours a week or more) and were worked according to local rules and agreements, which varied greatly. Not until 1495 was there a measure to regulate hours of work. Once the winter and bad weather started, hours worked were dramatically reduced. In frosty weather the pure lime mortars then in use hardened very slowly. All masonry work was covered with straw, and work ceased.

On large building programmes viewers ('visores'), or inspectors, certified the work, and checked accounts rendered by the clerk of works (*Clericus Operacionum*), the most important man on the site.

THE TUDOR PERIOD (1485–1603)

This was the first great age of brick in England. The material began to enjoy a very wide popularity, in contrast to its previous limited use. No longer considered inferior to stone, its use spread from East Anglia and the south-east into London and the Midlands. Cardinal Wolsey (1475–1530), chose brick when he began Hampton Court Palace in 1515. Brick became so highly regarded that rich courtiers and merchants chose to use it for their mansions. Its social acceptance was clear, although stone continued in normal use in the north and west of England. Brick was the primary building material for the castles at Deal and Walmer, the first time in England that brickwork had been used for engineering construction.

Tudor brickwork exudes confidence and one sees its use for show as well as utility, with the use of many extravagant and elaborate shapes for the cut and moulded openings. They are used for the Octagonal bays, towers and the richly decorated chimney stacks on the manor and gate houses such as Layer Marney, Essex (*c.*1523), and the inner gatehouse of Leez Priory, Essex (*c.*1536–7). As the brickwork was essentially walling in a Gothic masonry style, it possessed plinth and parapet, buttresses and gables. The Tudors favoured a more depressed arch, with straight sloping bricks rather than curved ones.

Diapers,* a flat-patterning of bricks of different colours, remained very popular on plain walling, but this technique now involved a more disciplined, regular arrangement. Overburnt or 'flared' headers presented dark, often shiny surfaces ranging from deep purple to slate in colour, laid carefully in quarter-brick offsets in mainly a modified English bond (which was virtually standard by then) or English cross-bond to form diamonds, lozenges, saltire-cross, chevrons, zigzags, keys and even hearts. This needed great care, and seriously impaired the bricklayers' rhythm and work-rate. (See figure 2.2) To cover up variations in shade and to give further emphasis to the diaper work, the predominantly red brickwork was often colour-washed in

---

* T. P. Smith has an interesting article 'The Diaper Work at Queen's College Cambridge', in The British Brick Society, *Information*, no. 55, pp. 20–23 (March 1992).

red ochre ('ruddle'), the coloured double-struck jointed joints being picked out again by painting ('pencillyng') with lime. Good examples of diaper work are to be seen at the Deanery Tower at Hadleigh, Suffolk (*c*.1489–90), the porch-towers of Hatfield Old Palace, Herts. (*c*.1480–90) and Hampton Court Palace (Base Court, 1514–29).

Windows, simple in form and proportion, were grouped in twos or threes with a stone or brick 'label' or head mould over them. The arch heads were flat, often cut from a single block of stone or moulded and rendered brickwork, the triangular corner spaces carved with a three-corner depression, faintly reminiscent of tracery. Larger domestic windows were of the perpendicular type, rectangular shapes formed by the stone or brick mullions and transoms.

The brick chimney

It is with the introduction of the brick chimney stack that the sixteenth century is largely associated. This was directly the result of the increased use of a new fuel, coal, whose foul smoke had to be quickly removed in flues. The flues were from 14″ × 9″ (350mm × 229mm), and wider, and at their upper ends chimney stacks, a riot of carved, moulded, and patterned brickwork, punctuated the roof-line. Chimneys of the bigger houses are often works of consummate skill which are a testament to a high level of craftsmanship.

Fireplaces up to 14′ (4.2m) wide and 5′ (1.5m) deep remained fashionable. At their back specially hard 'firebricks' were used, often laid in herring-bone or chevron bond patterns. Early fireplaces were on external walls because they were often later additions to buildings which had previously utilised a simple central hearth, with no formal flue arrangements. By the beginning of the sixteenth century many house owners wanted chimneys of brick, even if the house was timber-framed or stone, as a display of affluence. These chimneys were also much safer, and greatly reduced the risk of fire.

Terracotta (hard burnt clay moulded to provide architectural details), enjoyed a vogue from around 1520 to 1570. It was often executed by Italian craftsmen, and decorated brick buildings with architectural elements usually in stone, such as transoms, roundels and the acroteria on pediments.

During the reign of Elizabeth I a series of great country houses was built. The new educated class of lawyers, doctors and wealthy merchants, demanded more comfort and amenities from their buildings, and were anxious for their houses to be 'tricked-out' in all the latest fashionable details. The Renaissance or 're-birth' of classical forms, had begun in fourteenth-century Florence. Its effects on English architecture did not come directly from Italy, but from France, Germany

Figure 2.2 Tudor diaper work at Farnham Castle, *c.*1508.

and through the Low Countries, usually transmitted through the medium of builders' pattern books.

Asymmetrically planned early Tudor houses such as Compton Wynyates (*c.*1480–1528) now gave way to houses with more symmetrical façades and layouts, such as Longleat (*c.*1568) and Hardwick (*c.*1591). Windows became very large, with bays consisting of simple grids of mullions and horizontal transoms with diamond- or square-shaped leaded panes. Arches were less popular, window heads being preferred flat with either a Gothic label or Classical moulding.

Bonding patterns remained similar to those of the early sixteenth century, but the first signs of the adoption of Flemish bond appeared in this period. At Woodham Walter Church, Essex (*c.*1563), removal of long-established rendering revealed stretchers and headers, alternating as in Flemish bond with a course of stretchers in between, termed 'Flemish stretcher bond'. Gable walls were constructed so as to project above the roof, with stone copings set with 'kneelers' at the base and 'finials' at the apex. Some gables were connected by a parapet wall or balustrade. Chimneys were no longer the spectacular achievements of Henry VIII's reign, being mainly plain, circular, square or rectangular in section, although remaining tall and in stacks of pairs or threes built to resemble columns.

The Tylers and Bricklayers Company

In London the guilds were powerful and many sought the monarch's permission to be incorporated, being a legal requirement to facilitate

Figure 2.3 The coat of arms of the Worshipful Company of Tylers and Bricklayers, as displayed in the Bridewell Museum, Norwich. The extended arm held a brick axe similar to the two on either side of the shield (photograph reproduced by kind permission of J. Kenneth Major).

Figure 2.4 A tudor bricklayer building a wall while his attendant mixes mortar (from *Robert the Devyll*, printed by Wynkyn de Worde; reproduced by permission of Gwynfor Williams).

the holding of land and allowing the right to sue in cases of legal disputes. The London trade guilds were historically represented by the livery companies, so called because they formerly had a distinctive costume which certain members were permitted to wear on special occasions.

The existence of the Tylers and Bricklayers Company in the fourteenth and early fifteenth centuries is rather obscure, sometimes recognized by city authorities, sometimes not. However, in 1568 after a new set of rules and ordinances was approved by the City Corporation, their standing as a livery company was accepted. In the same year they approached Queen Elizabeth and were granted a royal charter of incorporation, some time after most of the other trades, such as the Carpenters (1477), and the Plasterers (1501). The delay was due in some measure to the struggle for recognition as a skilled craft, against the powerful stone masons, and the vested interests of employers, who did not want the the employment of bricklayers to be encumbered by guild rules and restrictions at a time when brick was becoming so important in the building process. (See figure 2.3)

It is worth noting some of the details contained in the royal charter. The 'area of search' was a fifteen-mile radius from the old city walls. Bricks for sale were to be 9″ × 4½″ × 2½″ (229mm × 115mm × 63mm) – the so-called 'statute brick'. No one could engage an apprentice until he was four years a freeman and none was to keep more than one apprentice until he had been a 'younger warden', when he became privileged to keep two. The master and wardens had to approve the employer to ensure he was 'able as well as cunning, sufficient to and for the instruction of the apprentices in ability and substance'.

During Elizabeth's reign a fundamental change took place regarding the responsibility for craft training. Hitherto, it had lain solely with the craft guilds, which laid down the conditions under which all trades should operate. Many new employers were refusing to be hampered by guild restrictions, and they transferred their activities to the outlying villages where they could exploit their workers without infringing regulations.

This abuse of employment regulations was a matter of grave concern to the government, which endeavoured to end it by several Acts of Parliament, notably the Statute of Artificers (1563). This regulated conditions of employment, and in the same year the Statute of Apprentices stipulated that no person was to exercise a trade unless he had served a seven-year apprenticeship to it.

Like most laws, the statute was open to abuse by some, who interpreted it as only applying to the towns or as being restricted to trades recognized as existing before 1563. This latter point was used by the judiciary in 1600 in a judgement which stated, in rather callous terms, that bricklayers did not come within the terms of the statute, as theirs was an art 'which requires rather ability of body than of skill' – a poor compliment indeed at the opening of the century that was to see the craft of the bricklayer flourish and produce work of consummate skill. (See figure 2.4)

THE STUART PERIOD (1603–1714)

In congested towns owners were encouraged to build their houses in brick instead of timber. The aim was to reduce the risk of fire. In 1605 James I issued a proclamation requiring all persons to build 'their fore fronts and windows either of brick or stone as well as for decay as by reason that all great and well grown woods are much spent and wasted, so as timber for shipping waxes scarce.'

Timber-framed houses

The majority of timber-framed houses with us today were built in the years between 1550 and 1642, incorporating large-section oak beams, prefabricated as wall-frames and roof-trusses by carpenters on the ground. In 1530 Palsgrave wrote 'my house is framed all redye; it wanteth but setting-up'.

Bricklayers were often called in to build a low foundation wall a few courses high, called a 'pinning', to prevent the wood from rotting through contact with the ground. Although initially 'infill' in the spaces between the members of the timber-frame was of wattle and daub, this was often replaced with brick, which was more weather-resistant and rodent-proof, and eventually a brick infill became a standard form of construction. The brickwork was often built in the geometric patterns in which the builders of these periods delighted, most commonly in herring-bone style, the bricks aslant to each other at 45°. This method developed its own internal tightening as the bricks locked together, and so strengthened the bond.

English bond or English cross bond remained popular throughout this period. Diaper work was now less well regarded, and the demand for patterning was partly met with bas-relief, geometrical 'strapwork' designs of Teutonic origin. Foundation walls, internal brickwork and the backs of external walls often continued to be mixed with random rubble or stonework, using local outcrops where available; this was partly designed to reduce brick costs. Dressed stone remained very popular for quoin blocks, openings, parapets balustrades and copings.

The Stuarts were great lovers of the arts and patrons of learning. Increased contact with France, Spain and Italy heralded a shift in architecture towards refinement of taste and the use of more varied materials. This fashion was led by Inigo Jones (1573–1652), who was looking to Italy as the source of the classical tradition of building. He was the first in Britain to be fully conversant with the laws laid down

Figure 2.5 A bricklayer at work, from an engraving dated 1695. The bricklayer wears an apron, common until the nineteenth century, and lifts his mortar from a shortened barrel, a practice which died out in the following century. His labourer carries his mortar in an early type of hod, a wicker basket (reproduced by kind permission of Hulton Deutsch).

by Andrea Palladio (1508–1580) in *Quattro Libri dell Architettura* (1570), giving emphasis to classical proportions and usage. Jones' work was thus classed as Palladian. From this point onwards the influence of the architect (from the Greek *architekton*, meaning 'builder-in-chief'), as opposed to the master builder, on the design and control of a new building, was becoming more significant. It was important that someone with understanding and knowledge of the subject was in charge, although details were traditionally decided by the client in consultation with his skilled craftsmen as the building progressed. Now within rigidly laid down convention, the architect would insist on the master bricklayer interpreting his drawings faithfully, with little scope being allowed for individual freedom.

These new methods were accompanied by changes in working practices. The tendency in the seventeenth century was to carry out work by contract. The contractor, usually a mason if the building was in stone or brick, provided the labour while the owner supplied the materials. Sometimes a master bricklayer might take the contract for a lump sum: in such cases he also undertook to find skilled craftsmen from allied trades. (See figure 2.5)

The Artisan Mannerist movement

The struggle between severely classical architecture and traditional styles of building manifested itself in a new provincial style which grew up around the Stuart court prior to the Civil War, and was based on the influence from northern European models. The Dutch influence was especially strong, made popular by the proliferation of pattern books which were often used by master builders. This led to a nationally influential style of architecture known today as 'Artisan Mannerist', so called because of the licence the builders (artisans) took with the rules of classical architecture. It existed in various forms in the years between Jones and the neo-Palladianism of the eighteenth century. Decorative gables were fashionable in a variety of 'Dutch forms' and skilful handling of brick to shape and build classical columns, pilasters and moulded openings all emphasized the advances in the use of the medium. The Dutch House, Kew Gardens, London (*c*.1631) is an influential example of the style. Others are Cromwell House, Highgate, London (*c*.1637–40), Broome Park, Kent (1635–38), Ball Park, Hertfordshire (*c*.1640) Tytenhanger Park, Hertfordshire (*c*.1655).

Fine craftsmanship in brick

The brickwork in the century from 1660 is considered by many authorities to be some of the finest artistic and skilful achievements in the world. Bricklayers, especially those in London where the centre of commercial and social activity lay, were keen to be recognized as intelligent, articulate and highly skilled. They had to be conversant with and able to reproduce the latest architectural fashions and craft practices. Among the most notable were Peter Mills (1598–1670), a master bricklayer, often referred to as an 'artisan architecht', who worked with Inigo Jones and was twice master of the Tylers and Brick-layers Company. He designed Thorpe Hall (1653–4), and houses attrib-uted to him in Great Queen Street, London, are said to have laid down the cannon of street design for the next two hundred years. Venturus Mandey (1645–1701) was the author of several esteemed books, includ-ing *Mellificium Mensionus: or The Marrow of Measuring* (1682). It is thought he advised Moxon in his book *Mechanick Excercises* (1684).

Finishing the mortar joints

Jointing, or applying a finish to the bedding mortar, was now widely practised in profiles to emphasize level and plumb on the irregular mortar joints. One style was the ruled joint where a thin-bladed jointer formed a groove running on a straight-edge to the centre of the joint. By the end of the period pointing (or the application of a superior strength mortar to the raked-out joints of weaker and slow setting bedding mortar) in similar profiles was rapidly accepted, especially for the most important elevations. Using a mortar coloured to match the bricks helped to minimize the impact of the joints, allowing classical detailing to be displayed from a broad façade, and not a series of busy units which could distract the eye. Tuck pointing was the ultimate development in this quest. In this the real joint was disguised and hidden behind a false joint which was formed by a ribbon of white lime putty and fine sand, and laid into a thin groove with a jointer.

Gauged brickwork

A second and more expensive solution was to use colour-matched red bricks of a clean sandy-textured clay, baked rather than burnt, which could be cut and rubbed to precise dimensions, for laying by dipping into a slurry of sieved lime putty and fine sand mortar, and laid with joints of $\frac{1}{16}''$ (2mm) or less. This class of brickwork, known as 'cut and rubbed' or gauged work, was introduced from Holland. The earliest known example of its use is at The Dutch House, Kew Gardens, London (1631). (See figure 2.6) It was improved and popularized by Sir Christopher Wren, an early example of his work being the entrance porches at Kings Bench Walk, London (*c.*1667).

Brickwork in the Mannerist styles allowed city bricklayers to display,

Figure 2.6 Kew Palace, London, formerly known as the 'Dutch House', has the earliest known use of both gauged brickwork and correct Flemish bonding.

with pride and confidence, craftsmanship founded on a sound knowledge of geometry and superb skill of hand. 'Turning' arches of precisely cut voussoirs, often with raised brick keystones; flat arches, decorated with carved 'cupid's bow'; scrolls; and fleurs-de-lys. Ornate aprons and other classical features included moulded cornices enriched with acanthus, anthemion and egg-and-tongue decoration and in some instances with carved *in situ* Corinthian capitals. All these devices were cut with the brick-axe, chisels and small hand saws, rubbed and moulded with an assortment of stones and files.

From this period, until well into the nineteenth century, many buildings had raised quoins with a slight 'batter' or incline, possibly to give added resistance to the thrust from the roof, but also influenced by the use of entasis in classical architecture.

Early building legislation

The Great Fire of London in 1666 caused extreme destruction. The ashes were barely cold when Charles II issued a Royal Proclamation, consolidated by the Building Act of 1667, regarding the rebuilding of London. It ordered that no more timber-framed houses were to be erected. In future only brick and stone were to be used. This Act was the foundation of the modern system of building regulation. It also instructed that no timber was to be positioned within one foot (304mm), of the 'foreside' of the jambs of a chimney; all joists at the rear of any chimney were to be 'trimmed' six inches (152mm) from the back; and no timber was to be laid in the 'tunnel' (or flue) of any chimney.

In the Building Act of 1670 the Bricklayers Company acquired from the Carpenters Company the chartered privilege of providing 'visores' (viewers) of new buildings. Bricklayers were now considered better qualified because of the predominance of brick in the reconstructed parts of the fire-damaged city.

The changing fortunes of the guilds

It is an irony that the hugely increased volume of work using brick should have brought disaster to the Company controlling the craft. 'Freemen' bricklayers were hopelessly inadequate in numbers to tackle the job of reconstruction, yet company rules excluded craftsmen from the provinces (or 'foreigners' as they were referred to). Parliament dealt quickly with this matter by decreeing, in the Re-Building Act of 1667, that all craftsmen who were not freemen of the City would, upon being set to reconstruction work, be entitled to the same privileges and 'enjoy the same liberty to work as freemen of the said City for and during their natural lives'.

Craftsmen flocked from the provinces to London to secure work under state protection. The Company was unable to insist on the previous conditions of servitude. 'Unfree' craftsmen were able to keep as many apprentices as they saw fit, and so obtained work which freemen of the Company would have undertaken if their rules allowed them the same flexibility. Despite new laws allowing more apprentices to members, it was a hopeless struggle. The Company was losing its monopoly, and its members were finding the benefits of membership minimal.

The Company was active in examining journeymen for evidence of apprenticeships in distant towns, to ensure they were proficient and to prevent them working in any other trade. Arguments arose, even in court, with 'foreign' bricklayers working their trade, and the open hostility did not cease until the long task of rebuilding neared completion and the labour demand contracted. This loosening of the regulations was a blow from which the Tylers and Bricklayers Company would never recover: the old restrictions within the guild system were dying out.

Some discontented freemen-bricklayers emigrated to the American colonies in the late seventeenth century, mainly because of a large slump in activity following the boom years. They took with them their traditions, skills and styles to states such as Maryland and Virginia, where a tradition for fine brickwork grew up. They also founded American branches of the livery companies. (See figure 2.7)

Figure 2.7 Hammond-Harwood House, Annapolis, Maryland, built in 1774, is an outstanding example of American colonial architecture, made possible by the emigration of many highly skilled craftsmen (photograph courtesy of The Hammond-Harwood House Association).

Another outcome of the enforced union of City and foreign bricklayers in the 1660s was the adoption of the high skills displayed in gauged brickwork and some pointing styles. At a time when news and fashions normally travelled slowly, these sophisticated techniques spread rapidly across the country when the foreign bricklayers returned home, enriching the craft nationally. This trend helped to pave the way for the building practices of the Georgian period.

THE GEORGIAN PERIOD (1714–1837)

The brickwork of this period was largely a development of the fine work of the post-Restoration period. Brick was now cheaper and more fashionable than any other medium, and well regarded in domestic construction. Through its skilful use by Wren and his contemporaries, it was considered a prestigious material for the best of mansions. Brickwork was employed in huge quantities by the new breed of speculators appearing in the city, such as Nicholas Barbon (1640–1698) and later Thomas Cubitt (1788–1855).

Georgian builders often combined coloured bricks for a reticent polychromatic effect, around door and window jambs, pilasters and on some quoins. A frequently used device was to place paler bricks to bond, down the centre, framed by the darker reveal or quoin bricks. Another method on some houses produced a chequer pattern, in the Flemish bond, by contrasting coloured headers to stretchers.

A popular bricklaying practice was the use of selected first-class bricks called 'fronts' reserved for the outer face of the most important elevation and randomly bonded into the load-bearing skin of inferior and cheaper 'place' bricks. This 'façadism', popular from the late Stuart period, allowed for the brickwork design to be constructed with fashionable conceits. There seemed to have been little, if any, consideration of the structural requirements. Isaac Ware in *A Complete Body of Architecture* (1756) reveals this enthusiasm for purposes of economy without an awareness of the structural consequences, when he recommended that the 'Grey stocks are made of purer earth and better wrought, and they are used in fronts of building being the strongest and handsomest to this kind; the place bricks are made of the same clay, with a mixture of dirt and other loam material and are more carelessly put in hand, they are therefore weaker and more brittle, and are used out of sight and where less stress is laid upon them.' This was a serious contradiction as he, like almost all designers and master builders at this time of high fashion, seems oblivious to the fact that the strong bricks were used on a non-structural façade, while the 'back-up' brickwork (party walls and piers between windows supporting the floor joists, because they were to be plastered over) was built from weaker bricks aided only by the wall thickness – a dangerous practice.

Although header bond was employed in the early eighteenth century, often to display grey, flared faces, it was expensive. Flemish bond held the field almost without rival for face work, especially when an expensive 'front' brick was used, because the greater proportion of stretchers allowed the majority of headers to be 'snapped', thereby gaining two faces from one brick. The side and rear elevations would be of second-quality bricks laid in a 'garden wall bond' version of the face bond.

The Georgian builder was also capable of deliberate bad practices, especially in the now popular terraced houses. One such folly was raising the front elevation and party walls as the building progressed but leaving the rear wall until the roofing stage was reached. Lengths of wood laid within the brickwork, or 'bond timbers' as they were known, were there not only to help to retain level and line, and to provide tensile resistance, but also to provide a temporary restraint.

Window arches were generally flat – then termed 'streight' until the early eighteenth century, but this was largely superseded by the fashion for segmental arches between 1710 and 1730. The dominance of the flat arch was occasionally challenged by semi-circular, elliptical and (less often) Venetian and ogee arches. Usually the internal brickwork was supported by a timber lintel, with or without a relieving arch. The use of the projecting window cill stone also dates from this time, the cill often being placed over projecting 'aprons' of gauged brickwork on the more important windows.

In the 1670s the vertical sliding sash window was introduced, rapidly replacing the casement and remaining the standard domestic window until the end of the nineteenth century. When first introduced, the frame was to the front of the brickwork. However, the Building Act of 1709 ruled that the frame was to be set back to a depth of 4" (102mm) from the façade. The comprehensive London Building Act of 1774 placed another constraint on window frames: the box of the sash was not only to be set back from the façade, by 9" (229mm), but also to be recessed into the brick reveals behind the window jambs.

As a fire precaution the Act of 1774 virtually prohibited the use of exposed timber work on buildings, stating that fronts were to be of brick, stone, burnt clay, artificial stone or stucco. This Act also transferred the duties of 'viewers' in London from the Tylers and Bricklayers Company to specially appointed district surveyors. By the late eighteenth century the Tylers and Bricklayers Company's fortunes were waning. Despite various attempts to maintain their status, the loss of craft control within London meant that many City bricklayers failed to pay dues expected of them.

Georgian bricklayers worked either for an agreed lump sum for the whole structure, or on piecework priced by the trade at agreed rates. Architects remained loyal to a master-builder and employed craftsmen whose work they knew, could trust, and could design around. In London a large percentage of a craftsman's work was given to fellow craftsmen in return for favours in the future, a system of work-for-work. It appears to have been a very effective bartering system, facilitated by the continuity of similar work and collaboration by craftsmen, with limited recourse to cash payments. Contracts were signed and sealed with mutual agreement in a perfectly legal way.

Payment 'by the piece' was the universal procedure in the later eighteenth century and price books were recognized: fees were based on a rate for each $16\frac{1}{2}$ feet of bricks laid. The schedules for the various craft works were prepared by a clerk of works; these were then priced by selected master craftsmen and after comparing by the architect and the clerk of works, the lowest tender was accepted. Upon completion the work was measured and priced-out at the ratio in the original schedule, in agreement with the master bricklayer concerned, and paid by the clerk of works. The bricklayer paid his labourer by time worked, but worked himself by the piece.

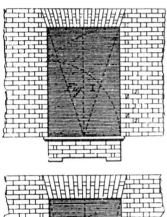

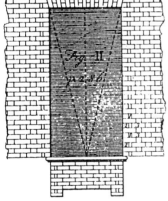

Figure 2.8 This plate from Batty Langley's *London Prices of Bricklayers' Materials and Work* (London, 1748) clearly illustrating the method for setting out the splay of the arch and how correctly to bond the 'streight arch' and the reveal to the rules of Flemish bond: 1 is a closer; 2 is a header; and 3 is a stretcher.

The influence of pattern books

Some architects, copying and adapting published designs of Palladio, Jones and many others, were able to provide builders with sufficient knowledge to erect a building to the satisfaction of the client. Publications also gave technical guidance to skilled craftsmen; examples include *The City and Country Builder's and Workman's Treasury of Designs* by Batty Langley (1740), and *The Complete Body of Architecture* by Isaac Ware (1756). (See figure 2.8) These enabled building owners to become more conversant with details of proposed works, a consequence of which was the erection of many fine buildings spoilt only by the repetition of detail. R. Campbell in *The London Tradesman* of 1747 warns of the perils of master bricklayers designing and building: 'A master bricklayer thinks himself capable to raise a brick house without the tuition of an architect . . . It is no new thing in London for these master builders to build themselves out of their own houses, and fix themselves in gaol with their own materials.'

The Brick and Window Taxes

By the middle of the eighteenth century brickwork was falling from favour as a face material, a decline which was not helped by the Brick Tax of 1784, imposed by William Pitt the younger (1759–1806), and repealed in 1850. This tax varied from 2s. 6d. (12.5p) to 10s. (50p) per 1,000 bricks without any maximum size limit. The Commissioners for Excise were responsible for its collection. A consequence was that for a time bricks were made larger (10″ × 5″ × 3″; 254mm × 127mm × 76mm) to reduce the tax liability, so a limit of 150 cubic inches was imposed for bricks of the standard rate, with a double rate for any bricks exceeding this size.

Another building tax in force throughout the Georgian period was the Window Tax, introduced in 1696 and increased in rate six times between 1746 and 1808 before being repealed in 1851. It is often blamed for the many 'bricked-up' or 'blind' windows, sometimes referred to as 'Pitt's Pictures', built during its period of enforcement. This is an understandable misconception. Certainly some windows were filled in to avoid the tax, but the majority were deliberately built 'blind' to maintain the architectural symmetry of the façade which, due to internal room arrangements, positioned walls inappropriate to a window opening. Another reason was that master builders insisted on adhering to pattern-book designs.

Brick facings fall from favour

A fashion in facing to emerge during the Brick Tax period (although not the result of it, as was previously thought) was the 'rebate', 'mathematical' or 'brick-tile', moulded so as to present a stretcher or header face of brick usually laid in mortar. It was attached by nails to oak battens fixed to the wall, either hung dry, or preferably bedded in mortar and pointed, to resemble fine jointed brickwork.

The desire for a stone appearance was met by the use of stucco (an Italian term for a particular mix of powdered marble and lime), an external rendering of differing patent mixes, ruled to suggest fine stone work. Stone was preferred for classical detailing but could only be afforded by the very wealthy, especially in the capital where there were no local quarries. Therefore, even when houses were not completely cloaked in stucco, features like cornices, quoin-blocks, capitals and voussoirs in arches were often stucco-modelled on a core of brickwork.

Terracotta came to prominence again during this period. The most famous factory was that founded by Eleanor Coade in the 1760s, producing the high-quality 'Coade stone' from 1767 until 1835. This artificial stone product was particularly prized for embellishments to openings, for arches with vermiculated voussoirs, rusticated with brick, and for a wide range of sculptured keystone motifs.

THE VICTORIAN AND EDWARDIAN
PERIODS (1837–1914)

The high level of building activity during the mid-eighteenth century had seen the complete disappearance of the medieval guild system, and the time-honoured hierarchy of master, journeyman and apprentice. By the beginning of the Victorian period, master bricklayers were relatively rare in London. Big businesses sprang up regulating wages and conditions of work, changing building from a craft-oriented industry to one of general contracting, a contractor estimating for a whole job. Diverse trades were employed by one master, who directed far more journeymen than could ever hope to become masters in their own time. This had early consequences in quality of craftsmanship for the embittered workers who had now lost control of their work, prices and traditions.

The housing speculator Thomas Cubitt pioneered mass production of building units such as window frames and doors, delivered to site for fixing only, in large development schemes such as Belgravia and Pimlico. However, not all speculators were imbued with such dignity and taste and many bought inexpensive land around factories for the construction of cheap high-density housing for the workers.

Most Victorian speculators began as craftsmen who sub-contracted other trades. Entry into the business was made relatively easy by the ready flow of capital seeking investment, and by builders' merchants extending generous credit. In 1878–80 (the high point of building activity) in the South London suburb of Camberwell, 416 builders were constructing 5,670 houses, helped by the emergence of large stockyards of bricks, mass production of joinery from foreign timber stocks and stone dressing under controlled conditions.

A shortage of architects and surveyors dragged down building standards, and subsequently the house designs. Terraces and estates went into a rapid architectural decline, and many unskilled labourers drifted to bricklaying from other worse-off trades, picking up enough knowledge to be profitable to the 'Jerry Builder'. This was an expression popular from the 1860s, given for the speculative builders who ran up insubstantial buildings of inferior materials and workmanship.

Despite hostility, the time-served craftsmen worked on the prestigious contracts or on the parts of a building requiring knowledge, experience and skill, but the rest of the trade was being flooded with cheap semi-skilled labour, content with lower rates than the craftsman bricklayer. These men usually worked on the parts of buildings where their lack of skill was less noticeable – inner walls backing-up the face work and sometimes flank and rear walls.

Bricklayers were assessed by, and rates of pay and type of work on the buildings were set by, the contractor. One common method, on buildings with cellars, was to place all the 'trowels' to work there, let the foreman bricklayer make his selection and give notice to any not coming up to the mark. Such was the demand for industrial housing, however, that many unsuitable men still found work on buildings.

The bad mortar era

The popularity of stucco, especially in the Regency period (1800–1830), meant that many brickmakers took advantage by selling poor-quality bricks, knowing that these were to be hidden behind plaster. Unscrupulous builders in pursuit of further profit also skimped on the quality of mortar by using inferior lime, and even the sweepings of lime stone roads called 'road drift'. The quality was often so bad that fires had to be lit against thin, propped walls to encourage the 'mortar' to stiffen.

Despite fines, the temptation for speculators to cheat when so much brickwork was being erected meant that such practices were not fully controlled when the fashion for face brickwork returned after 1840. Not until a number of collapses took place in the course of construction in the 1870s, followed by a huge public and political outcry, did enforceable Building Acts appear, such as the Public Health Act (1875) and new model bye-laws in 1877.

The rise of the engineer

Although once seen as incompatible, the aesthetic and functional elements of industrial architecture were combined as the engineer came into prominence. The design and building of tunnels, bridges and sewers for the industrial infrastructure were largely met by the use of cheap bricks. Sir Marc Brunel (1769–1849) was a civil engineer who devised an effective method of reinforcing and bonding brickwork by laying lengths of hoop-iron in every fourth or fifth course. Introduced c.1825, this technique rapidly replaced the use of bond timbers and was quickly adopted throughout the industry. Brunel's design for the brick bridge over the Thames at Maidenhead (c.1838), involved twin semi-elliptical arches each of 128 feet (39m) span with a rise of only 24 feet (8.5m), an amazing feat requiring a great understanding of load and support, combined with confident audacity.

The early Victorian bricklayer still worked with tools of iron similar to those of his medieval ancestor, with the plumb bob to level and

Figure 2.9 A bricklayer at work on his walls of 1½ brick in thickness, *c.*1836. Note that he still uses a level similar to his medieval ancestors which utilizes the lead plumb-bob (reproduced by kind permission of the Mary Evans Picture Library).

plumb his work. (See figure 2.9) By the end of Victoria's reign these tools were mainly of steel, and the spirit level had become commonplace for levelling work on the many machine-pressed regular bricks, although the plumb rule for checking verticals remained in common use for another fifty years.

The fall and rise of the craft and its guilds

Training through 'time-serving' varied little from the sixteenth century onwards. The Statute of Apprentices (1563) was not being enforced, being seen by the Government and employers as outdated and not suited to the new market place. This left apprentices and journeymen powerless to safeguard their positions and secure a livelihood.

In 1814 the clauses empowering the justices of the peace to fix wages and dealing with apprentices were repealed. The prevailing spirit of 'laissez-faire' meant that the building industry was not investing in its future, with provision for apprenticeships, and although a seven-year apprenticeship was theoretically operational, it could in reality be as short as four or five years. Everything was a matter of tradition rather than law.

Figure 2.10 A membership certificate of the Operative Bricklayers Society dated 15 July 1893. The design, painted in 1863 by A. J. Waudby, clearly shows a desire to be associated with the old craft guilds and for the craft itself to be seen as rooted firmly in skills linked with knowledge (photograph by D. Seddon, reproduced by kind permission of the Working-Class Movement Library, Salford).

The craft guilds and livery companies no longer had control over craftsmen. The Combination Acts (1799), introduced by William Pitt, meant that journeymen's clubs could be lawfully suppressed and members fined, or even transported, for conspiracy. Only the old 'companies' or guilds were allowed.

The guilds' introverted, medieval procedures were not appropriate for this new market place where the rush to build a new industrial economy was sweeping aside many old practices.

The Tylers and Bricklayers Company managed to recoup many of the financial losses of the eighteenth century, and this money was used wisely to keep a close alliance with the craft it represented. Although its powers of search and craft supervision had long since lapsed, it concentrated much of its effort in supporting the building trade training schools. In the 1870s and '80s, to ensure a future supply of much-needed bricklayers skilled in the craft, the company gave a £25 premium to master bricklayers willing to take apprentices. This sponsorship succeeded in salvaging many skills, badly needed for the next century, that might otherwise have been lost.

In 1878 the City and Guilds of London Institute was established by the Corporation of the City of London (the 'City') and certain of the London Livery Companies (the 'Guilds') for the advancement of technical education. In the 1890s, by examinations of apprentices and journeymen, it was hoped to bring skilled recruits to bricklaying. The Tylers and Bricklayers Company, in a substantial grant to the City and Guilds, helped to support the project by giving £20 towards medals and prizes to encourage industrious study.

The emergence of the newly legalized trade unions of 1870s meant overall conditions began to improve for building craftsmen and some sense of craft pride returned. The bricklayers had founded the Operative Bricklayers Society (OBS) in 1848. (See figure 2.10) Yet even as late as the 1890s the sociologist Charles Booth (1840–1916), estimated in his survey of workers in London that 55% of its bricklayers lived in poverty.

In 1834 a ten-hour working day had been secured; working until 4 pm produced a sixty-hour week. In 1862 payment methods changed from the day to the hour. By the 1870s a nine-hour, six-day week was standard. Security of work was tenuous: even in 1892 one hour's notice to 'stand off' was accepted practice all over London. By 1913 there was a revival of sub-contracting, and of small firms run by masters who insisted on piecework, and this led the unions to claim that 'conditions are worse than twenty years ago'.

Terracotta

Bricklayers worked with materials other than brick to maintain their place on the masonry of a building. Terracotta and faience, in red or buff colour, enjoyed a period of popularity, partly as a result of a series of strikes by stonemasons from 1840 until 1877. It provided a convenient architectural substitute for stone, which could be installed by bricklayers. For ten years from 1877 the OBS fought hard against the

masons' and plasterers' organizations to drive all but themselves off
this work, a struggle which was only abandoned because the plasterers were too strong. It was also during this period that tall terracotta
chimney pots – a cheap way of terminating a flue, gaining height
without brickwork, and improving the draught of chimney stacks –
became such a feature of the skyline.

A revolution in mortar

Despite the problem of bad mortar described above, the rapid development of natural cements (hydraulic limes), such as Roman cement,
provided mortars which set more quickly and were stronger, a change
vital to the speed of construction and strength of building which the
new industrial age demanded. Technical books of the period emphasized this, condemning the use of chalk (non-hydraulic) lime for
mortar. The mid-nineteenth century saw the introduction of artificial
Portland cements, which were to bring about a revolution in building
techniques, especially for use in concrete foundations, although they
did not significantly replace lime as the major binder in mortar until
well after the turn of the century.

Figure 2.11 Bricklayers at work in Salford, *c.*1805. This picture clearly shows the
favoured northern style of building 'overhand' off the planked floor joists and laying the bricks in the popular English Garden Wall bond. The bricklayers wear
bowler hats as a symbol of craft status; the cloth-capped apprentice is adjusting
the line and pin. Against the back wall rests the plumb rule, still an essential tool
for checking verticality (photograph D. Seddon, reproduced by kind permission of
Salford Local History Library, City of Salford Arts and Leisure Department).

Victorian bonding practices

The late Victorians rarely indulged in 'façadism', and instead bonded the facing bricks into their thick walls. On good contracts when building thinner walls, usually under the watchful eye of the clerk of works, they lapped and interlocked the bricks ensuring well-bonded brickwork. Many 'party walls', however, continued to be only occasionally bonded into the front and rear walls. Grouting was widely practised, often with a hot fresh lime liquid mortar.

In this period many bonds came into use. Flemish remained the most popular choice for premier elevations in the south of the country, while header bond and other variations became popular in the North West. English bond held universal appeal for its undoubted strength in civil engineering brickwork, with variations in domestic use in the North. (See figure 2.11) Stretcher bond started to make an early appearance on some cavity walls.

Salt-glazed bricks became very popular in the second half of the period, and were prized for their clean hygienic surfaces – ideal for use in hospitals, toilets, and in situations where their light, reflective qualities were advantageous, such as on platforms and walkways in underground railway stations. On external walls they were detailed for precision and for their self-cleaning properties in shops and public houses.

Patent bricks enjoyed some degree of popularity. 'Grippers Bricks', for example, were invented by Edward Gripper and specified by Scott for St Pancras Hotel in 1865–71. Caleb Hitch, a brickmaker from Ware in Hertfordshire, patented large interlocking bricks which proved over-complicated, many specials being needed to complete even a simple right-angled quoin. The standard-shape brick remained unchallenged due to its very simplicity and its adaptability in use.

The choice of brick by the railway builders may have helped hasten the repeal of the Brick Tax in 1850. What is certain is that the increase in production of regular, precise bricks in an increasingly wide range of colours and textures (much loved by the High Victorians), and delivered with efficiency using a widespread network of canals and railways, meant that brick was used for all types of work in all areas of the country. It must be stated, however, that this not only brought about the demise of regional variations, but also introduced bricks to parts of the country not entirely suited to their manufacturing method or durability.

The Victorian love of precision and calculated uniformity could now be realized on a grand scale as joints became thinner $\frac{1}{8}''$ (3mm) in the North, and $\frac{3}{8}''$ (8mm) in the South, due to the accuracy of the machine-pressed bricks.

Pointing remained the way to finish brickwork in profiles, although tuck pointing was now also being used as a device to hide the excessively poor consistency in the size of bricks used on terraced town houses. The 'weather struck and cut' style became particularly popular during the later Victorian period, black pointing being favoured on the red stock bricks.

The cavity wall

The preference for a cavity wall remained general among more forward-thinking designers throughout the period. In the early 1800s the use of Rat-trap bond, formed by laying the bricks on edge in a Flemish bond style, was one method. Another linked an outer half-brick leaf to an inner, one-brick thick, load-bearing leaf using a canted glazed header. Metal wall ties date from the 1860s and, by the turn of the century, were the most popular method on joining the two wall leaves. Bricklayers almost always took the trouble to cut the headers, so external bonding was traditional, and to seal the cavity where the outer and inner leaves came into direct contact, at door and window openings, with a variety of damp-proof materials.

On domestic buildings a variety of arches, usually gauged and of neatly cut or 'axed' rubbing bricks, or of quality soft stocks, were used over openings. The development of the reinforced concrete lintel towards the end of the nineteenth century not only superseded the internal timber lintel, but was often used externally in moulded 'artificial stone' beams, to excellent architectural effect. Brick arch construction was pushed to new limits, especially in civil engineering, where they were used to great effect on railway bridges and viaducts.

The 'Battle of the Styles'

This was a period in architecture of revived vernacular styles, often striving for a return to 'medievalism', rusticity and other traditional building forms as a relief from what was seen as the hard functionalism of the machine age.

The Gothic revival was foremost in the move against the prevailing classical architecture. For a while Gothic held the ascendancy, and it made extensive use of brick. William Butterfield (1814–1900) was an architect of the Gothic school particularly noted for 'polychrome', or multi-coloured brickwork. He preferred mass-produced bricks and 'specials' (bricks purposely moulded to various ornamental shapes by the brick manufacturer), because the range of colours available was wider than with the traditional, hand-made bricks. He established a way of handling brickwork that remained popular, particularly in the years 1865–1885. Keble College, Oxford (*c.*1867–83) is a striking example.

The first aim of William Morris (1834–1896) and of the Arts and Crafts Movement was for a return to the virtues of freely expressed craftsmanship which were, it was thought, being destroyed by mass production and the economics of capitalism. This led to yet another revival – the seventeenth-century style of the Dutch, the so-called 'William and Mary', and 'Queen Anne' styles popularized by W. Eden Nesfield (1835–1888) and Philip Webb (1831–1915). These were more suited to brickwork than the Gothic style had been. Another pioneer was the architect Richard Norman Shaw (1831–1912). These men studied the older English use of hand-made, mainly red, bricks and based their designs on traditional methods. Craftsmen bricklayers relished this long-awaited opportunity to display their craft skills at their best.

Gauged brickwork also came back into fashion, with the bricklayers making use of a bow-saw fitted with a twisted steel wire blade to cut the squared rubbing bricks clamped within profiled mould boxes, and dip-laid in the preferred hydraulic (greystone) lime putty mortar. Newnham College, Cambridge (*c.*1875) by Basil Champneys (1842–1935), is an excellent example of this type of work.

The Edwardian period, up to the beginning of the First World War, saw a sharp contraction in trade during which wage cuts were enforced. From 1911 to 1914 there was, however, a busy time for the building industry, with a large programme of commercial as well as domestic building – especially of large country houses for the wealthy. There was also a very rapid increase in house building in the suburbs, where brick again played a crucial role.

Such architects as Edwin Lutyens, Detmar Blow and Guy Dawber were looking especially at hand-made bricks, using them with great authority and originality. Their designs were safe in the capable hands of the Edwardian bricklayer. Their work demonstrated the success of the late-Victorian revival in apprenticeships and craft pride. Transferring their wide range of skills to all manner of brickwork, these were in many ways the last of the traditional craftsmen, familiar both with old ways and the new materials and methods. After The Great War the craft would never be quite the same again.

THE INTER-WAR YEARS (1914–1945)

Building sites were changing, especially in the towns and cities. Trenching machines and motor-driven tools began to appear. Site congestion led to reductions in extensive on-site workshops, and by the 1920s tubular steel was slowly replacing timber for scaffolding.

As building activity was fuelled mainly by the middle classes, styles initially followed Edwardian Baroque, and later pseudo-revivalist styles. This continued the popularity of the thin (2″, 51mm) hand-made bricks as well as standard stocks for premier elevations, with 'pressed' common bricks being used for flank, rear and inner walling, or behind rendering or 'tile-hanging'. An acute shortage of bricks, due to so many brickyards not re-opening after The Great War, meant that for the first time common bricks were reluctantly accepted on face-work on many municipal housing estates.

Flemish and English bonds were most common – even for brick and brick cavity walls, which were continuing to increase in popularity – with bricklayers taking the time to 'snap' headers to achieve a traditional appearance. The use of stretcher bond was also increasing by the outbreak of the Second World War in 1939. Mortars remained largely based on limes and mature coarse stuff, with pointing to finish. Cement-based 'instant-mix' mortars made large inroads towards the end on the 1930s, and jointing by striking the bedding mortar joint in a 'weathered' finish subsequent to laying.

By the 1930s decorative brickwork had declined in popularity, especially as gauged work, due to the loss of highly skilled men, the cost and the speed necessary to meet housing targets. Although some arches were still of cut and rubbed bricks laid in lime putty, a fashion for thicker mortar joints had evolved during the latter Edwardian period and remained popular. Lintels were being exposed on the face, and standard bricks laid upright as 'soldiers', either supported on a flat steel bar and/or cast with ties into a backing concrete lintel, became fashionable.

Windows in houses were set behind the rebated brick reveal, with a concrete or steel lintel behind the arch. Side-hung timber windows and steel framed ones were increasing in use, built into the brickwork with sliding lugs. Both were placed flush to the reveal.

Terracotta remained in vogue for the more expensive large works, and glazed brickwork also held its popularity. Towards the mid-1930s glass blocks were introduced and taken up with some enthusiasm because of their ability to transmit light, their reduction of glare, and good thermal insulation.

Despite the spreading use of concrete and steel, civil engineering still made use of brick. Mechanization had helped in this fight in several ways. Not only did mass production keep down the price, but increasing precision in the type and specification of the materials meant that brickwork's behaviour under stress, loading and climate could be calculated precisely, allowing a minimum of material to be used.

The availability of mass-produced steel towards the end of the nineteenth century was of great importance to brickwork for use in reinforcement in civil engineering work. Paul Cottancin used his patented system on a number of buildings around the turn of the century. Little happened until the 1920s, however, with the publication of the results of brick reinforcement tests conducted by Sir Alexander Brebner with the British Army in India during the 1890s. He concluded that reinforced brickwork could be designed to the theories of reinforced concrete, achieving otherwise unsuited designs such as cantilevers, and promising to herald a new age for brick, which was only truly taken up in England since the 1970s.

A changing craft

Hours of work for bricklayers remained long, up to $56\frac{1}{2}$ during the summer. The Union fought excessive hours, piecework or 'sweating', and the gradual return of the employment of unskilled men. In 1920 the National Federation of Building Trade Operatives (NFBTO), won a major triumph in securing a reduction in hours to eight per day, resulting in a 44-hour, $5\frac{1}{2}$-day week.

With the Operative Bricklayers Society (OBS), merging with other unions to form the Allied Union of Building Trade Workers (AUBTW) in 1921, there was no national voice for the craft. Many conscientious bricklayers were concerned for the future of the craft, heritage of skills, knowledge and standards of excellence, founded on the good-quality training of apprentices. This was particularly true of Brickwork Instructors responsible for theoretical education and refining practical skills of apprentices in the new technology colleges opening in major towns and cities.

From the inspiration of E. Lindsay Braley, the Guild of Bricklayers was founded in 1932, with the aim of forming an association of journeymen and apprentice bricklayers, to disseminate information and skills, and raise standards of craftsmanship and the status of the craft in the eyes of the public. (See figure 2.12)

The Tylers and Bricklayers Company still promoted the craft of bricklaying within its historical London area. In 1935 it awarded its first 'Gold Medal' to Sir Giles Gilbert Scott RA (1880–1960) and a 'Silver Medal' to the foreman bricklayer for the design and use of brick on Battersea Power Station.

Figure 2.12 The emblem of the Guild of Bricklayers, founded in 1932.

THE POST-WAR PERIOD (1945-1993)

In 1944 the *Housing Manual* was published by the Ministry of Health and Ministry of Works. It laid down requirements for strength, stability, thermal and sound insulation, and resistance to damp and fire. This influential publication became the guide for all subsequent standards in house construction for the next decade, and provided builders with a wealth of accumulated technical information which the local authorities, eager to be up to date, could both encourage and enforce.

By 1947 post-war restrictions on the private sector were partly removed and, providing a licence was obtained, private homes could be built at a ratio to local authority houses of one to four. This ratio varied in subsequent years before finally being lifted in 1954. By 1961 of almost 269,000 houses built 170,000 were for private owners.

The very influential Government *Houses for Today and Tomorrow* was published in 1961. It set the 'Parker-Morris' standards of construction. The Building Regulations of 1965 (revised several times since) became a system of controlling the planning and construction of buildings throughout England, Wales and Northern Ireland. Separate Building Regulations were drawn up for Scotland. They replaced the various local bye-laws in operation since The Public Health Act, 1815. Research, commercial and professional bodies also contributed to the development of the style and use of masonry to meet contemporary demands. The National Housebuilder Registration Council (NHBC), Building Research Establishment (BRE)*, British Standards Institute (BSI), British Ceramics Research Institute (BCRI) and the Brick Development Association (BDA), being the most influential.

New constructional practices emphasizing economy of material meant that brickwork underwent dramatic changes directly affecting traditional craft practices and, with it, much of the rich heritage of the craft. Brickwork became functional, in simple rectangular buildings, and was shorn of architectural enrichment. Cavity walls of brick, and later of brick and block, superseded solid walls for houses, or as a cladding to tall steel and concrete-framed buildings. There was a loss of various bond patterns and universal use of stretcher bond, all the more severe on the eye because of the general acceptance of less aesthetically appealing machine-made facing bricks. Regional variations in brick size, type and use completely disappeared in the push for increased output.

---

* Formerly the Building Research Station (BRS).

Thin, often more highly stressed, walls required quick-setting and rapid strength-attaining cement mortars, which quickly replaced slow hardening lime-based mortars. The ancient use of footing courses passed with the introduction of calculated concrete foundation design.

The need for pointing was effectively lost with stronger bedding mortars, and the uniformly toned bricks removed the need for colour washing. Jointing initially followed the pre-war 'weathered' style, but was succeeded in the 1950s by the ubiquitous 'bucket-handle' joint. This has been challenged to some degree in recent years by the 'raked-out', recessed joint.

The standardization and metrication of brick sizes in the 1960s formed part of a movement towards modularization. Allowing for dimensional co-ordination using standard components and assemblies, which led to a short fashion for larger than standard bricks, to work in with the widely accepted 300mm module as a means to increase speed in building. There was also more experiments with patent bricks such as the 'V' brick and the 'Calculon'.

These dramatic changes have affected the craft of the bricklayer. After the war the craft remained traditionally based. The older craftsmen had served their time in the Edwardian period, many preferring their old tools, like the plumb rule. These craftsmen influenced the younger journeymen and apprentices, who were now serving a five-year apprenticeship assisted by attendance at the colleges rapidly springing up all over the country in the 1950s. They still possessed a strong sense of craft pride, and a hierarchy of skilled craftsmen within and around the building, which was recognized and respected by their labourers.

The simplifying of brickwork, combined with the often unsupervised, sub-contractor (or 'subbie') in the 1960s, reduced the skill of bricklaying to little more than building a plumb quoin, and keeping the cross-joints perpendicular, having the disastrous effect of allowing the craft to become swamped by untrained bricklayers devoid of all sense of craft heritage, and driving off the trowel many time-served tradesmen the craft could ill-afford to lose. Of course, since the 1800s unqualified bricklayers worked on the trowel (generally drawn from builders' labourers, not general labourers), but this was hardly visible on mass brick walls. Today this is not possible, and the majority of the bricks laid are unfortunately on facework, meaning that the reduction in skill levels shows all too clearly and reflects badly on the craft.

Post-war developments in apprenticeship

The late 1940s revealed a picture of an industry resuming its pre-war arrangements, with a five-year period of building craft apprenticeship, although the payment of a premium to the Company or master bricklayer was no longer practised. The proliferation of Further Education Colleges made available a prescribed education and training for apprentices to supplement site training. Under the National Joint Council for the Building Industry (NJCBI) deed of apprenticeship, employers were obliged to release their apprentices to attend college at least one day a week. In many cases this pattern still exists, though proper indenture arrangements have become scarce.

The Industrial Training Act of 1963 implemented a series of measures regulating prescribed training. Of importance for construction was the setting up of the Construction Industry Training Board (CITB) to levy funds from industry to develop and provide training schemes. For a time their schemes for training apprentices were different to the City and Guilds, being aimed at skills competence, while the latter provided a more rounded education and craft training.

The simplicity of buildings led to the perception that bricklayers were now mainly required to be competent in simple assembly and fixing rather than to possess a full range of craft skills. By the mid-1960s, therefore, the period of apprenticeship had been reduced to four years and, in the 1970s, to three, with a consequent dilution of the training programmes.

New Training Initiative (NTI) in 1981 identified the government's training priorities for the foreseeable future. Out of this came the Youth Training Scheme (YTS), stating that all sixteen-year-old school leavers were to be offered work experience, whether employed or not. The already tenuous partnership between employer and college in providing apprenticeship training became discredited, the employer often unable to supply suitable experience whilst college education and training at the college became increasingly divorced from the reality of the modern site and its needs. Thus neither qualifications nor time-serving could confirm a bricklayer's competence in the craft.

A significant development in the delivery of training has been the introduction of the National Vocational Qualification (NVQ) system, designed to rationalize qualifications throughout industry, and to guarantee the competence of trainees by demonstrating that they satisfy specified performance standards.

The important consideration now is not how long it took to achieve, at what age, or where the skills were acquired. In effect, there is no set length of apprenticeship; to become qualified, it is only necessary to demonstrate job competence in the required units of construction.

Until proven, however, it would seem prudent to question and examine closely whether the product of a system not demanding a prescribed training period, minimum experience or adequate maturity

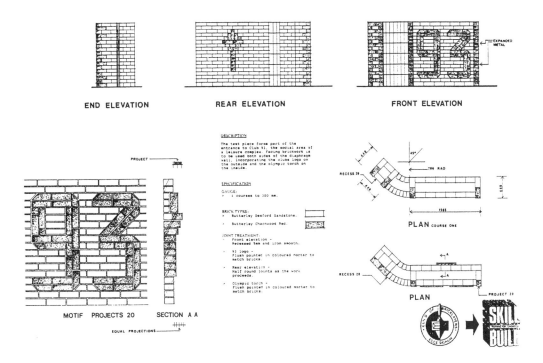

Figure 2.13 The 1993 National Skill Build final competition for the regional apprentice winners, to select the apprentice who will represent the United Kingdom in the International Youth Skill Olympics, held at Peterborough College (working drawing and photograph reproduced by kind permission of Barrie Roe).

– the cornerstones of our historical and traditional training methods
– does produce the skills required of true craftsmen.

The Guild of Bricklayers

The Guild of Bricklayers resumed activity after the war and was
quickly recognized for its wealth of expertise, so that by 1948 the City
and Guilds accepted them as an authoritative body of local examiners.
The office of Chief Examiner in Brickwork G&LI has always been filled
by a senior member of the Guild since 1946, the first being E. L.
Braley. Since 1953 the Guild has acted in an official capacity at all
major brickwork competitions held throughout the country.

In 1953 the Tylers and Bricklayers Company consolidated a long-
growing bond of friendship, presenting the Guild with a replica of an
eighteenth-century brick axe used by the Master of the Company.

Through the 1960s the Guild's membership and influence grew.
The list of past presidents reveals many authors of the standard,
practical and theoretical works for all who have studied brickwork and
bricklaying: masters passing on their skills and knowledge as in the
guilds of old.

Guild members became concerned at the termination of practical
examinations in the City and Guilds Craft and Advanced Craft examinations in favour of coursework assessment during the early 1970s.
Members felt this would lead to lower standards, contravening the
Guild's aim of maintaining a high level of craftsmanship. As a result,
the Guild in 1976 started its own regional apprentice competitions
supported by brick, mortar and tool manufacturers, furthering links
between the Guild and industry. Winners of each regional competition
go to the National Skill Build competition, the winner in bi-annual
years representing the United Kingdom in the International Youth
Skill Olympics. (See figure 2.13)

The Guild was approached by the Brick Development Association in
1987 to assist with the development and promotion of a new annual
award, 'The Quality Brickwork Award', now one of the major awards
in the construction industry. The aim is to recognize and reward
quality bricklaying in newly completed buildings.

Among its many other activities, the Guild of Bricklayers assists The
Worshipful Company of Tylers and Bricklayers, who continue to
promote excellence in the craft of bricklaying, with their 'triennial
award', for buildings which have been completed, restored or improved during the three years prior to adjudication.

HOPE FOR THE FUTURE

The move from brick as only a non-structural cladding on high-rise buildings of concrete or steel frames has gained momentum since the 1980s, utilizing the great potential for reinforced and pre-stressed brickwork. Structural brickwork, including modern brick masonry, ensures its use in an economical form to carry the loads of the walls and roof of a building and resist wind forces. It exploits the rich potential of brickwork, opening up the possibility of renewed enrichment.

Hand-made bricks and 'specials' are again popular, and there are indications of revivals in many traditional aspects of bricklaying for the skilled craftsmen-bricklayers too long starved of opportunity, to display the skills they are still proud to possess. Shortening the apprenticeship period, removing some areas of skill and theory from the curriculum to attempt to produce the multi-skilled workforce demanded by the market place, is seen by many as the way forward. Such an approach does not, however, address the question of how to train bricklayers to possess a wide range of knowledge and skills, equal to that which forty years ago would have been classed as no better than average.

It is by providing places for carefully selected apprentices, and by ensuring the right calibre of craftsmen, that we will be able to meet the many modern demands and be able to make use of traditional craft techniques. This will help ensure that the best of designs in good-quality materials are built, with skill, by craftsmen who have a pride in the noble craft of bricklaying.

3

The Manufacture of Bricks

Clays are fine-grained deposits laid down by deposition from still water at some time in the past; clay will contain certain constituents derived from the neighbouring land by the breakdown and disintegration of rocks through the processes of weathering. The main constituents are silica (60%) and alumina (20%). Iron oxide and salts of calcium, magnesium, sodium and potassium may also be present.

Although clay is primarily the product of the breaking down of rocks of various geological periods by weathering, and by the deposition of the fine grains under water, changing temperatures are also responsible for some mechanical breakdown of the rocks. High daytime temperatures followed by a rapid fall at night results in alternating expansion and contraction, greatly exacerbated by freezing, and leads to stresses which eventually crack the rocks.

The geological time chart of the principal building clays from their respective major geological divisions is shown in Figure 3.1. Important contributions are made to modern brick production from Mercian Mudstones (formerly known as Keuper Marl) (Triassic), Reading Beds (Eocene), Weald Clay (Cretaceous), and finally the alluvium and brick-earths of more recent times.

However, the most important are Coal Measures (Carboniferous), Oxford Clay (Jurassic) and the glacial clays of the Pleistocene. London Clay (Eocene) was once a very important building clay, but today is little used.

Eras		Time (millions of years)		Geological periods	Main building clays
T E R T I A R Y		24		Recent and Pleistocene	Alluvium Brickearth Glacial Clays
			− 25		
		35		Pliocene and Miocene	
			− 60	Oligocene and Eocene	London Clay Reading Beds
M E S O Z O I C		60		Cretaceous	Weald Clay Hastings Beds
			− 120		
		75		Jurassic	Oxford Clay
			− 145		
		40		Triassic	Mercian Mudstones
			− 170		
P A L A E O Z O I C	U P P E R	40	− 210	Permian	
		75	− 285	Carboniferous	Etruria Marl Coal Measures
		40	− 325	Devonian	
	L O W E R	25	− 350	Silurian	
		60	− 410	Ordovician	
		90	− 500	Cambrian	
PROTEROZOIC and 1500 ARCHAEZOIC				Pre-Cambrian	

Figure 3.1 Building clays and their geological background.

The characteristics of the various clay types can be summarized as follows:

♦ *Brick-earth.* Found mainly in Essex, this is a riverborne deposit which makes a brick of higher than average porosity. Red and yellow colours are common from this clay.

♦ *Carbonaceous shales.* Mainly found in Lancashire and Yorkshire, a clay high in iron which fires red in colour and produces a high-strength, low-porosity brick.

♦ *Etruria Marl.* This clay is worked in a belt of the West Midlands extending through Staffordshire and Shropshire. It is highly prized for producing bricks of very high strength and low water absorption. These are used to great effect on bridges and sewers – hence their name, 'engineering bricks'. Due to an extremely high iron content, the bricks will burn red or blue according to different firing methods, and have a wide vitrification range, allowing the bricks to 'glaze' without excessive shrinkage, a process almost impossible with other clays as extremely high temperatures would be required.

♦ *Gault Clay.* Only one Gault Clay quarry is now working in the United Kingdom, at Arlesey in Bedfordshire. This uncommon black clay has unusual properties, with a high proportion of free lime which under high firing bleaches out most other colours to produce light, almost buff, blue bricks which have relatively high water absorption.

♦ *Mercian Mudstones* (formerly known as Keuper Marl). The most widespread brickmaking clay after Oxford Clay, common in the Leicestershire area. Because it is particularly soft, it is desirable both for machine- and hand-made bricks. When fired it produces bricks of low strength and high water absorption. There are two types of clay with different iron contents: one type fires buff and the other red.

♦ *Lower Oxford Clay.* A unique clay with a high carbonaceous fuel content allowing it to be fired inexpensively. It is found from the Yorkshire coast to the Dorset coast, whilst in Cambridgeshire, Bedfordshire and North Buckinghamshire it is sufficiently near the surface to be accessible for brickmaking. A hard, shale-like clay which, in spite of its high water content (16–20%), can be ground and pressed into brick shapes. Used to make Fletton bricks in a manufacturing method known as the semi-dry pressed process.

♦ *Weald Clay.* Traditionally used for hand-made stock bricks although also used for engineering bricks, this clay is found mainly in Surrey and parts of Kent and Sussex. When fired the predominant colour is red, but there is a long tradition of adding coke breeze or coal slurry to give a black finish to the face.

ASSESSING CLAY FOR BRICKMAKING

The qualities and characteristics of clay, and an assessment of its suitability for manufacturing quality bricks, are determined by practical trials and scientific chemical analysis. One method is to test-fire a brick from a chosen clay. If the results are unsatisfactory, a complete chemical analysis may be undertaken to help to determine what additions would bring about an improvement. Few clays are found ready for use: most require certain preparatory processes before they are suitable for the manufacture of bricks.

The treatment of clays varies from firm to firm and brickyard to brickyard. However, because different clay types and the processes of manufacture vary, the practical operations followed in the manufacture of a brick, whether by manual or mechanical means, are general:

1. Clay winning and preparation.
2. Forming the brick.
3. Drying the brick.
4. Firing the brick.

The finished brick may be classified by the manufacturing method used:

1. Hand-moulded (clamp or kiln burned).
2. Machine-made, simulated hand-made (kiln burned).
3. Machine-made extruded, wire-cuts (kiln burned).
4. Machine-made pressed bricks (kiln burned).

Another classification is by the state of the clay dug for moulding:

1. Plastic.
2. Soft mud.
3. Semi-dry.
4. Stiff plastic.

Clay winning and preparation

The manner in which clay is won (dug) and transported to the brickworks varies according to the type and depth of the clay deposit and distance from the brickworks, and the financial resources at the company's disposal.

Some small yards still excavate by hand or with small machines, often seasonally, whereas larger companies working on volume production excavate all year round using a variety of heavy plant. The clay is taken to the brickworks by wagons on rails, by lorries or by conveyor belts, to be prepared for the moulding stage.

The preparation process involves crushing, grinding and mixing the clay in different ways, depending upon its nature and the subsequent shaping process to be employed. This is primarily to reduce the clay particle size, although in some processes materials are blended either to improve the quality or to add combustible materials to assist firing. Water content is carefully monitored to give a clay ready for shaping. The moistness of the clay can vary from very wet (over 30% moisture) to relatively dry (under 12% moisture).

Shaping the bricks

The method adopted will vary according to the nature of the clay used, its water content and the type of brick required. There are five systems, one being by hand, the remaining four being by machine, in which the raw material is forced into moulds by pressure. The five methods are described briefly as follows:

1. *Hand-made.* The traditional method of brickmaking, whereby the 'warp' or lump of clay is rolled in moulding and thrown by hand into a frame mould on a wooden stock, producing individual, attractive bricks of various colours and textures. Hand-made bricks usually have a single frog, but may be solid.
2. *Soft mud.* This is an adaptation of the hand-making method. Again, a clay with a high moisture content is used, dropped between two rotating rollers and mechanically thrown into metal moulds which, after excess clay is removed, reverse and release the brick, giving a simulated hand-made brick. Soft mud bricks generally have a single frog.
3. *Semi-dry.* The Fletton-type brick is manufactured using this process. A ground clay is fed into machines and pressed, four times in one cycle, into moulds by heavy hydraulic pressure. The facing bricks are sand-faced or machine-textured. The Fletton bricks have one frog and have sometimes been produced in two or three cells.
4. *Stiff plastic.* A similar process to semi-dry although the clay tends to have an inherently low moisture content such as the shale deposits of the North of England. After grinding, extra water is added to the clay dust before delivery to an extrusion pug which forces the clay into moulds, and is then pressed to shape. Sometimes a second pressing is deemed necessary for facing bricks. This method gives a dense, uniform-sized brick. With improved technological developments in the wirecut process this method has now been largely supplanted.

5. *Extruded wirecuts.* Apart from clays with naturally high levels of water, most clays are suitable for this process. Prepared clay is extruded through metal dies to give a long column of clay (with or without perforations) the correct width and length of the finished bricks. It is then textured by scoring or brushing and/or coloured by spraying. Finally it is cut to the specified gauge by a series of wires.

   Wire-cut bricks do not have frogs, although most contain a variety of perforations, or holes, formed during extrusion.

Drying

This is an important stage for hand-made, soft mud and some wire-cuts, where the moisture level is relatively high. It is vital that the bricks are dried to allow them to shrink as they release excess moisture. This prevents twisting and cracking in the kiln. It also enables them to develop a 'leather' skin, allowing them to be handled and stacked without deformation.

Drying can take place naturally outdoors in what are known as drying hacks, or in drying chambers where bricks are open-stacked on pallets so that a flow of heated air can pass over them. Alternatively the bricks can travel through heated tunnels on cars. Heating and levels of humidity must be carefully monitored to control shrinkage.

Firing

When the clay brick is fired at a sufficiently high temperature for a controlled length of time, chemical changes occur and these result in a harder and more lasting product. The properties can be summarized as follows:

1. The softness necessary for moulding is lost.
2. The clay shrinks.
3. Mechanical strength is greatly increased.
4. The material becomes durable and resistant to weathering.
5. Changes in colour occur.

The properties of these bricks and the nature of these changes depend upon the composition of the clay, the method of manufacture and the conditions during firing. (See figure 3.2)

Firing, the final and most important stage in the process of making bricks, takes considerable skill on the part of the person in charge, the 'burner'. He must be sure that the bricks have been properly 'set' in the kiln to give a good firing; know how fast the temperature can be raised without damaging the product; know how to combine the

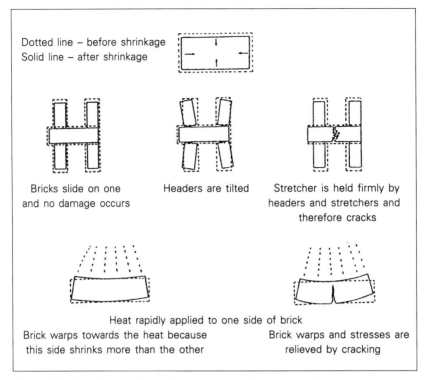

Dotted line – before shrinkage
Solid line – after shrinkage

Bricks slide on one
and no damage occurs

Headers are tilted

Stretcher is held firmly by
headers and stretchers and
therefore cracks

Heat rapidly applied to one side of brick

Brick warps towards the heat because
this side shrinks more than the other

Brick warps and stresses are
relieved by cracking

Figure 3.2 The effects on bricks if not properly dried or stacked.

natural carbon in some clays to reduce fuel consumption in the kiln; and know the correct temperature and oxidizing methods to employ to achieve the desired colour. In short, in his capable hands is the quality of the final product.

Setting the bricks

Arranging green bricks in an organized stacking system to gain uniformity of temperature and finished colour from a firing is known as 'setting'. There are a number of setting patterns designed to suit the particular bricks being fired and to maximize the efficient operation of the kiln.

Traditionally, kilns are loaded by hand. Many yards now use fork-lift trucks for setting the bricks outside the kiln, thereby gaining the advantages of setting and sorting under less cramped conditions, and a quicker load and unload, with less heat loss from the kiln.

The most common setting patterns are 5 headers on 2 stretchers, or double 5 on 2 (5 pairs of faced headers on 2 pairs of faced stretchers). Other patterns are also shown. (See figure 3.3)

In the process of firing the clay undergoes chemical and physical

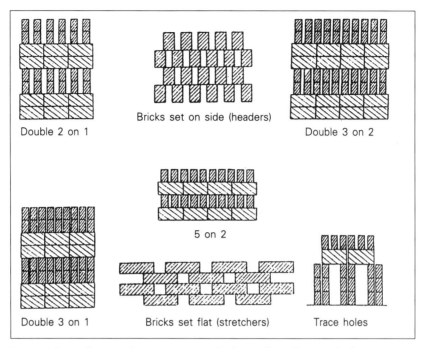

Double 2 on 1

Bricks set on side (headers)

Double 3 on 2

5 on 2

Double 3 on 1

Bricks set flat (stretchers)

Trace holes

Figure 3.3 A selection of setting patterns for firing, dependent on the burning characteristics of the bricks (reproduced by permission of the Brick Development Association).

changes which may be very complex. The most important is the production of a glass-like bond cementing the particles together, and giving strength to the brick, a process known as 'vitrification'. This reaction occurs between 900°C and 1,200°C. It is important to give most clay types a long baking at this temperature, for at least forty-eight hours, in order to burn out all volatiles, i.e. salts and limes. If this is not done the salts can appear on the brick face as a white mould when it is built into a construction, and this may not disappear for some time.

Fired colour

The colour of the burnt brick can be a complex area to study. However, a general rule is that it is the iron content which produces a range of colours, depending on the amount of oxygen within the kiln (oxidation). In a reduced atmosphere, used for the production of blue bricks, the colours will range from brown to blue, and black can even be produced. In a fully oxidized chamber the colour range will be from cream to yellow, red and brown.

Multi-coloured facing bricks are produced in some regions, such as Surrey and Sussex, by the addition of fuel to the clay blend. This produces a colour range which is only varied by the amount of fuel added – from silver-grey and pastel ranges to deep purple-blue and black.

In clays with a 5–9% iron oxide and a 10–22% alumina content, and with a negligible quantity of free lime, all shades of red are produced and the product becomes darker with higher temperature under oxidizing conditions.

Gault Clays can contain up to 20% lime, and despite 4–5% red ferric oxide are capable of being burned to produce almost white bricks. At 1,000°C Gault Clay heated in air yields pink to brown shades, and it becomes cream after a prolonged firing at 1,050°C due to the bleaching properties of the reaction of lime with iron oxide. This is reduced when sulphur oxide is present. With 1.5–3% iron oxide and about 25% alumina the fired colour will be buff.

Firing methods

There are four firing methods:

1. *Clamp.* A centuries-old method still in use today for stocks and hand-made bricks. It can vary in size although up to a million bricks can be fired in one setting. The method involves layers of fuel and closely stacked bricks, which themselves may contain fuel, generally in the form of ground coke. The outside is sealed with previously burnt bricks, with openings around the base through which the clamp is lit.

   Burning is not controllable, being dependent on the amount of fuel available. The fire spreads slowly through the clamp and is allowed to burn for up to six weeks until it goes out. The bricks vary considerably in quality and are graded before sale.

2. *Intermittent kilns.* These kilns are loaded and fired, then allowed to go out so they can be unloaded and prepared again for firing. Apart from clamps, intermittent kilns were the only method for burning bricks until the Hoffmann continuous kiln was introduced in 1858. Early intermittent kilns worked on the up-draught principle, being fired at the bottom of the kiln. The by-products of combustion escape through the open top: the Scotch kiln is one example. Because of the unevenness of the firing, the down-draught intermittent kiln was developed, combining flexibility with low capital outlay. Although limited in size and of high fuel consumption, they are still in use today: the 'top hat' and 'shuttle kilns' are examples.

3. *Continuous kilns.* These consist of a number of separate chambers connected so that kilns can be loaded, fired and cooled individ-

ually and simultaneously. The fire is never allowed to go out, and the production process is thus continuous.

The continuous kiln has gone through a series of developments to produce designs such as the Belgian and Buhrer kilns. The Hoffmann kiln is still used today as a much improved version. The Transverse Arch Hoffmann kiln is used by London Brick Company. One at its Stewartby works had eighty chambers and was capable of a weekly output of 3.6 million bricks.

4. *Tunnel kilns.* Tunnel kilns are a more recent innovation and a development of the continuous kiln, giving greater thermal efficiency and providing optimum conditions for computer quality-control of the firing process.

In an approximately 1,100-metre long tunnel kiln the fire is stationary. The bricks travel through set on railed cars, and speed of movement is carefully controlled so that the bricks move steadily through pre-heating, firing and cooling zones, the whole process taking approximately three days. Although developed in the first half of the twentieth century the tunnel kilns have only come into widespread use in recent years. An example of the modern tunnel kiln is the 'Kirton' at the Kirton works, capable of a weekly output of over 1 million bricks.

Fuels

Coal or coke are still employed, although oil (and more recently gas) are now widely used in the kilns, contributing to their greater control. Developments in the designs of kilns, including re-circulating gases, co-current flow patterns and cross-current tunnel kilns have all been evolved to gain versatility and greater efficiency in the firing process.

MODERN BRICK MANUFACTURING

Having examined the general principles of brickmaking it is appropriate to consider some individual modern companies which produce bricks by these different methods.

The plastic process

Michelmersh Brick and Tile Company employ the plastic process, producing high-quality hand-made bricks and specials throughout the colour range – orange-red, red-multi, dark multi and grey-brown. Their output is produced in metric and imperial sizes, as well as 50mm

Tudor bricks. Their expertise is valued for matching brickwork in restoration and conservation work.

On an outcrop of London/Reading Bed clay in Hampshire, bricks have been produced in the Michelmersh area since Saxon times. A brickworks has existed on the site of the present works since 1842.

Clay is excavated by mechanical excavator after removal of top soil, and work takes place all year round. The clay is then turned, by excavator, six times before being passed through a roller-filter mill. This consists of two revolving, perforated drums which force the clay through the perforations, collecting and rejecting extraneous materials such as stones and roots.

The clay pellets are stored in a 'clay barn' for a three-week 'souring' period. Using a rotation method, ensuring that the oldest clay is used first, the pellets are then passed, through a disintegrator which chops and turns the clay, on to two high-speed rollers. The first is set at 6mm, the second at 2mm. By the time it emerges the clay has been completely broken down.

Sand and coal dust, in carefully proportioned volumes, are fed into the clay and mixed thoroughly together in a dry state. This blend is fed by conveyor into a pug mill where water is added to produce the correct consistency for moulding.

The prepared clay is heaped to the right-hand side of the moulder, who scoops sufficient to form his 'clot', which is rolled in sand and thrown into the mould. This is a very skilled operation if the clay is to fill the mould completely. It is kept damp, and dry sand is thrown into the mould to help the shaped clay slide out. This process is known as sand-moulding. In earlier times moulds were of timber and the special moulds still are. Moulds for facing bricks, however, are now of steel. A moulder will make about 1,300 standard facings a day. Each has his own number in the frog board which is stamped into the frog of the brick, so that each brick is traceable to its maker. (See figure 3.4)

Moulded bricks are turned out of the mould on to pallet boards, fifteen to a board, with space between to facilitate drying. A standard facing brick contains nearly one kilo of water – necessary for plasticity during moulding – but which must be reduced to as low a level as possible before firing.

Stacks of bricks are taken by fork lift to tunnel driers where, during a seven-day drying period, waste heat from the kiln is recycled to reduce the moisture content. Each drier holds about 8,000 bricks.

At Michelmersh there are still two traditional beehive kilns. However, the development of transportable 'moving hood kilns' has given greater control, reduction in fuel consumption and improved firing times. Both types of kiln are fuelled by gas oil (33 sec).

In a firing cycle lasting thirty-six hours and reaching a temperature

Figure 3.4 'Striking off' the surplus clay on the top of the brick mould using the wire bow. The prepared clay is to the moulder's right, along with the sand. Note the stockboard with the raised 'kick' to form the frog in a standard brick to the moulder's left (photograph reproduced by kind permission of Michelmersh Brick and Tile Company).

of 1,050°C, the colour of the bricks can be adjusted by varying the air allowed to enter the kiln. The kiln is then put out and left to cool for four days to allow unloading. Emptying and grading the burnt bricks for quality and colour takes about two days.

Once the bricks are sorted they are stacked 400 to a pallet, and shrink-wrapped if requested, for delivery by the company's lorries, which are equipped for crane off-loading.

The soft mud process

At the Arlesey brickworks in the heart of Bedfordshire, Butterleys (founded in 1890) have been producing bricks by the soft mud, simulated hand-moulded machine process since 1984.

The overburden is removed to expose the prized Gault Clay, excavated by TB38 dragline. The clay is then transported to the working stockpile, where it remains for two to three days before being used. A continuous supply of raw clay is fed at regular intervals into box feeders outside the grinding shed. Other feeders are loaded with small amounts of 'grog' (crushed fired brick), which assists the drying of the moulded green bricks, together with a coal slurry, which aids good firing. These ingredients are integrated as they are transported by conveyor to the wet pan.

The clay is discharged into the wet pan, where two rotating wheels, weighing five and seven tonnes, crush the clay through a narrow mesh at the base. Simultaneously, water is added at a rate of $3-3\frac{1}{2}$ litres per minute and then the mixture is passed through a series of high-speed rollers which reduce the particle sizes. The prepared clay is held in a rotating clay store. Leaving the clay store it is fed into a mixer where it is blended with hot water to a moisture content of between 25% and 29%.

The mixed clay is taken by conveyor belt to the Hupert machine for making the bricks. Here it is cut to the correct quantity for moulding, forced between two converging rollers into a narrow gap, and then dashed into a synchronized steel mould. Approximately 6,000 bricks are produced this way every hour. (See figure 3.5)

Due to the very high moisture content the green bricks are set into drying chambers capable of holding 18,000 bricks, where they remain for forty-eight hours. Hot air is introduced gradually, and the temperature is raised from 40 to 115°C over two days and circulated by means of four rotating cones per chamber. Moisture content is reduced to 3%.

Upon drying the bricks are automatically transferred to the 'setting tables', and eventually set into a pre-defined pattern to ensure even firing and to minimize movement of packs. They are placed by setting

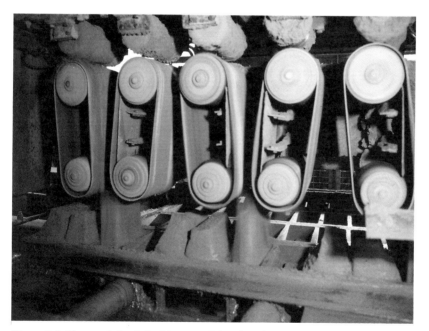

Figure 3.5 The revolving belts 'throwing' the clot of clay into the wooden moulds on the synchronized conveyor (by kind permission of Butterley Brick Limited).

machine onto kiln cars at 50,000 bricks per shift, and these move along a tunnel kiln called a Morando kiln fuelled by gas, 60% of which is recycled excess gas from the company's landfill programme. The remainder is natural gas.

Firing takes seventy-two hours in three zones within the kiln. In the first zone the bricks are pre-heated at a low temperature. As the cars are automatically 'pushed' along they enter the firing zone where the temperature reaches around 1,010°C, depending on brick type. The third stage is the cooling zone, where much of the heat is drawn off and ducted into the driers, which represents another sensible recycling of energy.

Three packers work as a team, grading the bricks. Any bricks which are cracked or chipped, or not matching in either texture or colour, are rejected and priced accordingly. The shrink-wrapped packs of 424 bricks are delivered by lorries with crane off-loading facility to the customer.

The semi-dry process

The semi-dry process is used for the vast output of London Brick Company Fletton bricks. The Stewartby works in Bedfordshire is the largest brickworks in the world and is the centre of a series of brickworks from Buckinghamshire to Cambridgeshire.

The overburden or 'callow', being too plastic for the semi-dry process, is removed. A walking dragline with a 12-cubic-metre bucket excavates clay from a 20-metre deep clay face, and discharges it into feeders which transfer it to a conveyor. It is then dropped onto vibrating metal bars, known as a 'grizzly', which separate the smaller pieces and retain large lumps. These then go to a machine called a 'kibbler' for crushing rocks. Any other waste is segregated and ultimately rejected.

The kibbled clay is transferred, with the other clay, into steel storage hoppers. At an automatically controlled rate of feed, the clay is passed into grinding pans, where it is crushed under rollers and passes through its perforated base onto a conveyor for grading on banks of electrically heated piano wire. The fine material passes on to the brick presses. The coarse material or 'tailings' return to the pans for further grinding. The finely ground clay moves into press hoppers. A reciprocating charger in each press first fills the back box with a measured charge of clay, and then two pistons, one above the other, compress the clay in a combined single pressing. There is a pause to expel air and excess clay, and then in a third pressing, the brick is raised, pushed forward and, falling into the front box, subjected to the same process. Every brick is thus subjected to four pressings. (See figure 3.6)

Figure 3.6 The Fletton bricks, having received their final pressing, move on to be 'blocked' in readiness for loading into the kiln for drying (photograph reproduced by kind permission of The London Brick Company Limited).

A moisture content of about 20% by weight must be removed before firing. All the kilns are of the Hoffmann continuous chamber type, which means that some bricks are in some chambers firing or cooling down, at the same time as others can be in separate chambers for drying.

Loaded by fork lifts, the stacked or 'blocked' bricks are then placed in the required position. Setting is carried out in two sections, 1,000 bricks at the bottom and 900 on the top. Reduction in weight after firing means that the entire stack can be drawn from the kiln in one operation.

Bricks are stacked for full circulation, and stand initially for one day in a warm chamber. Recycled hot air from other parts of the kiln is then drawn into the chamber for a five-day drying process, which is carefully controlled to ensure that full shrinkage has taken place before firing.

The stacking method will vary with the brick type being burnt, particularly for facings: the aim is to ensure complete firing and to prevent 'kiss' marks. Wickets are built of loose waste bricks and plastered with 'pug' at the entrance of the kiln. Pug, or grog, is finely ground bricks mixed with clay. The wickets are washed constantly when the chambers are on full fire in order to seal any cracks.

Because of the 5% natural fuel content in clay, no pre-heating is necessary and a fast build-up of combustion is possible. At 1,000°C cold air is deliberately poured into the chamber for several hours, to check this dramatic rise in temperature. In so doing a strong, well-vitrified brick is produced.

Because of this high fuel content, tests on each clay source are required to determine the calorific value in order to judge the correct conditions for burning. As these can vary, some bricks will be cheaper and others more expensive to kiln.

The temperature is further 'eased' or reduced to above 900°C for about thirty hours so that any residual carbon is removed. A low-grade coal referred to as 'smudge' is fed in through small openings in the roof to maintain temperature.

The 'wicket' to the chamber is then knocked down to allow combustion air to enter. Soon the bricks are ready for drawing.

The process from drying to firing and cooling the bricks takes about 11½ days. Once drawn the bricks are taken to the loading shed for grading and making up into blocks of 380 bricks for mechanical loading, and they are then distributed by LBC's own fleet of vehicles.

The wirecut process

In 1980 Armitage Brick Limited acquired the Accrington Brick and Tile Co. Ltd, in Lancashire, probably best known for its famous 'Nori' brick, although it produces a whole range of facings, engineerings, specials and pavers. A unique feature of 'Accrington' is the ability to produce chemically resistant bricks, and these are exported worldwide.

The Nori brick is made at the Whinney Hill works in Accrington. Here is one of the most modern brick factories in the world. Until the 1970s the stiff-plastic process was used, but improved technology has made possible the use of extrusion and wirecut process without any loss in quality, yet with increased production.

The lower Coal Measure clay shale is noted for its high silica and aluminium content, and is mechanically excavated. A blended stock pile is built up and left to weather for between twelve and twenty-four months. After this it is moved by a CAT 245 earth mover to a stock piling area adjacent to the works. Up to four months' supply of clay is kept in this area.

The raw material is fed through two serrated discs of an Eirich mill, which grinds the clay so effectively that the normal screening of particles is eliminated. Should it be required that the clay be highly dense and resistant to chemicals and abrasions, a high-speed roller grinds the material yet more finely.

After leaving the grinding process, clay is taken by conveyor to a mixer where water is added, raising the moisture content to 12%. The clay is then taken to a souring silo so that the moisture can work into all the material, increasing its plasticity. Once it is 'soured' more water is added, and it is mixed in to raise the moisture content to 16%, ready for moulding.

The clay is fed automatically into the extruder, which is mounted on adjustable jacks allowing exact alignment with the column of clay and the conveyor in the front of the die-mouth. This helps to prevent distortion of the clay column as it extrudes. The rate of extrusion is carefully controlled to ensure the correct feed to the cutting wires, which are altered to suit different sizes of product. (See figure 3.7) The cut bricks are placed mechanically on trays to be transferred to the chamber driers.

At the Accrington Nori factory there are eight double drying chambers, which are run on recycled waste heat from the natural-gas-fired kilns. They can be set individually for drying differently shaped and sized bricks. The process takes between twenty-four and seventy-two hours, depending on product type. On leaving the driers the trays are

Figure 3.7 Columns of extruded clay moving on to be cut to gauge by the cutting wires in a well-controlled, automated process at the 'Whinney Hill' works (photograph reproduced by kind permission of Marshalls Clay Products).

taken to the setting machine, where they are stacked in various configurations to enter the kilns.

Burning the bricks is undertaken in a 'keller' tunnel kiln, which can accommodate thirty-seven cars at any one time, with a further four cars in a pre-heating zone. Each car carries 4,800 bricks. The kiln achieves a maximum temperature of 1,040°C. All aspects of operating and monitoring the kiln are computerized so that different firing cycles can be programmed for each product. Firing takes about 3 to $4\frac{1}{2}$ days.

On leaving the cooling zone the kiln car is unloaded automatically by a machine. Bricks are carefully inspected, any inferior ones being rejected. The good bricks are stacked on pallets of 480, then shrink-wrapped for delivery by lorries with mechanical off-loading.

OTHER TYPES OF BRICKS

Besides traditional clay bricks other types have been developed for a variety of different, often specialized uses. The craftsman bricklayer should have some knowledge of them.

Calcium silicate bricks

Of the four manufacturers of calcium silicate bricks in Britain, Ryarsh Brick Ltd of West Malling, Kent, is the largest, with an annual production capacity of approximately 110 million bricks.

Calcium silicate bricks are manufactured to BS187, 1978, in highly automated factory conditions, many stages of production being computer-controlled.

The ingredients are approximately 90% silica sand (and a blended aggregate for flint limes) and 10% hydrated lime. Inorganic oxide pigments are added for facing production to give a stable and through-coloured brick. Sufficient water is added to facilitate the moulding of these materials in steel moulds under high pressure. (See figure 3.8)

The silica sand, which is obtained by opencast quarrying, and the other materials are combined in a pan mixer before releasing to the press, which works on a fill, press and eject basis, exerting a pressure of 30 tonnes, and making 2,100 bricks per hour. Texturing, when required, is made at the point of ejection from the mould.

Green bricks are automatically stacked on to transfer cars into a steam-heated autoclave, capable of holding 35,000 bricks. The bricks are 'cooked' at a temperatures around 180°C and at a steam pressure of $0.8-1.3 \text{N/mm}^2$ for approximately twelve hours. During this steaming process, involving heat and moisture, the chemical bonding

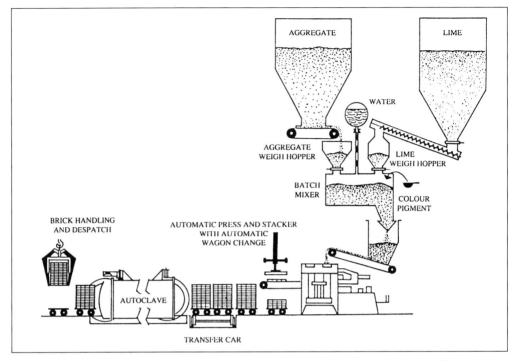

Figure 3.8 A diagram showing a typical plant layout in the manufacture of a calcium silicate brick (reproduced by kind permission of the Calcium Silicate Brick Association Ltd).

between the calcium oxide in the lime and the silica in the sand produces solid calcium silicate bricks. At this stage the bricks are ready for immediate use.

Concrete bricks

All concrete bricks are manufactured to BS6073: Part 1, 1981. In a highly automated process the raw material of dense aggregate cementitious binder and water are blended and compacted into moulds at very high pressure. Attention is given to achieving accurate dimensions and clean arrises. If a colouring is required, particularly for the range of facings, this is achieved by blending different aggregates and/or by adding colour-fast iron oxide pigments to BS1014, 1975 (1986). The normal face finish is plain and smooth today, although a number of roughened surfaces are manufactured by adjusting the steel moulds used in casting.

Upon extraction from the steel moulds the concrete bricks are properly cured to allow for hardening and shrinkage, problems common to all concrete products. The bricks are then ready for dispatch, and are sold shrink-wrapped on pallets.

4

Bricks: Properties and Classification

DEFINITION

A brick is a walling unit not exceeding 337.5mm in length, 225mm in width and 112.5mm in height. The form may be defined generally as a rectangular prism of a size which can be handled conveniently with one hand. It is normal to find that the length of a brick is equal to twice its width plus one standard joint, and three times the height plus two standard joints. These dimensions have evolved through the centuries and provide a unit that is easily bonded and gives a good appearance. (See figure 4.1)

It is usual to describe the thickness of a brick wall in terms of the number of brick lengths. In other words, by placing a brick stretcher-wise across a given wall one can indicate its thickness in multiples of stretcher lengths. Therefore a standard 102.5mm thick wall would be referred to as a half-brick thick wall, as it would only be half of the stretcher length. A 215mm wall built, for example, in English bond would be referred to as a 1-brick thick wall, a wall measuring 327.5mm in thickness would be termed a 1½-brick thick wall, and so on.

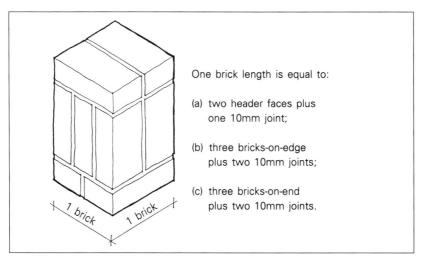

One brick length is equal to:

(a) two header faces plus
    one 10mm joint;

(b) three bricks-on-edge
    plus two 10mm joints;

(c) three bricks-on-end
    plus two 10mm joints.

Figure 4.1 The adaptability of standard brick dimensions.

SIZES

Bricks are designated in terms of their co-ordinating sizes and work sizes which are as follows:

Table 4.1 Sizes of bricks.

Co-ordinating size			Work size		
Length	Width	Height	Length	Width	Height
225mm	112.5mm	75mm	215mm	102.5mm	65mm

Co-ordinating size is also known as 'format', indicating the space allocated to a brick, including an allowance for a nominal 10mm mortar joint. (See figure 4.2)

Work size is the measurements of a brick specified for the manufacturing process, to which its actual size should conform within specified allowable deviations.

Most companies will manufacture various sizes of bricks to the client's specifications for repair and restoration work. This is especially so with the imperial-sized bricks found on many older buildings.

If the bricklayers are not to experience problems in working to the architect's measurements, it is essential that there are clearly defined limits to size variation within a consignment of bricks.

The limits of the sizes are expressed as limits on the overall measurements of twenty-four bricks sampled in accordance with clause 9 and measured as described in Appendix A. They should not fall outside the limits given in Table 1. In addition, the size of any individual brick in the sample must not exceed the 'co-ordinating size'.

In the UK there is a standard size for bricks – 215 × 102.5 × 65mm – but a manufacturing tolerance is allowed. The test for limits of size should be carried out by collecting a sample of twenty-four bricks from the batch in question. BS3921 'Standard for Clay Bricks' specifies three main methods of sampling:

1. Random sampling.
2. Sampling from a stack.
3. Sampling from a consignment of bonded packs.

This is to ensure as wide a range of bricks as possible. As the majority of bricks today are delivered in packs, many polythene shrink-wrapped, the method employed would be as follows.

Six packs would be selected at random, the band around one slice of each carefully removed and an equal number of not more than four bricks sampled at random from each of the opened slices. This will give the number required, with no consideration being allowed for condition or quality of the bricks. The bricks are dusted clean, and any blisters, small projections or loose clay particles adhering to any of them are removed. All the bricks are then placed in contact with each other upon a level, clean surface. The overall measurement of the dimensions is obtained using a steel tape to the nearest millimetre and the results checked against Table 1 from BS3921.

Table 4.2 Limits of size.

Work size	Overall measurement of 24 bricks	
	Maximum	*Minimum*
215mm	5235mm	5085mm
1025mm	2505mm	2415mm
65mm	1605mm	1515mm

Sizes of voids

The difference between solid, perforated, frogged and cellular bricks is defined according to their physical form in BS3921:

♦ *Solid bricks* do not have holes, cavities or depressions.
♦ *Perforated bricks* have holes not exceeding 25% of the gross volume of the brick. The holes are so disposed that the aggregate thickness of solid material, measured horizontally across the width of the unit at right angles to the face, is nowhere less than 30% of the overall width of the brick. The area of any one hole does not exceed 10% of the gross area of the brick.

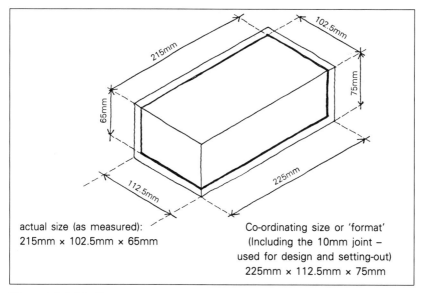

actual size (as measured):
215mm × 102.5mm × 65mm

Co-ordinating size or 'format'
(Including the 10mm joint –
used for design and setting-out)
225mm × 112.5mm × 75mm

Figure 4.2 Brick dimensions.

♦ *Frogged bricks* have depressions known as 'frogs' in one or more of the bed faces, but their total volume does not exceed 20% of the gross volume of the brick.
♦ *Cellular bricks* may have cavities not exceeding 20% of the gross volume of the brick, a cavity being a hole closed at one end.

Specification BS3921, 1985 'Specification for Clay Bricks' gives in detail the properties required of clay bricks and when used in conjunction with the 'British Standard Code of Practice for Use of Masonry, BS5628: Part 3, 1985 Materials and Components, Design and Workmanship', provides the basis for correct specification of clay bricks and brickwork.

Clay bricks vary considerably in physical properties and appearance. They may generally be said to perform well in the following respects:

♦ Aesthetic appearance.
♦ Durability.
♦ Resistance to rain penetration.
♦ Compressive strength.
♦ Fire resistance.
♦ Sound insulation.
♦ Low thermal and moisture movement.
♦ Economy.
♦ Versatility in application.
♦ Low maintenance requirements.

QUALITIES OF A GOOD BRICK

1. *Shape.* Good bricks will be consistent in size and will conform to the standard BS3921. Individual bricks in a consignment can vary within allowable tolerances, leading to differing joint sizes.

2. *Well burnt.* A well-burnt brick will be fired throughout its thickness and show a uniform texture internally when cut across. Under-burnt bricks are not durable and tend to weather quickly and disintegrate.

3. *Ring.* When struck with another brick, or with a trowel, good bricks emit a clear ringing sound. A poor brick gives a dull sound.

4. *Water absorption.* The water absorption of bricks varies considerably according to its type. A soft rubbing brick will naturally absorb much more than a dense, vitrified engineering brick. This property is not significant in determining frost resistance or resistance of brickwork to rain penetration.

5. *Compressive strength.* Clay bricks vary in strength from about $7N/mm^2$ to well over $100N/mm^2$. Where brickwork is to be structural (i.e. subjected to the loads of floors and roofs or other forces) bricks of adequate strength must be specified. In many instances, however, bricks are used well below their load-bearing capacity.

6. *Strength and density* (water absorption). Strong bricks of low water absorption, within prescribed limits, are known as engineering bricks. They are made from clay which, when fired, produces a hard, dense brick with a smooth shiny face. Traditionally they are used for civil engineering applications.

7. *Materials.* Clays for bricks should be composed of well-blended materials which will produce a good-quality product. If lime, which is sometimes added, is not finely ground it will cause 'lime blows'. This occurs when particles of burnt lime (quicklime) near the surface of the brick expand in contact with rainwater, blowing small and unsightly conical holes in the face of the wall.

8. *Soluble salts.* Some clays contain naturally occurring salts which clay treatment does not remove fully. When rainwater soaks into the brick these salts are dissolved and migrate in solution to the face of the brick as it dries. Upon reaching the air these salts crystallise in a white powder in a process known as efflorescence. Although not harmful, this is most unattractive until it weathers away in rainy weather. In persistent wet conditions some soluble salts can cause chemical reactions which change mortar (see later under 'Durability').

9. *Blemish free.* From the brickworks to the completed wall, bricks

may be handled many times. If this is done carelessly, a large percentage can be spoilt, with damaged arrises and chipped faces. This means that they cannot be used for facing work, but only on work which will not be seen, and this is an expensive waste.

10. *Colour.* Unless the brick is fired or textured for a multi-coloured face, it should be of uniform colour. Different batches of the same bricks can produce a variation in tone of colour which must be monitored if one is to avoid 'banding' in a wall. If consistency

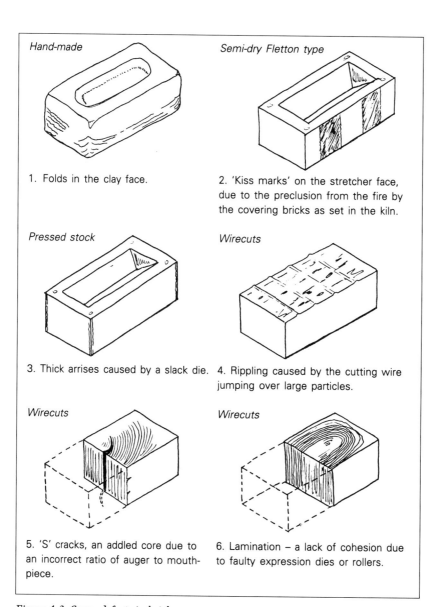

Hand-made

1. Folds in the clay face.

Semi-dry Fletton type

2. 'Kiss marks' on the stretcher face, due to the preclusion from the fire by the covering bricks as set in the kiln.

Pressed stock

3. Thick arrises caused by a slack die.

Wirecuts

4. Rippling caused by the cutting wire jumping over large particles.

Wirecuts

5. 'S' cracks, an addled core due to an incorrect ratio of auger to mouthpiece.

Wirecuts

6. Lamination – a lack of cohesion due to faulty expression dies or rollers.

Figure 4.3 Some defects in bricks.

cannot be guaranteed then all the bricks required should be purchased and delivered simultaneously. As an extra precaution, if the bricks have come in packs, when laying it is essential to mix from at least three packs to blend any variations in colour.

DEFECTS IN BRICKS

With the high standard of quality control available today, from the most basic hand selection carried out by small brick producers to the most advanced methods of computer control and test sampling at large brickworks, the chances of receiving defective bricks when one has paid for quality should be small. However, all bricks should be examined on delivery – although this is somewhat difficult today when so many bricks arrive in shrink-wrapped packs. It should be a standing instruction to the labourer and bricklayer to discard inferior bricks if they find them.

An under-burnt brick is generally softer than its counterparts, while an over-burnt brick will be harder, darker and often smaller. It may also be more brittle. Defective bricks may be laminated, crazed or 'cobwebby', or full of 'S' cracks. Others may have patches of burnt lime or stones showing or may be deformed by over-burning in some way.

Bricks which have distorted due to lack of care in drying, poor clay or blend, error in kiln placement, or over-burning, are known as 'crozzles'. 'Scum' is due to soluble salts in the clay or a deposit in the kiln caused by insufficient drying in the pre-firing stage. (See figure 4.3) In all these instances the bricks should be stacked to one side for possible use as hardcore or to be removed as rubbish. They should not be used in any walling of importance.

DESCRIPTION

The methods by which bricks are described are numerous:

1. *Method of manufacture* – extruded, wirecut, pressed, hand-made, etc.
2. *Uses* – commons, facings, engineerings.
3. *Place of origin* – Staffordshire Blues, London Stocks, Accrington 'Noris' etc.
4. *Surface texture* – sand-faced, glazed, rustic etc.
5. *Colour* – reds, buffs, blues etc.
6. *Raw material* – marl, gault, shale etc.

CLASSIFICATION OF BRICKS

The following brick classifications are generally recognized:

1. *Commons.* These have no special claim to aesthetic distinction and
   are defined as 'suitable for general building work'. Thus the term
   'commons' is applied to many varieties of clay bricks which fall
   outside the 'engineering' or 'facing' classifications. (See figure 4.4)
   They are widely used for foundations and as a backing for rendering, plaster or colour wash. Until the increase in popularity of
   lightweight blocks over thirty years ago, they were also popular
   for the inner leaf of cavity walling.
2. *Facings.* Specially made or selected to give an attractive appearance when used without rendering or plaster or other surface
   treatment of the wall. They combine attractive appearance with
   structural strength and good resistance to exposure. Today facing
   bricks are available in a wide range of colours, textures and
   strengths for use above ground level.
3. *Engineerings.* These are generally classified as either Class A (having a minimum crushing strength of $70N/mm^2$ and a maximum
   water absorption of 4.5%), or Class B (with a minimum crushing
   strength of $50N/mm^2$ and a maximum water absorption of 7.0%).
   They are further sub-divided into facings and commons according
   to their appearance. They are dense, strong, semi-vitreous bricks
   possessing both the required strength and absorption properties.
   There are numerous excellent load-bearing commons and facing
   bricks which even exceed the defined limits for a Class A engineering, but which are not classified as such because their water
   absorption exceeds the specification.
       Their name derives their use in civil engineering – construction

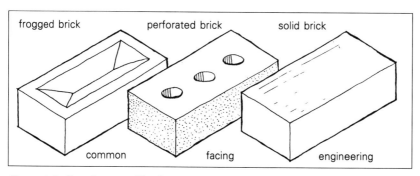

Figure 4.4 Classification of bricks.

of bridges, sewers aqueducts etc. – particularly during the nine-teenth and early twentieth centuries. They are still in demand today, for civil engineering work and also for engine pits, power houses and damp proof courses.

PROPERTIES OF BRICKS

Durability

Bricks are assessed for durability in BS3921, 1985 (Specification for Clay Bricks). Clay bricks are classified separately for frost resistance and soluble salt content; this produces six designations which are given in Table 4.3 of the Standard and defined in clauses 5.1 and 5.2.

Table 4.3 Durability designation.

Designation	Frost resistance	Soluble salt content
FL	Frost resistance (F)	Low (L)
FN	Frost resistance (F)	Normal (N)
ML	Moderately frost resistant (M)	Low (L)
MN	Moderately frost resistant (M)	Normal (N)
OL	Not frost resistant (O)	Low (L)
ON	Not frost resistant (O)	Normal (N)

Frost resistance

The degrees of frost resistance of a brick define its ability to withstand the potentially destructive effects of frost attack. This can occur when the brick is subjected to saturation and then repeated freeze–thaw cycles leading to expansive forces as the water freezes. The resistance of bricks to frost action varies, and therefore bricks should be used in accordance with their durability.

The frost resistance of a clay brick is generally determined by experience of its use. There is no British Standard Test for measuring frost resistance. However, reference is made in the Foreword to a test developed by British Ceramic Research Limited, which brick manufac-turers could use to assess their products. The test is carried out on a panel of brickwork involving 100 freeze–thaw cycles. Bricks surviving this severe test are deemed to be frost resistant.

The British Standard then goes on to describe three classes into which the manufacturer may place his products:

(F) *Frost resistant.* Bricks durable in all building situations, including those where they become saturated and subject to repeated freez-ing and thawing.

(M) *Moderately frost resistant.* Bricks durable except when in a saturated condition but subjected to repeated freezing and thawing.

(O) *Not frost resistant.* Bricks liable to be damaged by freezing and thawing if not protected as recommended in BS5628: Part 3. These bricks are considered suitable for internal use, or as a base for imperforate cladding.

Soluble salt content

The clays used for manufacturing bricks often contain naturally occurring soluble salts of calcium, magnesium, potassium, sodium and sulphate. These salts vary according to the geology of the clay. In the durability classification the level of soluble salts is defined as low (L) or normal (N).

(L) To qualify for a 'low' classification the salts content shall not exceed the following:
Calcium 0.300%
Magnesium 0.030%
Potassium 0.030%
Sodium 0.030%
Sulphate 0.500% by mass.

(N) For classification as 'normal', there is no limit on soluble salt content.

This classification has important implications for architects and specifiers in relation to the durability of finished brickwork, because soluble sulphates can damage cement mortar if the brickwork is subjected to prolonged wet conditions. Consideration must also be given to sulphates in the soil, and the prevailing ground conditions. Although the phenomenon known as efflorescence may be caused by soluble salts in L and N classification bricks, it is not necessarily related to the liability to efflorescence of the bricks. However the standard provides a test for, and limit of, efflorescence.

In any event sulphate attack can only occur in brickwork if three conditions combine. These are:

1. *Water.* Although this will be present during constructional use of the brickwork, that will not be the cause. Rather, prolonged wet conditions are necessary – from ground water or the effects of rain on the exposed brickwork.

2. *Tri-calcium aluminate (C_3A).* Found in Ordinary Portland Cement (OPC) in quantities of between 8 and 13%.

3. *Soluble sulphates.* These may be present naturally in the bricks or the ground.

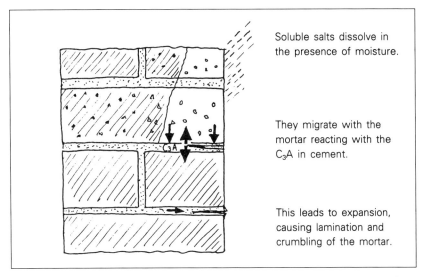

Figure 4.5 Sulphate attack.

If the brickwork remains in a very wet state then soluble sulphate salts will dissolve and migrate to the mortar joints on the surface of the walling, reacting chemically with the tri-calcium aluminate in the cement. This produces an expansive reaction which will manifest itself initially as a lightening of the colour of the mortar, followed by a horizontal cracking of the joint. Eventually the mortar will crack and crumble, and this decomposition may even cause the wall to lean or bulge, and to become weak and unstable. Sulphate attack takes some time to develop and is generally not evident within the first two or three years of a new wall being built. (See figure 4.5)

To avoid sulphate attack, the following points should be observed:

1. Use a frost resistant, low salt content brick conforming to the FL designation.
2. Use a sulphate-resisting cement in a good-quality cement-rich mortar which will be more resistant to saturation than will a leaner mix.
3. Design, build and maintain the brickwork so that it does not remain saturated for long periods.

Tests for soluble salts are carried out on a random sample of ten bricks. The test involves crushing and analysing the brick chemically.

Efflorescence

Efflorescence, formerly referred to as saltpetre, is the term used to describe the white powdery deposit of crystallized soluble salts on or near the surface of the brickwork. It is quite common to see some signs of efflorescence on new facework after the walling has dried out for the first time, but it rarely persists as it is washed away by wind and rain. Where it is more persistent or is heavy it can be very unsightly, but it is harmless. (See figure 4.6)

Although mainly due to the presence of soluble salts in the brick, it can also manifest itself in the joint, and this implies that the soluble salts are present in the sand of the mortar. This emphasizes, however, that the joint is the conduit through which the wall breathes. The salts are generally chlorates or sulphates of calcium, magnesium, potassium or sodium. All these are natural to building clays. They can also be present in the subsoil, and can rise up the brickwork through capillary action. Bricks which have been poorly stored, resting on the ground and open to the weather, can become contaminated with the minerals in the soil. The use of household detergents as a plasticizer can also contribute towards efflorescence, as they generally contain common salt. Only proprietary and properly formulated masonry mortar plasticizers should be used.

Efflorescence forms as the dissolved salts migrate to the surface of the wall while it is drying out. As the moisture content drops so the concentration increases until crystallization occurs either within the pores of the brick or on the face. Manufacturers are required to state the liability to efflorescence of their bricks, sampled and tested within the procedures laid down in the BS3921.

Although the test gives an assessment of liability to efflorescence the result has little direct relationship to the occurrence of efflorescence in brickwork, as the salts causing the condition may derive from other

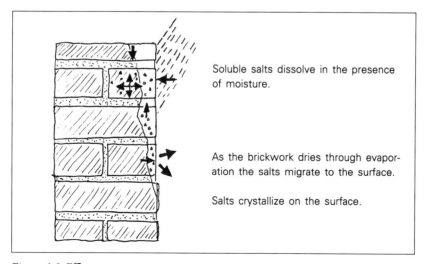

Soluble salts dissolve in the presence of moisture.

As the brickwork dries through evaporation the salts migrate to the surface.

Salts crystallize on the surface.

Figure 4.6 Efflorescence.

sources such as the mortar materials, site contamination, or even sea spray in coastal locations.

The liability of bricks to efflorescence is increased if bricks become saturated in the stack or if unfinished brickwork is left open and becomes wet. Thus, although proper specification of a brick, considering both frost resistance and soluble salt content, is vital at the design stage, designers should also specify that the brickwork should be covered to protect it from saturation during construction. Wide eaves, good copings, and sills give a valuable 'umbrella' to the wall and also minimize the likelihood of efflorescence. Site control over workmanship plays a vital part in this: bricks stored off the ground and kept covered and free from contamination; newly built work protected from wet weather for at least a week after construction; and scaffold boards turned up to prevent splashes of driving rain causing a 'band' of efflorescence at lift heights, can all help to control the problem.

Treatment of efflorescence

Under most circumstances it is best not to use acid or brick cleaners as this may only exacerbate the problem. The wall can be brushed clean using a bristle brush (never a wire brush), and light washing with clean water may help, but efflorescence is best left to weather away naturally.

Compressive strength

The compressive strength of bricks must be stated accurately. It must in no case be less than the strength for the appropriate class of brick given in Table 4.4.

Table 4.4 Classification of bricks by compressive strength and water absorption.

Class	Compressive strength N/mm^2	Water absorption % by mass
Engineering A	70	4.5
Engineering B	50	7.0
Dpc course 1	5	4.5
Dpc course 2	5	7.0
All others	5	No limits

NB: Clay bricks are available with compressive strengths ranging from about 7N/mm^2 to in excess of 100N/mm^2

The compressive strength of a brick is normally assessed by testing a sample of ten bricks. The average crushing strength of the ten bricks is quoted as the characteristic crushing strength of the consignment. Any frogs in the brick are filled with mortar before testing.

Compressive strength is especially relevant to a structural engineer when calculating structural brickwork strengths in accordance with the recommendations of the Structural Masonry Codes of Practice. It is not an indicator of the frost resistance or durability of the brick.

Water absorption

Clay brick manufacturers must state the water absorption levels of their products when sampled in accordance with Clause 9 and tested as described in Appendix E of BS3921. These levels must in no case be greater than those given for the appropriate class of brick in Table 4.4.

Water absorption is a measure of available pore space and is expressed as a percentage of the dry brick weight. This varies in clay bricks from 1% to 35%. Many people hold the mistaken belief that the lower the absorption the higher the degree of frost resistance, but this relationship is an unreliable guide. There are stocks and certain hand-made bricks which, by virtue of their pore structure, are often more frost resistant than machine-made bricks with a similar, high water absorption. Although high-strength bricks are generally found to have low values of water absorption this is not always a simple and consistent relationship. The classification of water absorption is used in calculating the flexural strength of masonry walls (i.e. their resistance to bending) because it is related to mortar bonding. The mortar strength is included in this calculation.

Water absorption is used to classify engineering and dpc bricks. Damp proof course 1 bricks are recommended for use in buildings, whilst damp proof course 2 bricks are recommended for external use (refer to Table B of BS5628: Part 3, 1985).

Water absorption is further used as a method of assessing how a particular clay brick may affect the action of water penetration through a wall. A wall of highly porous bricks can have what is known as an 'overcoat' effect. In this, some rain runs down the face but more is absorbed. Eventually water penetrates by the action of wind or heavy rain. However, a wall of bricks of low porosity will have a 'raincoat' effect: more water runs down the wall face, although water on the joint is increased.

In both cases good workmanship ensuring solid well finished mortar joints (bed joints and cross-joints) will resist wind-driven rain effectively. Even so, in heavy persistent rainfall water penetrates the outer leaf and drains down inside the wall cavity. It will then be conducted out by cavity trays and weep holes provided for that purpose.

Calcium silicate bricks

Calcium silicate bricks are manufactured to BS187, 1978, in highly automated factory conditions in which many stages of production are computer controlled. The bricks have a consistent structure with no soluble salts or sulphates in their composition. Therefore, mortar attack and efflorescence can only come from external sources such as soil contact or sea-water spray. This combines with the consistent high strength now available to give good frost resistance, making them ideal for foundation work.

The sizes of the bricks are as for clay bricks, and the tolerances are in accordance with BS187, 1978. The regularity of dimensions in size and shape of the bricks gives enhanced consistency of laying. The light reflective qualities, added to dimensional accuracy, give appeal for decorative internal brickwork, although the majority of facing bricks are still used for external applications. The inherent properties give global applications for use in hot and cold climates. They have been successfully used in places as diverse as the Middle East and the Antarctic island of South Georgia.

A comprehensive range of colours is available, and these can be adjusted in tone to match any colour shade which the client requests.

Classification

Calcium silicate bricks are designated by BS187, 1978, according to their compressive strength and appearance into the following classes:

Table 4.5 Compressive strength of calcium silicate bricks.

Class	Minimum mean compressive strength (wet) of ten bricks, N/mm^2	Minimum predicted lower limit of compressive strength, N/mm^2
7	48.50	40.5
6	41.5	34.5
5	34.5	28.0
4	27.5	21.5
3	20.5	15.5

Concrete bricks

Concrete bricks are available in three categories:

1. Facing bricks of $20N/mm^2$ strength, to provide an attractive appearance for use in all forms of construction, internal or external.

They are available in a wide range of colours including multi-colours, and in smooth, rustic, split, pitched or weathered finishes.

2. Engineering bricks of 40N/mm² strength can be used in particularly aggressive conditions where sulphate resistance and low water absorption are of paramount importance, such as in retaining walls, special applications below dpc level, and in structural applications. Inspection chambers can also be constructed with these bricks.

3. Common bricks are manufactured in a wide range of strengths, densities and cementitious content to satisfy the structural and durability requirements of BS5628: Part 3. They can be used above or below ground level, although if intended for fair-face work or painted finish, it is essential to specify the bricks before ordering.

The size of a concrete brick is as for clay bricks. However, the fact that the brick can be made to such fine tolerances does enhance its use on walls which are fair-faced on both sides. Metric modular bricks as well as imperial sizes are made by some manufacturers to specific order.

5

Mortar

Mortar – from the French *mortier* out of the Latin *mortarium* – consists of a binding agent; a mix of lime and/or cement, or refractory materials; a filler or aggregate (usually sand); and water. Sometimes there are additional ingredients for specific purposes, such as plasticizers. Air-entraining agents, retardants, or colouring pigments may also be incorporated. Mortar is mixed to a workable consistency by the addition of water, to serve as a soft bedding and jointing material which will take up the irregularities of bricks and fill voids. Mortar therefore binds the bricks together, is used as an aid for levelling irregularly sized bricks, gives a certain measure of impermeability to the weather, and adds to the overall appearance of the finished brickwork.

A comprehensive understanding of the range of traditional and modern mortars, as well as their respective materials, properties and characteristics, is essential to the modern craftsman, in order to ensure that he selects and uses the correct materials and mixes for the particular task at hand. A lack of understanding, combined with loss of the traditional skills needed to make a quality mortar at site level, irrespective of type, has led increasingly to a reliance on standard specifications. Until this is recognized, the present situation will prevail: products are sold because of their ease of use rather than on merit. This will further exacerbate the decline in traditional craft skills which are important not only for the specialist conservation market, but for infusing the highest quality into modern building construction.

Properties of a good mortar are:

1. *Adequate strength.* Mortar should have strength compatible with the bricks it binds in resistance to compressive loading – it should

never be harder than the bricks which will be bedded in the mortar, and should preferably be slightly weaker.

2. *Durability.* When fully set it should be resistant to extremes of weather and pollution.

3. *Porosity.* This should be similar to the bricks it binds, especially in old brickwork.

4. *Workability.* In its fresh state the mortar is easy to work and will not fatigue the craftsman unduly. A good mortar is 'fatty', leaves the trowel cleanly, holds together when being worked, and stiffens slowly.

5. *Aesthetically pleasing.* As mortar represents between 15–25% (depending on the bond) of a wall face, it affects the appearance of the overall brickwork. Therefore, consistency of colour and joint finish is essential.

There are several types of mortar relevant to the varied tasks which they are called upon to perform – traditional lime mortars are normally reserved for restoration and conservation work, gauged mortars (cement : lime : sand) for general brickwork, and cement mortars with air plasticizers for a large percentage of modern site work. Ready-mixed mortars are also used to an increasing extent, either as lime : sand ('coarse stuff') mix to be gauged on site with cement, or ready-to-use (retarded) cement mortars.

In order to avoid confusion, such a broad subject needs to be considered in two separate parts. Part One will be devoted to the history, preparation and use of traditional lime-based mortars. Part Two will deal with modern cement-based mortars which are used on the vast majority of new buildings and general brickwork. In recent years there has been a return to the use of lime as a plasticizer in certain applications and a final section will consider some of these modern, lime-based mortars.

PART ONE

TRADITIONAL LIME-BASED MORTARS

Binders are materials used with water to unite the fillers into a workable mix which will ultimately harden to hold the masonry together. Apart from Portland cements, which appeared from the second quarter of the nineteenth century, the principal binders in traditional mortars were limes of the non-hydraulic as well as semi- and eminently-hydraulic types. Natural cements (for example, Parkers 'Roman' Cement) are essentially similar in composition to hydraulic limes, but different in colour. The characteristics of these binders are now discussed.

LIMES

Lime, in its variety of forms, is derived mainly from chalk or limestone. Sea shells, coral, marble or other forms of calcium carbonate are also suitable. Chalks vary in quality and composition across the country, from white chalk lime to 'greystone' lime, each in its turn producing its own class of building lime.

On mass masonry where no tensile stress was incurred by the mortar, pure lime mortar was generally used. Where early hardening and acquisition of strength were of greater concern pozzuolans were introduced. During the nineteenth century hydraulic limes were increasingly employed to give mortars the strength and relatively quick set much desired by Victorian builders. A 1:2 or 1:3 hydraulic lime and sand mix is equal to 1:7 or 1:8 cement and sand mortar, although the former would be more workable.

Before 1945 lime remained the principal binder for mortars, especially in rural areas, although cement was gaining in popularity. The desire for speed, the employment of less knowledgeable artisans and aggressive marketing by cement companies, all contributed to the decline in the use of lime and traditional mortar techniques.

Although it would be unfair and untrue to say that cement mortars have not been and are still not successful, their use in the repair of old buildings has often proved to be unsuitable. Because they are less permeable they do not allow a wall to 'breathe' freely. Also, dense impermeable joints tend to trap moisture in the surrounding, usually soft, stock bricks, thus increasing the rate of their deterioration. Lime-based mortars are more elastic than cement-rich mortars and can accommodate minor structural movements without cracking. Pure lime mortars are usually light in colour and soft in texture, quite different in character from cement mortars.

The process of producing lime for mortar initiates what is referred to as the 'lime cycle'. By burning the raw materials (calcination), calcium carbonate ($CaCO_3$), in a kiln (traditionally a coal- or wood-fired 'clamp') to a high temperature, 900–1,200°C, carbon dioxide (CO_2) is driven off to form calcium oxide (CaO) or 'quicklime', formerly known as 'living', 'lump' or 'caustic' lime. (See figure 5.1)

After burning, the lump of quicklime would be the same shape but much shrunken. After picking over to discard under- or over-burnt pieces, it was then taken through a process known as 'slaking' ('slacking'), or 'blowing'. This involved combining the quicklime with

Figure 5.1 Loading flare kilns at Totternhoe, Bedfordshire, in the 1930s, with grey chalk lump lime in preparation for burning or calcination. Flare kilns such as this were in use from 1650 until 1938 (photograph reproduced by kind permission of the Totternhoe Lime and Stone Co. Ltd).

water so that a vigorous reaction took place. Great heat was generated, and the lime swelled and split, gradually breaking down to a powder or, with excess water, a fine mass of slaked lime 'putty' (calcium hydroxide $Ca(OH)_2$). The slaked lime was then mixed with the aggregate and water to form a mortar which, upon hardening (carbonation), returned the lime to calcium carbonate. This process produced a material which was as stable as the original stone. (See figure 5.2)

The setting action of a lime mortar is determined by the type used. Thus:

♦ Pure lime mortars harden in two stages:
   1. Initially stiffening on losing water to bricks and evaporation, accompanied by some shrinkage.
   2. Carbonation, i.e. chemical combination of the slaked lime or calcium hydroxide with carbon dioxide in the air, in the presence of moisture. The rate of carbonation or 'induration' tends to be slow and is affected by the pore structure of the mortar and surrounding materials.
♦ Hydraulic lime mortars stiffen initially on the loss of water to both masonry and evaporation. There is then a chemical reaction between water, lime and reactive siliceous minerals, i.e. calcium silicate and aluminates, which varies in time and strength with the class of hydraulic lime used.

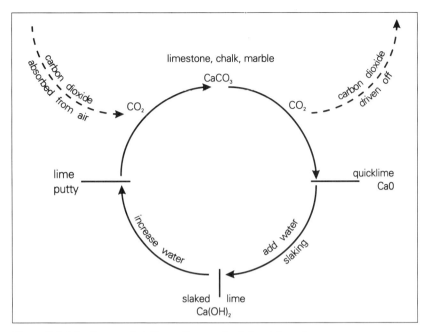

Figure 5.2 The lime cycle (after a diagram by John Ashurst).

It was John Smeaton (1724–1794) who in 1756, during investigations into limes for the construction of the Eddystone Lighthouse – where he required a binder capable of setting under water – divided limes into three classes:

1. Non-hydraulic (will not set under damp conditions).
2. Semi-hydraulic (will partially set under damp conditions).
3. Hydraulic (will set under damp conditions).

Non-hydraulic (white) limes are traditionally known as 'pure', 'fat' or 'rich' lime. Non-hydraulic lime is of high calcium content, and is produced from a white chalk, or a pure carboniferous limestone. It should not contain more than 5–6% impurities. Chalk limes slake very rapidly, and harden slowly in mortar, being entirely dependent on external agents for the setting action.

The majority of historic mortars are based on non-hydraulic lime as the principal binder. However, pure lime mortars built into thick walls never harden in the interior; the crystallization of the exterior of the joint when set prevents access of carbon dioxide to the inside of the wall. These chalk lime mortars were rarely pure in the modern sense, however, for they often contained impurities from the burning process – wood ash or coal cinders for example – which conferred early setting properties to the mortar.

By the end of the eighteenth century most writers on the subject were advocating either that pure lime mortars should be mixed with a variety of pozzuolans (additives to impart a 'hydraulic set') or that a hydraulic (stone) lime should be used. Certainly, by Victorian times chalk limes were considered unsuitable for constructional brickwork, and were mainly reserved for plastering, although they were still employed for some bricklaying mortars – especially in areas where they occurred naturally.

Today there is a large revival in the use of non-hydraulic lime mortars; their excellent working properties, good water retention, and bonding qualities, are recognized to be of the utmost importance in the repair and restoration of old buildings.

The value of pozzuolanic additives was first realized by the Greeks and Romans, who discovered that adding suitable materials or 'pozzuolans' to slaked non-hydraulic lime would impart a hydraulic set. These pozzuolans, fine siliceous materials, are capable of reacting with lime when mixed, forming calcium silicate cementing compounds. Such additives are called pozzuolans after Pozzouli, a region in Italy where a natural source (volcanic ash) of such material was mined.

Pozzuolans may be naturally occurring – examples include volcanic ash, diatomaceous earth, santorin earth or 'Trass' (formerly known as Dutch Terass). However, the Romans had no natural pozzuolans in Britain and therefore used crushed tiles or bricks as a synthetic pozzuolan. This gave them a hydraulic cement in mortars for binding masonry on waterlogged ground, as well as for work on drains, baths, aqueducts etc. This expertise in producing fast-setting, durable mortars was lost after the departure of the Romans. With the need for stronger and quicker setting mortars in a rapidly changing building industry and with the increasing interest in the techniques and knowledge of the ancients during the Renaissance, the direct use of pozzuolanic additives was slowly revived.

In the late sixteenth and early seventeenth centuries, Dutch trass began to be introduced into Britain. Trass was actually mined in Germany but processed in Holland where it was used in the construction of sea defences. After visiting and studying the marine structures in Holland, Smeaton at first felt that trass would be the ideal pozzuolan for the mortar to be used in the construction of the Eddystone Lighthouse. However, after various experiments on, and development of, cements, he chose another Italian pozzuolan, from Civitavecchia, mixed with Aberthaw lime. Joseph Gwilt in *The Encyclopedia of Architecture* (1888) states 'Various additions are made to mortar, in order to increase its hardness and tenacity; such as coal and wood ashes, forge scales, roasted iron ore, puzzuolana, and the like'.

Modern synthetic pozzuolans can also be materials like pulverized fuel ash (PFA) and high temperature insulation (HTI) brick dust powder from finely ground refractory bricks fired at temperatures of less than 150°C.

PFA is a waste material from power stations. When pulverized coal is blown into a stream of air and combusted, 75% of the resultant ash in the flue gases is extruded as pulverized fuel ash. When mixed with lime PFA imparts pozzuolanic properties and renders the mortar hydraulic. It should be noted that PFA will vary in sulphate content and therefore a low sulphate should be specified. It will also vary in colour and grading, and therefore pozzuolanicity. HTI is a refractory brick dust which is a waste product of the brick manufacturing process; as such its performance as a pozzuolan is variable.

Semi-hydraulic (grey) lime

Sometimes termed 'poor' or 'lean' limes, semi-hydraulic limes contain impurities in the form of clay and other useless matter. They have a slower slaking rate – up to two hours – and harden in mortars much more slowly. They are sometimes used as a plasticizer with cement : sand mixes, or with sand only on internal non-load-bearing walling. They are no longer produced in Britain.

Hydraulic lime

Hydraulic or 'greystone' limes are made from limestone which contains certain proportions of clay, the minerals in which (e.g. alumina, silica and iron oxide), not unlike the process in Portland cement, combine with the lime during calcination. This endows it with the properties of being able to set under wate,r and in places from which air is excluded, or without external agents. Capability in this area determines whether the lime is described as 'eminently', 'moderately' or 'feebly hydraulic': these terms are derived from their setting times.

- *Feebly hydraulic* (0–8% clay content). Setting time of 15–21 days, ultimately becoming as hard as a block of soap.
- *Moderately hydraulic* (8–18% clay content). Setting time of 5–15 days, ultimately becoming as hard as the softer varieties of building stones.
- *Eminently hydraulic* (18–25% clay content). Setting time of 1–4 days, and at the end of six months becoming similar in hardness to the harder kind of limestone.

Because hydraulic limes set by combining chemically with water they can be used for underwater or hydraulic engineering works. Blue Lias lime was an example of an eminently hydraulic lime which was used for foundations, basements, underwater work and engineering brickwork. Blue lias lime was quarried in the limestone belt across England from the South West to the East Midlands, and in South Wales; at Aberthaw, Watchet, Barrow and Rugby.

Feebly or moderately hydraulic limes, although certainly used before the eighteenth century if a source were close to a proposed building, became widely used from Georgian times in brickwork mortars, especially in London where speculative builders needed to work at speed.

Today hydraulic lime is no longer produced in Britain, which is regrettable as it played a significant part in the masonry of many of our structures from the late eighteenth century onwards. Despite the plentiful sources of the raw material, the large variation in quality and variety meant there was ultimately a failure to agree a British Standard. Traditional sites were Lyme Regis, Whitby, Arden (near Glasgow), Dorking, Halling, Merstham and the district around the River Medway. Hydraulic limes may still be obtained from France, Italy, Switzerland and Portugal.

NOTE
Hydraulic, or any of the burnt slaked limes, must not be confused with modern hydrated limes; they neither look nor perform similarly.

The end of the eighteenth century saw a massive building boom prompted by the Industrial Revolution, and the building of great engineering works using bricks and mortar. The construction of tunnels, bridges and harbours all demanded a dependable hydraulic binder. Although hydraulic limes and limes with pozzalanic additives were widely employed, the small-scale production from the local kilns was unable to cope with this new and huge demand, and was not well enough organized to meet the competition from the new quick-setting binder, cement.

Natural 'Roman' cements

Patented in 1794 by James Parker of Northfleet, Roman cement was actually a hydraulic lime containing a considerable quantity of clayey material. Calcining (burning) nodules of argillaceous limestone, called 'septaria', at a low temperature resulted in a rich brown hydraulic cement. It had a very quick set of about fifteen minutes after mixing with water. Until the middle of the nineteenth century the term 'cement' generally referred to Roman cement. After that period it was commonly understood to mean 'Portland' cement, which rapidly took its place. Roman cement was only about one third as strong as modern Portland cement. It was used extensively in the nineteenth century, especially for pointing, and in repair and restoration work.

The name Roman cement was a misnomer, as it certainly had no connections with the ancients. Although they did use the right type of limestone, with septaria, on some works they added powdered tile as a pozzuolan, not realizing that if they had burned the septaria they could have produced an equally satisfactory hydraulic cement. The name, it seems, came from the colour and its apparent similarity to the tone of Roman mortars. It was often referred to as 'brown cement', and ceased to be produced in the early 1960s.

There were similar brown-coloured cements ('Sheppey' and 'Medina' cements), produced in a like manner to Roman cement and, like it, made from septaria nodules. These were produced at Harwich, the Solent, Weymouth, Calderwood, Rugby and Whitby. 'Medina' was considered superior to Roman cement.

Cement

Natural cements are in reality eminently hydraulic limes. What we today call 'cements' are truly synthetic. Experiments with limes and pozzuolans by Smeaton in 1755 had led to the discovery of cements with quick-setting hydraulic action, ideal for the new constructional demands. Patent holders, investors and industrialists were quick to realize that if an effective system of mass production and fast delivery could be established, they would be able to supply a highly lucrative market against little competition from the localized limestone kilns.

Cement was further enhanced by its production being relatively cheap. Manufacturing took place next to the quarry which supplied the raw material, chalk or limestone. It was therefore more economical to move and handle only the finished product, rather than the coarse starting material.

Further developments of patented cements, technological progress and product competition by the late nineteenth century, led to aggressive marketing and meant that ultimately the use of lime as the major binder was simply pushed to one side.

Historical development of artificial cements

In 1824, a Leeds bricklayer, Joseph Aspdin, patented a true 'Portland cement', so-called from its supposed similarity of appearance to the stone of that name. It was one of a series of new synthetic cements derived from an initial patent taken out in 1811 by James Frost. By lightly burning crushed chalk and clay together, he developed the general rules for this new binder.

Aspdin's early Portland cement was manufactured in Wakefield, using crushed and calcined 'hard limestone' mixed with lime and clay, which was then ground into a fine slurry with water. This mixture was then fired in beehive shaped brick kilns, broken into lumps and fired a second time. This burning took months at a time, and as temperatures were low it was probably not of great quality. Aspdin's son, William, continued to expand and develop his father's company, establishing premises along the River Thames and in Gateshead. However, it was Isaac C. Johnson (1811–1911) who was to develop Portland cement into a product not too dissimilar to that used today. It was he who noticed the importance of vitrification in the burning of the raw materials. He had taken over Aspdin's old Gateshead kilns and observed that, when ground down, the over-burnt lumps in the kiln produced a slower setting and a better final product. In 1845, after further research, he launched a refined Portland cement marketed as 'Johnson's Cement' from Swancombe in Kent. From this period onwards the manufacturing process was to advance in its calcining and processing methods so that by the 1860s cement quality was very similar to that produced today.

Initially cement was calcined in an intermittent, vertical, brick or 'beehive' kiln, similar to that used for burning lime, with the raw materials placed in layers alternating with fuel – wood, coal or coke. However, this kiln was troublesome as it had to be recharged after each burning, and during the recharging the kiln would cool down. Much fuel was inevitably wasted in reheating it.

A modified kiln of this type, called a 'Dietsch kiln', came into use around 1880. This had a narrow firing zone and was lined with refractory bricks as it fired at a much higher temperature. The kiln was loaded as before, with the dry raw materials and the fuel in the upper part of the kiln. The resultant clinker fell into a lower chamber to be removed by a moveable grate, and this was cooled by forced draught control from a gate at the base of the kiln. Both of these methods were termed the 'dry process' of manufacture.

A third method of producing Portland cement was by what is called the 'wet process'. This method was possible due to the perfecting of a rotary kiln in the 1890s. This enabled the raw materials to be fed into the kiln as a wet slurry. As the inclined kiln rotated the slurry gravitated to the firing zone where it was calcined to a clinker. This method is essentially the same as the one employed today.

Aggregates

Sand was, and remains, the most frequently used aggregate. Today the choice of sand for lime-based mortars remains of the utmost importance in securing a quality mortar. The sand should be coarse and sharp, well graded, with not too may 'fines', or dust, as the lime provides the fines. Sometimes in matching a historic mortar the aggregates may ultimately be a blend of two types of aggregates.

The importance of aggregate in securing a good mortar must not be overlooked, as a well-graded one will compensate for a poor lime in helping to achieve a set. The sand, as well as being an economical filler, gives a ready passage to air when mixed well with the lime, allowing absorption from the atmosphere to take place and facilitating the setting action. Building sand was traditionally classified into three main groups:

1. *Pit sand.* Angular, porous and sharp in grit, pit sand has to be washed to remove impurities although very often used 'as-raised' from the quarry. Considered the best sand for mortar.
2. *River sand.* Although cleaner, it had a rounder grain and so a mortar more suitable for plastering. It also required thorough washing.
3. *Sea sand.* Disliked because of the contamination of salt, and be-cause it was rounded in grain. The salt content made it liable to attract dampness, and so if used it had to be very well washed to remove the salt.

Road drift was another source of sand. It was obtained from the sweepings off the roads and was considered by some a good alter-native, provided it was carefully washed to remove vegetable and animal matter. However, all too often it was not washed, and during the 'bad mortar era' in the second half of the nineteenth century complaints of 'road drift' being mixed with old 'fallen' chalk lime, and forming only a pretence of lime mortar, abounded.

The advent of the mortar mill at the end of the seventeenth century gave rise to many substitutes for sand, such as crushed brick and sand stone, which, if properly mixed, produced excellent mortars. The mixer consisted of millstones and a container into which the ingredients were fed to be ground to the required consistency.

W. Frost in *The Modern Bricklayer* (1931) testifies to the strength of crushed brick as an aggregate: 'the bricks were crushed on the job, and were mixed with lime (no sand being used), in the mortar mill. The proportion of lime was below the average, yet the mortar proved quite satisfactory. Indeed, when part of the brickwork had to be cut away it was found the mortar had developed amazing strength within a month or two!' Crushed brick (from soft stocks) and/or tile was mixed with lime (ideally hot and freshly slaked, according to some authorities), and sand in a ratio of 1 part lime, 2 parts crushed brick and 1 part sand. When mixed to a workable gauge it was commonly known as 'pan mortar' and was considered an excellent material. The dry brick rubbish of old walling, broken down and sifted, was employed on a large scale in London after the war, using waste bricks from bomb sites for the huge rebuilding programme.

Crushed lime or sandstone were sometimes used, either alone or with sand. Metallic sand sold in coarse or fine powder as required was introduced in about 1843. It was mixed with blue lias lime for joining bricks and stone, or for moulded work.

Mix ratios

The master mortar maker was heir to a long tradition of technical knowledge and understanding of materials. He knew how to blend the materials to get the best results for the craftsmen bricklayers, who had themselves, since the days of their apprenticeship, developed an innate knowledge of their materials and a comprehensive grounding in their correct use. Thus they maximized the capabilities of the materials in the days before there were any legislative standards or guarantees as to their performance.

The binder : aggregate ratios have always varied considerably, with mixes ranging from 1:1 to 1:4. Richard Neve in *The City and Country Purchaser and Builders Dictionary* (1762, pp. 198, 199) illustrates this with examples of varying mortar ratios used in and around London, often in different parts of the same building – footings, inner and outer walls. To a very large extent these ratios were, and remain, determined by the type of aggregates and the need to obtain a workable mix. It is interesting to note that the common use of a 1:3 specification for a lime : sand ratio is based essentially on the voids by volume in a dry sand.

Water used for mixing mortar was always expected to be clean, and free from clay, soil, salt or organic matter. Today it is described as being potable – fit for drinking – and if in any doubt one should refer to BS3148.

Additives

Additives are mixed into mortars either to impart particular physical properties to the fresh or hardened mortars (such as frost resistance, water proofing, or plasticizers to improve workability), or to give a coloured finish to the mortar.

From the mid-thirteenth century natural organic substances were employed. These included casein from milk, the whites of eggs, boiled linseed oil, fresh blood, keratin from horses' hooves, tallow from animal fat, beeswax, malt, beer and urine, all intended to assist set or plasticity. Beer and urine acted as plasticizers; waxes, fats and oils would help in resisting moisture penetration, and sugary materials helped to retard carbonation or set, and reduce the amount of water required. From the mid-nineteenth century bitumen was also used, alone or with lime, to make a mortar for marine works as well as for covering the tops of arches and vaults to prevent the passage of moisture.

Pigments

Before the 1950s the colouring agents used in mortars, especially for pointing were natural, from mineral or vegetable sources. The following colourings and their origins are those recommended by Peter Nicholson in his book *The New and Practical Builder* (1823):

> Lamp black is properly the soot of oil collected as it is formed by burning but generally, no other than a soot raised from the resinous and fat parts of the fir trees.
>
> Yellow ochre is a natural mineral which is found in many places but of different degrees of purity. In the UK it is chiefly excavated in Oxfordshire.
>
> Venetian red is a natural ochre, rather inclining to scarlet.
>
> Spanish brown is a natural earth, found in the very state and colour in which it is used.

NOTE

In conservation work the colour of replacement mortars should be derived principally from the colour of the aggregates themselves. Pigments alone should not be relied upon to achieve a satisfactory colour match. Where pigments are used to colour mortars these should be based on mineral oxides.

Mixing traditional lime mortars

In conservation and restoration work it has long been recognized that, as far as possible, one should carry out all work with authentic materials which are in harmony with the original. Traditional lime mortars for brickwork are no exception, although it is to be regretted that many of the techniques for its preparation and use have been lost to the vast majority of site personnel. This lack of knowledge and skill has led to its correct use being seriously impaired, yet its preparation and application are quite straightforward, providing that basic, long-established rules are followed.

Mortar analysis

Mortar analysis may be required for important listed buildings. This procedure can be as simple as an experienced person giving an accurate visual examination, or as complex as a highly sophisticated physical and chemical laboratory analysis. While a simple analysis can assist the preparation of a specification for an appropriate conservation mortar, factors such as the degree of exposure to which the new mortar will be subjected, and the condition of the brickwork, will be more significant for its design.

Mixing area

This should always be as near as possible to where the bricklayers are working. Traditionally a flat timber mixing platform or 'stage' was constructed on which to gauge and mix the mortar. This consisted of a number of scaffold boards (often twelve) about 12 feet (3m) in length, with four stakes driven into the ground to keep the boards in position and close at the joints, allowing only the minimum of water to escape.

Today this can be formed using 20mm-thick sheets of shuttering plywood. A stage should be constructed even if machine mixing is used, in order to prepare the materials which are to be introduced into the mixer, and to receive the turned-out mixed materials. At the end of a day's work the mixer and stage should always be washed clean, no matter what type of mortar has been prepared.

Gauging the materials

Careless measuring, especially by the use of the shovel, should always be condemned. Traditionally, timber gauge boxes without bottoms were employed, and their use is still recommended. All gauges for sand were based on the cubic yard, with different-sized boxes for the half- and third-yard, as well as others if necessary to suit the proportions of the various materials. Today we base our measurements on the cubic metre. (See figure 5.3)

In the days when lime was the principal binder it was always the first material specified. A mix ratio of 1:3 indicated 1 part lime to 3 of sand. Even with the inclusion of cement with lime, in the later nineteenth century, a 1:1:6 meant 1 part lime to 1 of cement and 6 of sand. Today, however, even in traditional mortar, a 1:1:6 indicates a cement : lime : sand mix. The binder always comes before the aggregate, so a lime mortar of one unit of lime to three units of sand is always written 1:3, never 3:1.

Traditional lime mortars can be divided into two groups:

1. Lime : sand.
2. Cement : lime : sand (gauged mortar).

LIME : SAND

When lump or non-hydrated lime is used it must first be slaked. Traditionally this was done either by slaking the lime with the sand, or by adding the slaked lime to the sand, in the specified proportions. The former method is rarely, if ever, practised today.

From the seventeenth century, for bricklaying mortars, slaking the lime with the sand was the most common method, as can be clearly seen in studying old texts. This was especially so with the advent of the popular use of hydraulic limes. The very large volumes and turnover of mortars necessary to supply large gangs of bricklayers working on thick-walled structures, and particularly on speculative building and engineering projects, demanded an organized system of mortar production. This involved rapid slaking and mixing, and the material was allowed to stand as a 'coarse stuff' for a few days only before use as a hot lime mortar: all took place under the watchful eye of the master mortar maker.

Feebly and moderately hydraulic limes are capable of being slaked from the lump with sand like pure lime, although this takes longer, and they can also be kept for several days as a coarse stuff before use, at which point they must be knocked up again. A pure lime coarse stuff, well covered, will keep for years and is considered all the better for this maturity.

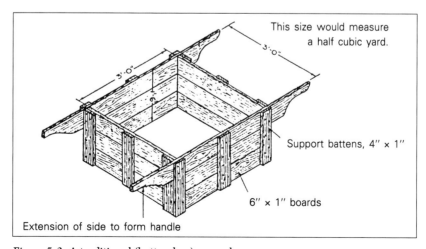

Figure 5.3 A traditional (bottomless) gauge box.

Slaking the pure lime in a bin or pit, and then mixing with the aggregate in the correct proportions, is a practice of great antiquity. While sites and demand remained relatively small, with plenty of room for storage, and while the bricklaying season was short (March to October), it was a method which worked effectively.

By the eighteenth century, however, in the speculative building environment of the large towns and cities, the demand for mortar was large, and space on site was in short supply. Slaking in a pit or bin was fast becoming a method of storing matured slaked lime for the plasterers, and for use in some areas of specialized bricklaying. Today it is widely practised for producing small amounts of pure lime mortars for use in restoration work on historic buildings.

Mixing pure lime mortars

Slaking lime putty

The lime, which should be fresh from burning – hot lime was preferred by many old craftsmen – should be stored on a hard standing (not combustible) and covered with sheeting to keep it clean and dry. If this is not done the lime can start to 'air' or 'wind' slake by absorbing moisture from the atmosphere. When this happens it is known as 'fallen lime'. It is therefore prudent to minimize this problem by commencing the slake as soon as possible after delivery, .

This process can be achieved in a number of ways. A traditional method, commonly employed, was either to slake initially in a galvanized tank and then pour through a sieve into a wood-lined lime pit, or to slake directly in the pit and, when ready for use, sieve it into the mortar. Once cooled, the lime pit would be kept covered to keep the lime clean. (See figure 5.4)

In both methods, water is placed first to a depth of 300mm and then, using a clean shovel, the lime is added (never the other way around as the lime would spit) slowly up to half the depth of the water. The water : lime ratio is about one volume of lime to eight volumes of water, although this depends upon the type of lime. The lump lime should be monitored carefully as it is added to discard discoloured or noticeably heavier lumps.

The whole mass is periodically stirred using a hoe-like tool called a 'larry' (the operation is in fact termed 'larrying') until the visible reaction subsides. Larrying is very important, as it agitates the quicklime, suppressing skin formation which would prevent further slaking. When it occurs, this is referred to as 'drowning', and careful monitoring is important.

To speed up the slaking process, hot water can be used initially. The

Figure 5.4 Slaking lime to a putty. The operatives are pouring cooled lime putty through a large sieve to settle and mature into the wood-lined lime pit. A roll of thick gauge polythene is next to the pit to cover the lime putty. In the background, on a boarded work area, some lump lime has been broken down ready for slaking, while nearby steam is given off as the lime reaches boiling point at the height of the slake in another galvanized tank.

lumps may also broken be down into small pieces and, if one is slaking in a tank, the process can be 'kicked off' by placing a gas burner under the tank to bring the water to the boil. This is very effective, but with high calcium lime it will not be necessary.

Once the slaking process subsides, after about twenty-four hours, a cloudy suspension called 'milk of lime' will set over the soft mass which is now termed 'lime putty' (or putty lime). If the slaking is being done in a tank, it is at this stage, when cool, that the lime is poured, by removing a bung or opening a tap at the lower end of the inclined tank. It is run through a fine sieve (5mm approximately) to remove core and large coagulations) into the lime pit to mature. If it is left too long in the tank the lime will thicken, making sieving harder. The pit must be kept covered with water throughout this maturing, which should be a minimum of two weeks to ensure that the lime is thoroughly slaked. However, the properties of lime putty improve the longer it stands, so ideally it should be left to mature for as long as possible before use. The clear water which collects on the surface of the stored putty is correctly termed 'lime-water'.

Today it is often more convenient to purchase lime putty from specialist suppliers, who will deliver the lime putty (and pre-mixed coarse stuff) in re-sealable plastic tubs.

The slaking of quicklime is a hazardous process, and it is incumbent upon the operatives to ensure that they have full eye protection (not only to protect from any 'spits' but also from the possibility of quick-lime dust reacting with eye moisture). Full gauntlet gloves and protective clothing should be worn. It is also advised that a barrier cream is applied to exposed skin. An eyewash bottle containing clear water is an essential standby.

Methods of mixing lime mortar

The traditional method – by hand

Upon a clean platform or stage the sand was measured by the 'yard', having been passed through a ¼″ (5mm) screen. As the sand was usually 'as-raised', it was often naturally mixed with stones or gravel. The large screen would be fixed at an angle, with a prop placed at the back to keep it firmly in position. The mortar man then shovelled up the unsifted sand and threw (or 'punched') it against the screen. Because the screen was inclined, the fine sand passed though it and formed a heap which could be removed to stage, while the waste stones rolled slowly down the face of the screen to form another heap. In the past these stones were used in concrete. (See figure 5.5)

The sand on the stage was then pulled out to form a large ring. The lump lime was then placed into the middle, with the pieces broken as small as possible to help in gauging and to speed up the slake. It was then sprinkled with sufficient water, from a watering-can or hose with a rose attached, to slake it. Some of the sand was drawn over the lime to keep in the all-important heat, and it was then left in this state until the lime was thoroughly slaked, when the generation of steam ceased. This stage of the process varied according to the type of lime used.

Although some people would then mix the sand and lime at this stage, and barrow it away as coarse stuff for later 'screening', many would first screen the slaked lime. This was done in exactly the same manner as with sand. A similar-sized mesh was used, giving a powder which passed through as fit for use. The core (from the French *coeur* – heart), material which would not pass through the screen, was rejected for the purpose of mortar and used instead for filling in the sides of foundations and under timber floors.

The screened lime was returned to the sand ring, to which water was added, and the whole mass was then stirred with a larry until a thick cream-like consistency was obtained. If the mortar was being mixed with pure lime putty, the procedure from this point was exactly the same, the lime putty introduced from the gauge box into the ring and again mixed with water. The sand was then gradually drawn in and thoroughly mixed with the lime by using the same tool. The mortar was then barrowed away to stand for some days before use.

Figure 5.5 A man 'punching' the materials for making lime mortar through the large inclined screen to remove large unwanted particles (print, *c.*1866, by kind permission of Richard Filmer).

When required it was returned to the stage again and well beaten up with larry and shovel.

Traditionally it was found that mortar, well chopped, rammed and beaten, produced a more plastic and workable mix without the addition of extra water. Isaac Ware's *Complete Body of Architecture* (1756) refers to a French proverb which states that the only moisture which should be added to a mortar is the sweat of the labourer's brow. Vitruvius recommended that the mortar should be beaten with wooden staves before being used. Smeaton reckoned it a fair day's work for a labourer to mix and beat up two or three large hods of mortar for use. Although the latter was an exceptional example, and not widely practised because this would be insufficient for a brick-layer's daily consumption of mortar on thick walling, recent trials have confirmed the importance of a really vigorous mixing. It was in this hand-mixing action that the term to 'knock up' mortar originated.

If, after thorough knocking up, the coarse stuff is too sloppy for the intended use it can be spread on an absorbent surface and allowed to de-water prior to reworking. If it is too stiff, a very little water (added in the form of a fine spray) may be added to increase workability, but one should also consider increasing the binder ratio (e.g. from 1:3 to 1:2) if the mortar lacks cohesion.

When as many batches of coarse stuff as required had been prepared and 'banked', it was then covered with straw and damp sacking. The expression to 'bank' is equivalent to the use of the term for a fire, i.e. to make it burn (heat) slowly by covering it up. Nowadays banks of coarse stuff can be covered with underlay felt or polythene sheeting. Plastic bins with airtight lids can also be used for storing coarse stuff. It must be kept damp and, like lime putty, improves with keeping. This allows the ingredients to integrate fully and mature, and when it is knocked or beaten up again gives a cohesive, 'fatty' mortar, which is extremely workable.

Although hydraulic lime would slake after a long period, it was often impossible to wait that length of time, especially on sites where it was used for footings, foundation brickwork and basements as well as civil engineering work. It was therefore often sold as a ground powder, in which state, after exposure, it became 'air-slaked'. Blue lias lime was generally mixed 1:1, 1:1½ or 1:2. The lime and sand were screened, measured and shot upon the stage, the sand first and the lime on top of it. These were then mixed together in a dry state and then with sufficient water to form mortar which was stiff so that the lime did not escape with surplus water. This class of mortar, like cement mortar, could not be stored and had to be used within four hours.

Machine mixing

By the late seventeenth century a horse-powered mortar mill was employed on large works to mix mortar. After the mid-1850s machine mixing was possible, generally with the aid of a steam-driven pan mixer, into which the coarse stuff would be introduced. This eliminated the need to beat, ram and chop the mix and greatly speeded up mixing time, output, and consistency in the overall quality of the mortar. The mill was first revolved with the materials in a dry state, and water was added as the materials progressed towards their proper consistency. Nowadays paddle or roller-type pan mixers may be used. Roller pan mixers are very efficient but care has to be taken to ensure that the coarse stuff is not over-worked or crushed. The clearance between the rollers and pan base can be adjusted in some models to avoid the latter problem. (See figure 5.6)

A delay in adding any additional water is very important to give time to assess the true consistency. It is therefore prudent to wait and allow a dry mix to reach its true state after five minutes of mixing. Lime

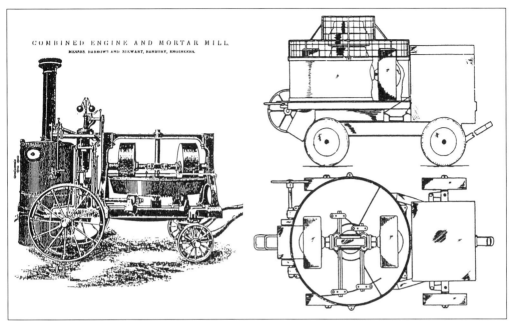

Figure 5.6 A Victorian steam-driven mortar mill, taken from *The Engineer*, 1876; and (right) its modern counterpart, a Liner Rolpanit roller pan mixer (print, by kind permission of Multi Marque Production Engineering Ltd).

mortars need to be mixed for almost twice as long as cement mortars. When used, pozzuolanic additives, accurately gauged and mixed with water to form a slurry, should be added during the final reworking.

When prepared in this way and presented to the craftsman brick-layer, lime mortar will retain water very well, and will not be inclined to dry out in use as modern mortars do. It will possess excellent workability, clinging to the trowel, yet spreading and furrowing cleanly in preparation for bedding bricks.

Health and safety

Quicklime is highly hygroscopic and hence its use with water can be dangerous. Full eye protection and protective clothing, including a barrier cream on exposed skin, are advisable. A condition known as 'bricklayer's itch' was relatively common in former times: it was a cutaneous disease produced on the hands of bricklayers through repeated contact with lime. As there is a possibility of dust getting into the eye and reacting with its moisture, it is advisable to have an eye irrigation unit at hand. Only a person skilled in this work and conversant with the materials should be allowed near the slaking area. Hydrated lime is an irritant similar to cement, and the precautions outlined on pages 131–2 should be followed.

CEMENT : LIME : SAND (GAUGED MORTARS)

Traditionally this was known as 'compo mortar', as it was a 'composition mix' of the old slaked lime : sand and the new cement : sand mortars. In general non-hydraulic lime was mixed with sand, as described before, to form coarse stuff which, after a period of maturing, would be reworked and mixed with cement for immediate use as a gauged mortar. It is worth mentioning here that 'gauged stuff' for a bricklayer (as opposed to a plasterer) was traditionally a 1:3 Roman cement or Portland cement to sand mortar, used for filletings and setting chimney pots.

The conventional gauging of the cement : lime sand varies from $1:\frac{1}{4}:3$, $1:\frac{1}{2}:4\frac{1}{2}$, 1:1:6, 1:2:9 and 1:3:12. However, many craftsmen preferred only a 'dusting' of cement to give ratios nearer to $\frac{1}{8}:2:9$ and $\frac{1}{8}:3:12$ respectively. Recent research has shown that the addition of very small proportion of cement can adversely affect strength and durability, rendering the gauged mortar inferior to a part-lime mortar. In historic brickwork, where gauged mortars are used, mixes will typically be in the range from 1:1:6 to 1:3:12.

Mixing

By hand

Coarse stuff should be prepared as previously described. With the coarse stuff heaped on to the stage the gauged volume of cement is placed on top. The whole heap or mound should then be shovelled or 'turned', with each shovelful being added on top of the next, until a new mound is created. The process should then be repeated, shovelling always from the bottom and sprinkling onto the top, until the mound is returned to its original position. This action is repeated one more time to fulfil the site saying 'Always turn a mix three times'.

This gauged mix is then hollowed out to form a ring and a minimum of clean water added (in the form of a spray) and left for a short while to allow the mix to soak most of it up. An experienced mixer can gauge this with unerring accuracy and rarely adds any more water after this stage. The whole mix is now thoroughly integrated using either a shovel, a larry, or both. This gauged mix has to be used within two hours of mixing, otherwise the cement will stiffen and begin setting. On no account should the mortar be re-tempered after this time as to do so would seriously affect both strength and colour.

By machine

The coarse stuff should be placed into the mixer pan and the cement added in the correct proportion as a slurry. The final water should be held back until the true moisture content of the mix has been determined, after mixing for at least three minutes. It should then be mixed for a further two or three minutes.

Avoid using modern artificial plasticizers: they do not enhance workability. Masonry cement should not be used with gauged mortars as it is intended for a totally different modern mortar.

The advantages of traditional lime-based mortars

1. They are flexible and will take up slight movement and settlement in the brick walling.
2. Although weatherproof, they are not impermeable and therefore allow the brick wall to 'breathe' and dry out after long wetting periods, thus reducing the vulnerability to frost damage.
3. They are more porous than dense cement mortars and do not, therefore, concentrate harmful cycles of salt crystallization at the surface of the bricks.
4. They are highly workable and cohesive and can be used more cleanly than modern cement mortars.
5. Because they are light coloured they are aesthetically more pleasing, without the dullness of modern cement mortars.

Disadvantages of traditional lime-based mortars

1. Although quicklime or prepared lime putty is relatively inexpensive, the costs of transporting them from the limited number of suppliers, and of the more labour-intensive preparation, are quite high.
2. As there is no initial chemical set, it is a slow process of carbonation which leads to hardening.
3. Because of this slow cure, a frost occurring within one month of construction could cause problems with the mortar, which is why the traditional bricklaying months were from March to October.
4. Unless correct procedures are followed in the selection, preparation, mixing and use of lime : sand, and in bricklaying, problems can occur. This type of mortar is less tolerant of poor workmanship.

To conclude: traditional lime mortars are relatively straightforward in use, but require patience and skill, assets which are sadly lacking on modern sites. If used properly, the result will be a light- coloured, soft-textured, porous mortar, ideal for the mainly hand-made bricks which it binds. Dense, brittle and darker cement-rich mortars are not compatible with traditional materials for restoration work and should not be used as a substitute for them.

Traditional lime mortars are not encouraged for the majority of modern work, although modern lime : sand and Portland cement mortars are appropriate.

PART TWO

MODERN CEMENT-BASED MORTARS

Today's mortars serve slightly different functions from their pre-decessors for, besides the aesthetic and durability considerations, they have important roles to play in transferring the compressive, tensile and sheer stresses inherent in modern brickwork.

By definition, cement is a general term denoting a powdered binding material which, when added to water, takes on a plastic consistency with adhesive properties and a hydraulic setting action. It is processed in a number of ways with varying materials and additives (although

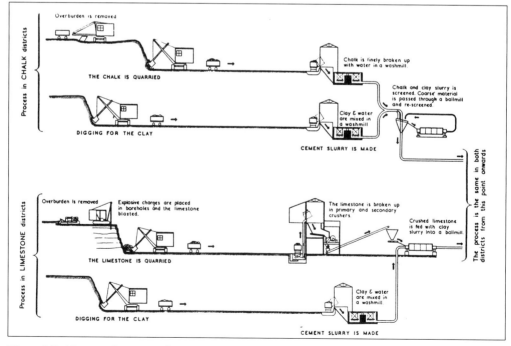

Figure 5.7 Above and opposite: diagram showing stages in the manufacture of cements (reproduced by kind permission of the British Cement Association (BCA)).

chalk and limestone remain the most important), to produce a strong, dense binder for a variety of purposes and situations.

Ordinary Portland Cement (OPC) mortars stiffen initially by loss of water to the bricks, and by evaporation, with some shrinkage. The hardening is then a process of chemical reactions between the cement and water, resulting in the liberation of lime and the formation of a glue-like colloidal complex, cementing itself or the sand mixed with it. The rate of hardening is affected by the temperature and pore structure of the surrounding masonry.

Ordinary Portland Cements (OPC)

These are manufactured to conform to BS12 and are the most widely used cements in modern mortars. During the last thirty years developments in production and quality control in highly sophisticated plants have led to the manufacturing of a cement vastly superior to that first patented by Aspdin. Although production has altered considerably, modern methods are still known as the wet process and the semi-wet process, the semi-dry process and the dry process, . (See figure 5.7)

♦ *Wet process.* The chalk and clay are mixed with water before entering the kiln as a slurry. However, much energy is then consumed

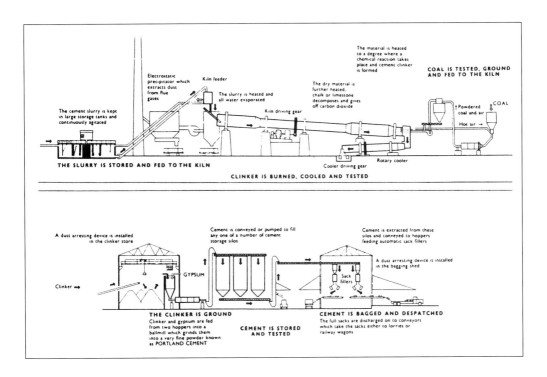

while boiling off the water before the formation of the cement. This is therefore becoming less popular because of high energy costs.

♦ *Semi-wet process.* This takes the slurry and passes it through the filter presses, which squeeze the moisture out. It thus saves fuel during firing in the rotary kiln.

♦ *Semi-dry process.* This takes a dry raw material and adds a small amount of water to create a granule which is fed to a pre-heater and a short kiln.

♦ *Dry process.* When the raw material is harder and drier, as with limestone and shale, it is initially ground to a fine powder to form what is known as a 'dry meal'. Once again this method saves fuel in the kiln.

Whichever process has been selected, the raw materials are then introduced into the inclined rotary kiln at the top end. Here, at a temperature of up to 140°C, using pulverized coal as the fuel, the raw materials are converted to cement clinker. The clinker is then ground and blended with about 5% gypsum (to retard the initial set), and produces the final cement powder.

Other types of cements for mortars

White Portland cement

The manufacture of this type of cement also complies with BS12. It is a mix of chalk and china clay, fired by fuel oil instead of coal. It has setting characteristics and strength development similar to those of OPC, although it is more expensive. It is often specified with silver sand to give a pale joint finish, and for mortars, where its neutrality does not affect the finished aggregate colour of the joint.

Masonry cement

This is manufactured to comply with BS5224 and is a blend of between 75–80% OPC, 15–25% inert mineral filler and air-entraining agent, which acts as a plasticizer and gives greater water retention. This cement gives a highly workable masonry mortar when mixed to correct proportions with sand and water. The addition of lime or liquid plasticizer is neither required nor desirable. It should not be used below ground level in clay soils because of its vulnerability to sulphate attack.

Sulphate-resisting Portland cement

This has a low tri-calcium aluminate (C_3A) content and is made to comply with BS4027. It is specified for mortars which will be subject to the aggressive action of sulphates such as those to be used below ground level in some clay sub-soils. It is not quite as strong as OPC and is darker in colour. Where very high levels of sulphates are anticipated, super-sulphate resisting cement should be used.

High alumina cement

This is sometimes known as 'lightning' cement because of its rapid strength attainment and it is manufactured to BS915. Sometimes it is specified for mortars needing heat resistance and refractory properties, or for its resistance to aggressive chemicals and mild acids.

Alumina cement must not be mixed with hydrated lime, although ground chalk or limestone may be used as a plasticizer.

Hydrated lime

Today, when lime is employed in the majority of modern cement-based mortars it is as a dry hydrate purchased in 25kg moisture-resisting bags. It is manufactured in well-controlled factory conditions where it is steam-heated to hydrate the lime mechanically. Impurities are separated at this stage, and blended back during the ball-mill grinding process.

It is a welcome development that lime is again gaining popularity, as a natural alternative to modern chemical plasticizers, and if used correctly it will give good results. However, it is best used not straight from the bag, as is the usual method, but soaked in water to a putty for twenty-four hours, or more if possible, to improve its plasticity and adhesiveness. Only 'high calcium' hydrated lime should be used for this purpose. In this instance, because of its high purity, 95% CaOH, the results are far more favourable, and not dissimilar to those of a traditional slaked lime.

MIXING AND USE OF MORTARS

Health and safety

Cement powder and hydrated lime in normal use will cause no ill effects, although it is obviously wise to avoid inhaling and ingesting dust by taking sensible precautions. When mixed with water, however, alkalis are released and therefore contact with the skin should be avoided by the use of a suitable barrier cream. If not, dermatitis may result, and prolonged skin contact can result in 'cement burns', with ulceration. Mortar on unprotected skin should be washed off using soap and water within one hour. Should cement or hydrated lime enter the eye, it should be irrigated immediately using copious amounts of clean water and medical advice sought.

Delivery and storage of cements

Cement is normally delivered to site in 50kg sealed bags. On big sites it may be delivered by tanker in loads of 20 tonnes, to be blown into storage silos: this method is much cheaper. When delivered it must be stored off the ground on pallets in a covered environment, preferably a weatherproof shed. This prevents a phenomenon known as 'air setting', whereby the moisture in the air causes the formation of hydrated lumps of cement. Cement is therefore best used fresh. After eight weeks it will start to air set, despite covering, and as such will have a strength loss of 20%.

It is best to order what is required for no more than three or four weeks' work at a time. As new supplies arrive they should be used in the order in which they are received, and each delivery must be kept separate to avoid confusion. Stacks should be no higher than eight bags (1.5m) to avoid compaction and the phenomenon known as 'warehouse set'.

Sand

There are several terms commonly used to describe sands. These are:

1. *Clean sand:* contains a small percentage of small grains.
2. *Dirty sand:* contains excessive amounts of clay, silt or organic contamination.
3. *Sharp sand:* consists of angular, coarse, harsh grains.
4. *Soft sand:* consists mostly of fine and clayey particles.
5. *Loamy sand:* contains excessive amounts of organic matter.
6. *Clayey sand:* contains excessive amounts of 'fines', usually clay.
7. *'As-raised' sand:* this is a traditional expression for unwashed and ungraded pit sand for laying mortar, delivered as it is quarried or 'raised' from the pit.

Grading of sand

BS1200 should ensure an aggregate of 5mm or less with no more than 8% silt. This should be ideal for most bricklaying mortars. Sand can be tested for grading by passing it through a nest of sieves to BS410. If well graded, equal amounts of sand should remain on each of the six sieves. In a 'well-graded' aggregate, as opposed to a uniform sand, the lesser-sized particles fit between larger particles, thus helping to ensure an even distribution of binder paste and reducing air in the mix.

Excessively fine sands present a greater surface area to be coated with the binder, and demand more water to give a workable mix. This results in shrinkage and a reduction in the strength of the hardened mortar.

On walling requiring a high strength mortar, even BS limits may be insufficient. In such cases, after mortar strength tests a different aggregate, such as sand from sieved and crushed rock, or a higher mortar specification may be deemed necessary.

The sand should be washed to free it from deleterious matter. Cleanness can be tested on site by some simple field tests. One is to rub some sand between the fingers and thumb. If it stains or 'balls' easily then further investigation is recommended.

This can be done by examining a sample under a magnifying glass to identify impurities such as clay balls, coal dust or other undesirable matter. If this content is deemed excessive further testing by a 'Field Settling' or 'Silt Test' is advisable (see figure 5.8).

The choice of sand will obviously affect the finished colour, both of mortar and of the brickwork, so continuity of sand source is essential. In some sand pyrites may cause a rust stain to emerge on the finished joints. BS1200 accepts that this is difficult to guard against: examination of previously built brickwork which used the same source of sand might be beneficial.

To conclude, use only a specified sand from an approved supplier, keep it clean and dry, and do not allow contamination from other building materials, soil, plant or site vehicles. All this can be achieved by suitable covering.

Water

The water used for mixing mortar should be from an approved source and be potable, clean and free from any deleterious matter. Tap water is normally satisfactory. Should the water be of doubtful quality, refer to BS3148.

Modern additives

Plasticizers

These can be in powdered or liquid form and must conform to BS4887. With the decline in the use of lime mortars after the Second World War, chemical plasticizers came on to the market to improve workability

Objective:	To determine the cleanliness of building sand.
Equipment:	One clean glass bottle or jar with lid.
Materials:	Sand (to be tested); Salt; Water (clean, fit for drinking).
Procedure:	Add one teaspoon of table salt to half a litre of clean water and stir to dissolve. Take a glass container and fill with salt solution. Fill with a representative sample of sand to a height of 100mm and replace the lid tightly. Shake the container vigorously, tap the sand to level it and place it on a flat, stable surface and allow the contents to settle. After a period of three hours a layer of sediment or silt will have formed on the top of the sand. Deposits of clay take several hours to settle, leaving the water dirty. An excessive quantity of iron oxide will show as a red cloudiness which does not disappear. To determine the percentage of clay and silt, their total depth is taken from the total depth of the sand. It should not exceed 8mm or 8%. If it exceeds this limit, the sand is probably too dirty for use.
Note:	These field tests are only a guide, their interpretation dependent on wide experience, and may require proper laboratory testing. Samples of sand approved by the architect should be kept on site for reference. A poorly graded, dirty sand may make a nice workable mix, but it will be weaker than designed due to irregular setting, poor adhesion and shrinkage cracking in the finished mortar, and therefore should not be used.

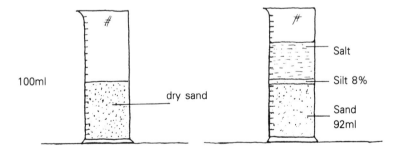

Figure 5.8 Field settling test.

of cement mortars. It is essential that the manufacturer's recommendations on proportions are carefully followed as these admixtures reduce strength. A positive effect, however, is that they can improve frost resistance during and after setting.

Plasticizers or 'workability aids' (also known as 'surfactants', an abbreviation for 'surface active agents') act to reduce surface tension in the mortar by 'entraining' air as micro-bubbles into the mix. This allows the surfaces to retain greater moisture and thus improves workability. They can be used with all cements except masonry cement. Plasticized mortars should not be mixed in a pan mixer as this technique fails to entrain sufficient air.

NOTE
Washing-up liquid must never be used as an alternative to a proprietary plasticizer as it generally contains undesirable chemicals. It also entrains large and uncontrolled air bubbles into the mix, resulting in a weak and less durable (and perfumed!) mortar.

Antifreeze admixtures

These are generally based on calcium chloride, and are intended for concretes. They should not be used in mortars. They work by accelerating the chemical set of cement and create heat, but the amount of heat generated in a mortar bed is negligible and it therefore imparts little, if any, frost resistance. They may also be deliquescent (attract moisture) and so encourage dampness in the hardened mortar. This, in turn, may encourage corrosion of ferrous metal wall ties and other brackets and fixings bedded in the mortar.

Modern colouring agents for mortars, which are covered by BS12 as well as BS1014, are made in a wide range of lime-resistant colours, and are used to colour white- or OPC-based mortars. Up to 10% by weight of the cement content has been added at the grinding process stage. Carbon black, however, must not exceed 3% because of its fineness, which can affect the strength of the resulting mortar mix.

Colouring agents are best pre-mixed on site by weight, with the cement, or alternatively at the ready mixed lime : sand mortar plant, where a strict control can be exercised, and a consistent colour virtually guaranteed. Synthetic iron oxides do not fade and it will be important to discuss this matter with the manufacturers or suppliers.

Should site mixing be called for it will be of paramount importance to follow strictly the manufacturer's instructions. Once a mix has been established producing an acceptable colour (normally by test panels which meet with the architect's and/or client's approval), it is best to change nothing. Altering cement or pigment proportions invariably alters the colour of the mortar and results in differing shades on the finished brickwork. Sources of cement, sand and lime should also be kept consistent.

Batching and mixing

Care must always be taken to ensure that the architect's specified mix is maintained throughout the construction of the brickwork. The use of a shovel as the standard measure of cement : lime : sand is wholly inadequate. Cement and lime are dry fine powders and will not stand high on a shovel as will sand. It therefore follows that sand will occupy a greater volume and this will result in a weak and 'lean' (little cement) mix. During damp weather building sand will also 'bulk' up and this can affect the volume by as much as 30%. Therefore if in doubt a test for bulking should be carried out (see figure 5.9).

Measurement by weight is preferred and is always used at a ready-mixed mortar batching plant. However, in the vast majority of cases where mortar is prepared on site it is by volume batching. Timber gauge boxes which stand on a timber base are used. The materials can then be accurately gauged and ruled off level on the top. The boxes are then lifted away, and the materials shovelled into the mixer. (See figure 5.10)

The foreman bricklayer should closely monitor the preparation and mixing of the mortar, ensuring that the operative executing this task is both able and well informed, and that all the materials are kept clean and protected from the effects of the weather.

In order to give the intended results in strength and aesthetics, it is important not to depart from the mortar mix as specified by the designer, and the specification must never be altered except after full consultation with the architect. The mortar itself must be of the correct strength and to design specifications. Although there are five classes of mortar mixes given in table 15 of BS5628: Part 3, 1985, there is a discrepancy in this and only specifications from (I) to (IV) are for use.

Table 5.1 Classes of mortar mixes.

Designation	cement : lime : sand	masonry cement : sand (includes plasticizer)	cement : sand plus plasticizer
(I)	1:0:3 to 1:¼:3		
(II)	1:½:4 to 1:½:4½	1:2½ to 1:3½	1:3 to 1:4
(III)	1:1:5 to 1:1:6	1:4 to 1:5	1:5 to 1:6
(IV)	1:2:8 to 1:2:9	1:5½ to 1:6½	1:7 to 1:8
(V)	1:3:10 to 1:3:12	1:6½ to 1:7	1:8

Objective: To establish the percentage of volume increase in building sand due to the absorption of water. This test is based on the fact that although damp sand bulks, saturated and perfectly dry sand occupy the same volume.

Equipment: A straight-sided glass jar (if possible graduated to help read measurements);
A glass jar;
A rod;
A ruler.

Materials: Sample of sand (randomly selected).

Procedure: The sand to be tested is poured into the jar until it is level at two-thirds full, without being compacted. If the jar is not graduated, measure down the centre to the base of the jar with a ruler and note the depth,150mm.

This sand is now emptied into the clean second jar, ensuring all is transferred. Half-fill the graduated jar with clean water. The sand is replaced into the graduated jar, rodding to expel air, until all the sand is contained and then it is levelled off.

A new measurement is now taken. If we consider the sample to be damp, it will be noted that it has sunk, for example to 125mm. We calculate the bulking as a percentage using the following formula: $\dfrac{(150-125)}{125} \times 100 = 20\%$ bulking.

Conclusion: That any volume of sand used in this instance would need to be 20% more than the dry specification.

Note: A test for bulking should be carried out at the commencement of work, after a new delivery of sand and following any serious alteration in the weather, for example hot sunshine or rain.

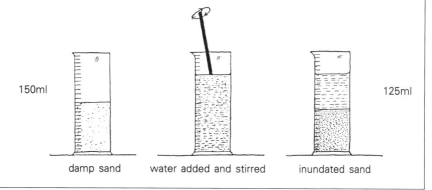

150ml   125ml

damp sand   water added and stirred   inundated sand

Figure 5.9 Testing the bulking of sand.

MODERN LIME MORTARS

As has already been stated, lime has been enjoying a revival in use as plasticizer in modern mortars and is generally seen in three different types of mortars.

1. On-site mixed cement : lime : sand.
2. Ready-mixed lime : sand mortar (LSM) (for gauging with OPC).
3. Ready-to-use cement : lime : sand mortar (CLM)(retarded).

On-site mixed cement : lime : sand

This will take the form of a dry powdered hydrated lime (BS890) gauged with cement and sand to form a plasticized mortar, 1:1:6 being the most common mix (designation III). Generally, the cement and lime will be measured in powdered form as they are put into the mixer simultaneously. The amount of lime can, however, be increased by up to 50%.

Mortar is much improved if the lime is dry mixed to gauge with the sand and allowed to stand for a minimum of twenty-four hours before mixing as a coarse stuff.

Mixing by hand

This is usually reserved for small amounts of mortar to be used quickly. However, the basic rules should be followed. The gauged dry ingredients should be placed on to a hard clean surface. The cement, lime and sand should then be turned with a shovel three times to integrate them fully. The dry mixed materials are then drawn out from the centre to form a hollow ring into which sufficient water is added (usually between 15–18%) to achieve a workable mix. This water is allowed to soak into the mix which is then turned over at least twice again. It is then ready to be served to the bricklayer and should be used within two hours. (See figure 5.11)

Mixing by machine

The sequence recommended in BS8000: Part 3, 1989 and BDA publication BN1, is to load out about three-quarters of the sand or pre-mixed lime/sand and water; while mixing gradually add lime and/or cement and continue mixing; then load remainder of sand or pre-mixed lime/sand and further water to achieve required workability.

Figure 5.10 Accurately batched materials for mortar in gauge boxes (reproduced by kind permission of R. J. Baldwin).

In general, a machine mixing time of 3 to 5 minutes (after all constituents have been added) should be suitable. Wide variations in mixing times between different batches should be avoided.

Ready-mixed lime : sand mortar (LSM)

This complies with BS4721, 1981, when tested by methods given in BS4551, 1980, and should be used in accordance with BS5628: Part 3. It is manufactured from washed well-graded sand and lime putty, and can be supplied ready pigmented. These ingredients are accurately gauged by weight and mixed under strict mechanical control, and are intended to be used only after gauging on site with cement and sufficient water for workability.

The supplier should be consulted before ordering, to ascertain the correct grade of mortar for the intended brickwork and for advice on site batching. This type of 'coarse stuff' is delivered in bulk, generally by tipper lorry and should be tipped on to either a clean 'banker' board or a clean concrete base, and then sheeted while not in use to protect against rain and weathering. This is particularly important with coloured mortars. If allowed to stand uncovered in periods of hot sunshine it will also crust and need crushing before mixing.

If different strength LSMs are in use, they must be stored in separate bays and clearly marked as to ratio to avoid batching the wrong mix.

Figure 5.11 Hand and machine mixing (by kind permission of Blue Circle Cement).

The colouring of LSMs is by the use of synthetic iron oxides, eighteen basic colours in six shades giving a wide range of choice and guaranteed by the manufacturers against fading. One tonne of LSM gauged with OPC on site will lay approximately 1,000 bricks.

Ready-to-use cement : lime : sand mortar (CLM)

CLM is generally marketed as a standard 1:1:6 mix which can be retarded for up to 36 hours, requiring no further machine mixing. Other mix specifications can be supplied. This type of mortar is normally delivered by specialized vehicles and discharged into clean site containers (generally 0.3m³), which are usually provided by the company on a buy or hire basis. These containers prevent wastage or contamination, and give some degree of weather protection. They should be stored under cover on site, on a hard standing. Once again, differing strengths must be clearly identified. (See figure 5.12)

CLMs are becoming increasingly popular on sites with restricted space. They allow more room for plant and materials, reduce wastage, increase bricklaying production and ease handling. Obviously these advantages are further enhanced by the fact that these are strictly controlled batched and tested materials.

This type of mortar is sold by volume. One cubic metre will lay between 1,300–1,700 Fletton-type frogged bricks, or 1,700–2,400 solid or perforated bricks.

CEMENT : SAND MORTAR

Generally a cement : sand mortar with no plasticizer is reserved for use on high-strength brickwork using dense engineering bricks (usually at a gauge of 1:3) to give compatibility with the bricks. It is also sometimes specified for load-bearing brickwork below ground level. When used without a chemical plasticizer the mortar can prove to be harsh, inclined to stiffen quickly on the board, and with only low workability, which seriously limits the output of the bricklayer.

The addition of a chemical plasticizer will greatly enhance workability but its use must be monitored carefully. It is best added to clean water which is contained in a large tub or barrel. The plasticizer should be added according to the manufacturer's recommendations,

Figure 5.12 Ready-to-use coloured cement : lime mortar (CLM) being discharged into insulated containers with coded liners indicating the day of delivery.

and then gently stirred to ensure full absorption. A plasticized 1:6 cement : sand mortar is broadly comparable in strength to a 1:1:6 cement : lime sand mix.

In general when one refers to cement : sand mortars, the cement is accepted as meaning OPC, although white and sulphate-resisting cements are used as alternatives. Masonry cement must not be substituted as it has specific properties for mixing with sand.

Modern cement mortars are basically in two forms: those mixed on site, by hand or machine; and ready-to-use cement sand + retarder (CSM).

On-site mixing

Many problems arise with on-site mixing of modern cement mortars. These are due, in the main, to poor gauging of materials, and the use of too strong a mortar for the intended walling. Whether mixing by hand or machine, all the ingredients should be accurately gauged and proportions strictly monitored.

With a plasticizer in the gauging water the mix may end up wetter than may be intended, so the addition of extra water should be delayed. Prolonged machine mixing, where air-entraining plasticizers are used, may also lead to excessive air entrainment and thus to a reduction in adhesion and durability.

Ready-to-use cement : sand + retarder (CSM)

This is a well-controlled factory-mixed mortar which can be retarded for up to thirty-six hours and requires no further machine mixing. Any CSM specification can be supplied to order.

The mortar is sold by volume, delivered by specialized vehicle and is discharged into clean site containers (0.30m³) which are supplied by the company on a buy or hire basis. As with the retarded CLMs, storage should be under cover on a hard standing, away from possible contamination. These mortars also have the advantage of increasing bricklaying production and prove popular on sites of restricted space, although they suffer from the disadvantage of forming too strong a mortar for most brickwork.

One cubic metre will lay 1,300–1,700 Fletton-type frogged bricks, 1,700–2,400 solid or perforated bricks and between 700–1,200 solid blocks with a nominal size of 440mm × 215mm × 100mm.

There are other mortars for specialized areas of brickwork, such as glazed, firebrick and gauged work, but these will be dealt with in other chapters.

6

Tools and Accessories

Bricklaying tools and accessories changed very little between the fourteenth and the opening of the present century; all but a few remain essentially the same. What have changed are materials, design and the evolution of new techniques that invariably evolve in a time of great technological development. (See figure 6.1)

A bricklayer's tools are neither numerous nor complicated, but are of the greatest importance in the pursuit of first-class work. Once they are 'broken in', a craftsman knows their 'feel' and capabilities, and they become an extension of his hands. It is therefore essential that a bricklayer selects and handles his tools with good knowledge and great care if he is to carry out work that will reflect only credit on him.

To make a sound judgement in his choice of tools the craftsman will consider the type of work he will be engaged in:

1. New work.
2. Alterations and extensions.
3. Maintenance, repair and restoration.

Tools are generally classified according to their use.

♦ Laying tools and accessories.
♦ Cutting tools and accessories.
♦ Levelling and measuring tools.
♦ Jointing and pointing tools and accessories.

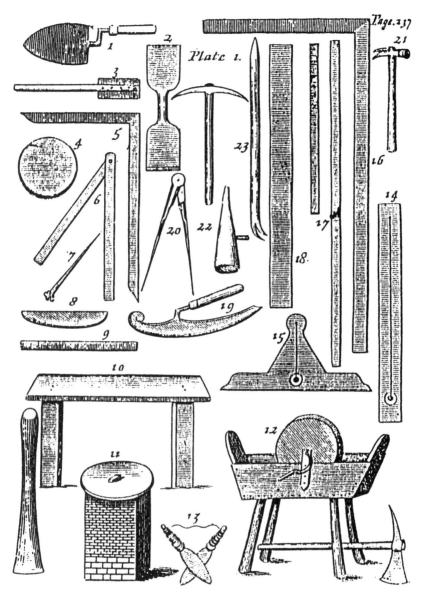

1. Brick trowel.
2. Brick axe.
3. Tin saw.
4. Rubbing stone.
5. A small square.
6. A bevel.
7. Scribe.
8. Float stone.
9. Small ruler.
10. A banker.
11. Brick pier for rubbing stone.
12. Grinding-stone.
13. Line and pins.
14. A plumb rule.
15. A level.
16. A large setting-out square.
17. Ten-, five- and two-foot rod/rule.
18. A jointing rule.
19. Iron jointer.
20. Compass.
21. Claw hammer.
22. Rammer.
23. Crow bar and pick-axe.

Figure 6.1 A plate depicting tools used by the seventeenth-century bricklayer, from *Mechanick Excercises or the Doctrine of Handy-Works* by Joseph Moxon (1703).

♦ Complementary tools and accessories.

The most important rules for all tools are that they should be:

(a) Robust, made of good-quality materials to high standards.
(b) Durable, able to withstand many years of use and give good service.
(c) Kept to their intended use, not used as a substitute for another tool.

LAYING TOOLS

Brick trowel

Recorded as early as 1295 as a 'truell' at Cambridge Castle, from the Latin *trulla* meaning a ladle or skimmer – an appropriate description since, well into the seventeenth century, mortar was placed in tiny baskets or shortened barrels.

It is a specially shaped flat steel-bladed tool for cutting, lifting and spreading the mortar required for laying bricks, flushing-up and applying various joints. Trowels provided with a cutting edge can be used for obtaining a rough-cut into 'bats', soft or common bricks, on brickwork which is not to be seen.

As one of the bricklayer's main tools, it is important to have a wide understanding of the trowel – how and why it is so made and shaped – so that a purchase is based on knowledge as well as feel, and so that it may serve the bricklayer well over many years.

Brick trowels are produced in a range of sizes from 10″ (250mm) to 13″ (325mm) long. In former times, for thicker walls requiring large

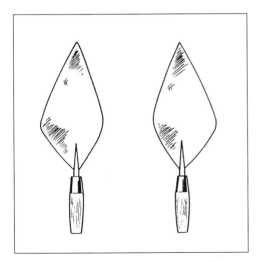

Figure 6.2 Right- and left-handed trowels.

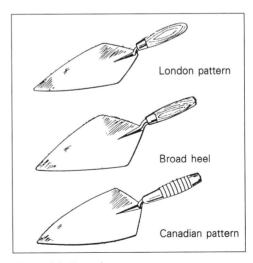

London pattern

Broad heel

Canadian pattern

Figure 6.3 Trowel patterns.

volumes of mortar, blades could be up to 15″ (375mm) long. Trowels are 'handed', for either a right- or left-handed person: holding the trowel blade vertical in front and looking along the trowel from the handle, one can see a distinctive hump along one side. On a right-handed trowel this curve will be on the right-hand edge of the blade. (See figure 6.2) It is deliberately forged like this to allow for cutting and trimming soft bricks. The left-hand edge, being straight, is for scooping or 'lifting' the mortar from the spot board. This cutting or 'bolstered' edge was formerly reinforced to withstand the cutting stresses. Today, however, improvements in the heat-treating process enable hardening across all of the blade without the risk of it being stiff and becoming brittle and cracking.

Traditionally trowels were made in 'patterns' with varying styles of handles. (See figure 6.3) For example, the 'London' trowel, popular in the South; it had a range of lengths from 250mm to 300mm by 112mm to 130mm wide respectively, is narrow-bladed, and is lighter in use. It is generally fitted with a turned ash handle with a rounded end. The 'tang' is enclosed within a steel ferule fitted to the handle which prevents it splitting, and does not protrude through. Ash is preferred as it is light, pliant, resists impact, puts up with rough usage and constant scouring, wears very smooth and does not splinter readily. It is the best timber for virtually any kind of handle and is especially suitable for the bricklayer's trowel where the up-ended handle is often used to tap the brick into position. (See figure 6.4)

The 'broad heel', popular in the North, is found in the same lengths as the London pattern but 25mm wider across the width or 'shoulder' in each case, giving a greater mortar capacity. It usually has a 'through tang and capped' handle of ash. The end of the tang, having been drawn out through the end of the handle, has a bright steel cap

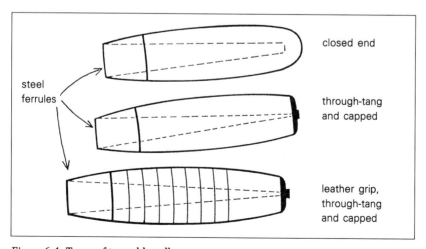

Figure 6.4 Types of trowel handles.

riveted over to hold and secure the handle in place. When a bricklayer prefers to use the end of the handle for adjusting his brick into place, the steel cap can be a valuable asset in preventing wear.

Increasingly popular today is the lightweight American trowel, more correctly termed 'Canadian' or 'Philadelphia' pattern. It is wide-bladed, not handed, and is primarily intended for the American 'overhand' practice of laying. The blade is symmetrical, with straight sides from where the tang rises to the widest part of the blade: each side then gradually curves to the point (or more correctly, the 'toe'). It is 275mm long by 140mm wide, and does not possess a cutting edge. Canadian patterns can come with long ash handles with a non-protruding tang, or a through-tang handle bound with circular sections of leather which serve as a grip, giving a comfortable rest in the hand and more readily able to absorb moisture.

A trowel of first-class quality is manufactured from high-carbon tool steel to very high standards by a process of forging, rolling, stamping, hardening, tempering, grinding and polishing, giving a blade that will finish hard yet be springy in use. The steel for the blade is cut to the diamond shape diagonally from the bar. After being brought to a bright red heat the stub, which will form the tang, is drawn out from one point of the diamond to receive the handle. After tempering, the blade is ground and glazed, and the handle fixed. (See figure 6.5)

The 'frog' is the thickened triangular projection where the tang begins to protrude from the blade: an elongated triangular shape indicates that it is a solid forged towel. A welded tang has a rounded end and a distinctive step between tang and blade.

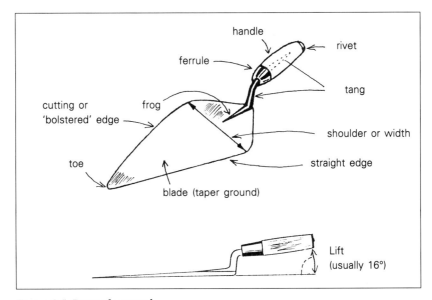

Figure 6.5 Parts of a trowel.

The 'tang' is the extension of the blade to which the handle is fixed. On a trowel of good quality it will have been forged as an integral part of the blade. The height of the tang along the 'shank' or 'neck' up to the hand governs the 'lift' and, therefore, knuckle clearance when lifting mortar from the spot board.

It is essential that the tang is well formed, to produce a strong trowel able to withstand the stresses of heavy use. On a cheap trowel the 'tang' looks weak, and has a hollow where the heel has been stretched round, creating a weakness.

The 'lift', 'hang', and 'weight' of a trowel are very important. The lift is the degree of inclination (usually 16°) of the underside of the handle in relation to the surface the trowel blade is resting on. Too flat a lift results less clearance for the knuckles when the handle is gripped, and the use is therefore more cumbersome. If the lift is correct there is sufficient clearance, so that it eases the weight of the mortar in readiness for spreading. The 'hang' of a trowel is difficult to describe, but is the quality of the rest (or 'hang') in the hand, and while the blade should be fairly stiff towards the point, the weight is governed by the hang and should suit the strength of the bricklayer.

Quite often a trowel is too pointed at the 'toe', a problem referred to as 'all point', and some bricklayers, rather than waiting for this to wear down, prefer to 'round' it. This is traditionally achieved by rubbing on York stone with water. Alternatively the point is cut off by laying the blade flat on a metal surface and giving it a hard blow with a cold chisel. It is then rounded on the stone or preferably a grinding wheel.

Purchasing a trowel

When selecting a trowel always ask for a choice of several, even if they are of the same size and pattern, for although they are mass produced there is some handwork in finishing, so that minor differences occur. This produces an individual tool. The one selected will feel right in your hand. Consider only a good make. A young apprentice should never use a trowel longer than 250mm, as it will hinder the development of his 'wrist' and mortar control. Traditionally a stiff blade with a good ring to it was preferred, although the lighter trowels with flexible blades are increasingly popular. It is my experience, however, that these prove difficult for a novice bricklayer and are best left until mortar control is mastered. Whichever is chosen, select a solid forged trowel in preference to one with riveted or welded tangs. On good quality trowels the blade will have been taper-ground to give balance and flexibility. Inferior trowels have only superficial grinding markings to the surface, and will feel 'dead' to the craftsman.

Care of the trowel

Should the wooden handle work loose, examine the tang. Sometimes it is insufficiently jagged, and jagging with a chisel will effect a cure. Once the handle is removed and the hole has been cleaned, the hole can be filled with bitumen, rubber, the shredded exterior of a golf ball or some other material with a low melting point. The tang is heated and inserted into the bitumen and left to cool. When refixing, be sure that the ferrule seals properly for a tight fit.

An old, badly worn trowel can be re-cut to shape (about 150mm long) to form a 'jobbing' or 'buttering trowel', ideal for fireplaces, fireclay work, small repairs or other jobs where a large trowel would prove unwieldy.

At the end of a day's work a trowel should always be washed clean. An old craft practice was to keep a small lump of quicklime in the tool bag and also to smear the trowels with lime mortar before leaving off work, as it was well known that both practices helped to prevent rusting. A later method was to give the trowel a 'dusting' of damp cement rubbed with a clean rag and, when dry, to polish with a dry rag. Sometimes mortar builds up at the shoulder: this can be rubbed off using a piece of soft brick with water as an abrasive. Once dry a trowel can either be rubbed with an oily rag or smeared with a thin coat of vaseline.

Line and pins

Pins are used in pairs of forged steel about 150mm long and 4mm in thickness. The top usually has a circular head about 25mm in diameter and 3mm in thickness (some older versions had what was called an 'anchor' head). Under this is the neck or shank of the pin, about 75mm in length and 5mm in thickness leading to a flattened blade about 25mm in width and 3mm thick, usually ground to a point. (See figure 6.6)

The shank is used for winding on the line. The circular top prevents it from slipping off, and also serves as a head for hammering the pin into hard mortar when working on old brickwork. It is best to wrap adhesive tape around the shank to prevent the line slipping. This was also done in the days before 'chroming', to prevent rust getting into the lines.

Line is obtained in 'hanks' of 30–40m in length (traditionally 12 yard 'knots'). It can be wound fully on to one pin only, with a clove hitch every 5 metres to prevent the line fully unwinding should a pin drop whilst working at height. Alternatively,

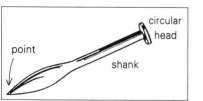

Figure 6.6 A line pin.

the line can be wound up to half its length on one pin and the remainder on the other pin. If this is done the line is wound left over right on one and right over left on the other. Ensure that the line always travels over the top of the pin when stretched to guide the bricks when laying. *Pakthrede* (stout twine or thread) is recorded at Westminster in 1532 for the 'brickleyers lynes'.

Care of lines

During repeated use lines become very twisted, and this causes them to curl on the pins. To remedy this the lines should be left to hang, pins down, from a rafter so that they spin, and thus unravel the twists, and the lines return to normal.

  If a line is broken its proper repair is of the utmost importance. A line should never be tied together, because a knot prevents accurate lining-in. Therefore a line should be spliced as follows:

1. At a length of 115mm in from one end and 75mm from the other end, unravel a small part of the twine to form a hole or a loop. Thread the ends of the line into each hole. (See figure 6.7)
2. Pull the ends of the line so that the twine closes up the hole and tightens on the line.
3. About 35mm away from the connections on either side, unravel another small hole and thread in the loose ends.
4. Pull the line tight on either side to secure the splice. Cut off any loose ends.

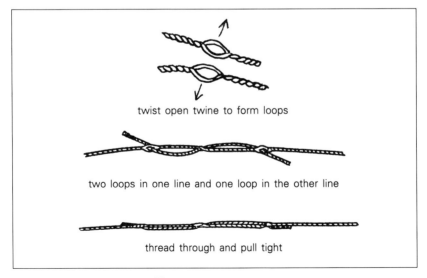

twist open twine to form loops

two loops in one line and one loop in the other line

thread through and pull tight

Figure 6.7 Splicing a snapped line.

Corner blocks

Also known as line bobbins, corner blocks are preferably made from hardwood measuring 100mm × 50mm × 40mm (although sizes vary). In common designs a halving is cut, and into the thicker part of the block a 2mm wide saw cut is made down the centre to the depth of the halving. Some prefer to have another saw cut at right-angles to this for tightening the line.

Used in conjunction with the line and pins, blocks are employed on external right-angled quoins and stopped-ends to line-in the walling in between. The line is drawn down the length of the block and wrapped around twice and then pulled tight from the block resting in position at the other end of the wall. The line tension causes the blocks to be held tight against the quoins, avoiding the need for pin holes in the mortar. The blocks are easily raised as the wall is being built, eliminating the need for line adjustment. Today corner blocks are also manufactured in plastic and in lightweight alloy.

Tingle plate

Made from thin sheet metal, copper or zinc, a tingle generally measures 100mm × 75mm × 3mm and has two 10mm × 10mm notches cut out. either side of the centre. leaving three level 'teeth'. The tingle is used to prevent 'line sag' on a long length of walling. It is positioned on a brick laid to gauge, levelled and plumbed at the mid-wall point, sitting across the brick with its teeth extending over the wall face. It

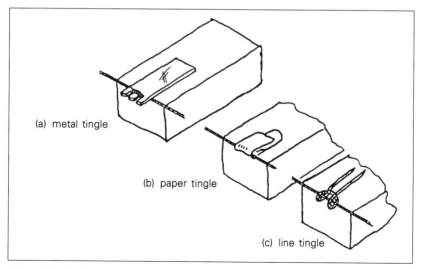

Figure 6.8 Tingles

is then weighted down with a brick, the line being fed under the outside tooth, over the inner and under the outer again. Thus the line is held true to level. It is usually employed from distances of 7 metres upwards. An improvization is to use a piece of paper or, better still, a string in the form of a loop, or loops, through which the line is threaded. The tingle is bedded in a little mortar and weighted down by a piece of brick. (See figure 6.8)

CUTTING TOOLS

Brick axe

A 'bryke' axe for the 'bryklayers' is recorded as costing 8*d.* at Windsor in 1533, and such tools are frequently mentioned in old documents – especially under charges for sharpening on the grindstone. The brick axe fell out of use during the nineteenth century. (See figure 6.9)

The early iron axe depicted by Moxon in *Mechanick Excercises* (1703) (see figure 6.1) resembled two wide bolster blades with average dimensions of 5″ (127mm), in width and 12″ (306mm) in length, with a round central grip of 4½″ (115mm). It weighed about 3lb (1.36kg). The later axe, illustrated by Nicholson, is considerably bigger and heavier. (See figure 6.10) It had narrow 3″ (76mm) blades, 25½″ (645mm) in total length, with a similar sized grip to that shown by Moxon, but it weighed about 6¼lbs (2.83kg). Clearly its purpose had altered.

Figure 6.9 A selection of iron brick axes to the Moxon specification (photograph reproduced by kind permission of Richard Filmer).

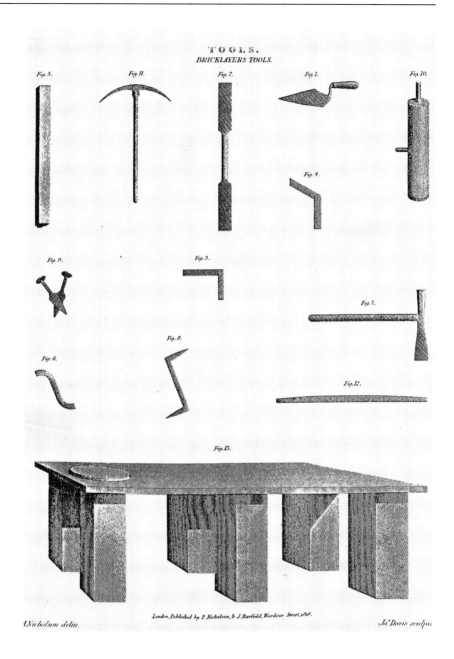

1. A brick trowel.
2. A large brick axe.
3. A try square.
4. A bevel.
5. A pointing rule.
6. A jointing iron.
7. A brick dresser.
8. A pointing pick.
9. Line pins.
10. A rammer.
11. A pick axe.
12. A camber slip.
13. A banker.

Figure 6.10 A plate depicting tools used by the early nineteenth-century brick-layer, from Peter Nicholson's *The Builder's and Workman's New Dictionary* (1824).

Both axes are well balanced, the double end giving a spare once the first edge had dulled. The earlier axe is intended both for chopping away the waste after scoring the outline with a tin saw, and, in the hands of skilled men, for fine-shaping the brick in the chopping block; this was often before a final rubbing smooth with the hand or float stone. This is emphasized by Moxon when he states. 'Others use no stone at all, but cut the brick exactly to the pattern with their Brick ax, leaving the Ax strokes to be seen on the brick, which, if they be streight and paralleled to one another look very prettily and is the truest way of working.'

The later axe, being large and heavy, was not intended for fine shaping: its size negates such use. It was designed to cut as large a waste portion of brick as possible, something which was important because of the large amounts of 'axing' (or cutting) of brick arches in the cutting-sheds of the nineteenth century.

Figure 6.11 The large 'Nicholson' type brick axe can be seen leaning against the cutting bench, as the brick cutter finishes the brick on the chopping block (taken from The Operative Bricklayers' Society membership certificate, 1865).

In Nathaniel Lloyd's *A History of English Brickwork* (1925, pp. 72–3) is a description by Arthur Leach FSA of the brick axe in use:

> A tool with two chisel shaped ends, used by bricklayers for cutting bricks for gauged arches. The lines having been first marked on the brick by a species of small saw, the axe is then taken by the middle and held in a perpendicular position, its edge is then applied to the brick where marked, and both being raised together, it is struck smartly on a block of wood, by which the brick is cut into shapes. The rough edges of the brick are then rubbed on a piece of grit stone.

The block of wood referred to is the chopping block, an inclined 90° seating for the brick being shaped. A shallow cut would be made in the brick with the tin saw to prevent the face spalling and help to give a sharp cut. The blade of the axe would be set into this cut, and both brick and axe would be slid up the back of the chopping block around 20–30mm and allowed to drop down together. The impact at the base of the chopping block was sufficient to cut the brick neatly and cleanly.

There is an attractive picture depicting a brick cutter at work in a cutting shed on the union membership certificate of the Operative Bricklayers Society (OBS), painted by the artist A. J. Waudby in 1865. The operative is fine-trimming a voussoir, held by his left hand in the cutting block. Although a lump hammer and bolster are clearly evident on the cutting bench, against it, and giving ample evidence of its size, lies a brick axe. (See figure 6.11)

It is from about this time that the brick axe fell out of use, being superseded by the scotch, although the earlier, smaller axe remained in use until the 1950s as a brick cleaner for chopping off old lime mortar. There was also a similar axe, fitted to a handle and resembling a wood axe, which was usually referred to as a 'brick dresser'.

Brick hammer

This consists of a steel head, shaped square at one end and flat-bladed at the other. There are two styles of hammer: the traditional long-headed type, ideal for plumbing adjustments while the level is in position; and the modern short-head type, with a larger head and broad blade tapering down to about 2mm, for rough cutting and trimming hard bricks and 'axing' soft bricks to the sizes required. As the cutting edge wears, it is re-sharpened on a grinding wheel. (See figure 6.12)

Scutch hammer

The 'Scotch' and blade, 'Scutch', or 'Scutcher' became popular from the mid-nineteenth century with the introduction of steel. It replaced

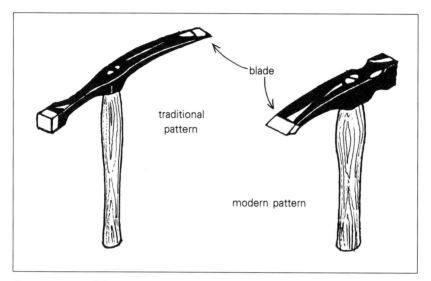

Figure 6.12 Brick hammer.

the iron-bladed brick axe, an important change because of the in-creased use of harder machine-pressed bricks. The scutch consisted of three distinct parts: stock, blade and wedge. The stock was a shaped handle of ash. The head was about 25mm in thickness, 50mm to 60mm in width and 75mm long. A slot about 25mm × 12mm was machined into the head at an angle of about 35°. Into this slot was fixed one of four steel blades, each designed for a different cutting function, varying from 250mm to 350mm in length and 25mm in width and 3mm in thickness, and tapering to differing points at each end. Often old files were re-worked into replacement blades because of the suitability of the steel. Blades were secured by a hardwood wedge about 75mm in length, tapering from 20mm to 3mm. (See figure 6.13) The origin of the term 'Scotch' is obscure, although it is known to be of late medieval origin and means 'to make an incision, cut, score or gash'. To 'scutch' is to strike, whip or slash.

Comb hammer

This is a development of the scutch hammer. Instead of a long blade there is a slot into which either toothed or plain-ended steel blades are inserted by tapping in with a hammer. It is ideal for hard pressed bricks. Once blunted, the blades are removed by striking on the angle with a hammer, turned round and re-fitted. The comb hammer can be used for trimming rough-cut bricks or arch voussoirs which need accurate dressing. (See figure 6.14)

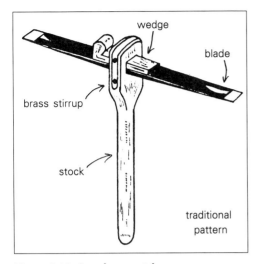

Figure 6.13 Scotch or scutch.

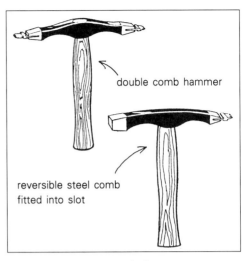

Figure 6.14 Comb (scutch) hammer.

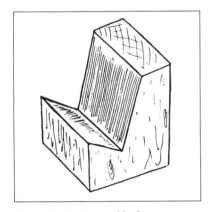

Figure 6.15 Cutting block.

Cutting block

Also known as the 'chopping block', this was a familiar sight in the cutting shop. It was used in conjunction with the brick axe or scutch for holding the brick securely while trimming it to shape. Traditionally made of a hardwood such as elm, in a size to suit one or more bricklayers, it was cut to form a seating of 90° which inclined the brick at an angle between 45° and 60°. By holding the brick while being trimmed with repeated cuts from the axe or scutch, it allowed greater precision and prevented the brick from rounding and damaging the arrises. (See figure 6.15)

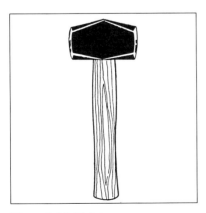

Figure 6.16 Club hammer.

Club hammer

Also known as the lump or mash hammer, like all hammers consisted of a 'drop forged' punched shaped steel head with a hickory or ash handle. The head is normally flat and chamfered to help to prevent injury to the hand from a careless blow. Head weights vary from 1kg to 3kg, depending on the work to be done. (See figure 6.16)

Care of hammers

Should the head loosen it must be tightened, because it could dislodge in use and cause a serious injury. A loose head is usually the result of slight shrinkage of the wooden handle. The steel wedge must be driven in further or replaced if it has fallen out. A hammer should never be allowed to stand in water to make the handle swell and tighten, as this will eventually rot the wood and could cause it to break at the point where it enters the hammer head.

Bolster or boaster chisel

Also referred to as a 'blocker' or 'kicker', this is used in conjunction with the club hammer for accurate brick cutting. A bolster consists of a shaped piece of steel, with a flattened blade at one end and a handle at the other. The blades are manufactured from bar, drop stamped and spread under rollers. The shape is cut out, marked, hardened, tempered, ground and polished. Bolsters were originally made with a round handle but today an octagonal shape is preferred, and it is sometimes encased with a rubber grip and guard.

   Blade widths vary from 50mm to 112mm, and preferably should be as wide as the brick to be cut. Lighter bolsters are for standard bricks, and the heavier patterns for engineering types. (See figure 6.17)

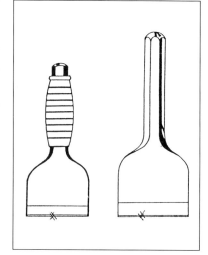

Figure 6.17 Bolsters.

Care of bolsters

A bolster should only be used for its intended purpose or it will become distorted. The blade must be kept sharpened to obtain good clean cuts. It is important to prevent the head of the handle becoming 'mushroomed'. This results from excessive wear, as the steel spreads from continued impact to the point where it splits and rolls under itself. This is dangerous as, when struck, a section of steel could fly off at high speed. The head should be re-ground.

Cold chisels

'Colde chiselles' are referred to in an inventory of 1444. Traditionally round in section, today they are always hexagonal and vary in length from 100mm × 3mm to 450mm × 20mm. When the head is struck

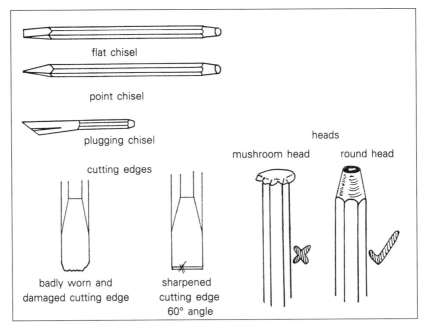

Figure 6.18 Cold chisels.

with the club hammer, the forces travel down the centre of the chisel and it is therefore more effective around the centre of the cutting edge. If the outer edge or corner is used, fracture can be expected even in the best of chisels. Often the user drives a chisel into the brickwork until it becomes wedged and then proceeds to hit the shank to loosen it. This may mean that the trapped blade fractures at the hardening line. A sharp edge is essential for best results with minimum effort. (See figure 6.18)

The blade must be kept sharp and the head carefully ground. Re-working of chisels on a 'gryndelstone' and their being 'battered' by the smithy is recorded at Sheppey in 1365.

Bat and closer gauge

This is made from timber, and used for marking bricks for three commonly used cuts – half-bat, three-quarter bat and the closer or quarter bat. Its use ensures regularity of cuts and saves much time measuring with rule or tape. (See figure 6.19)

The brick is placed for cutting and the gauge positioned to the 'stop' of the cut required. It is then scribed on both sides to give a clear mark ready for cutting. When different types of bricks are used, separate gauges should be made to suit their manufactured sizes. This would also be true if both hand- and machine-made bricks were in use.

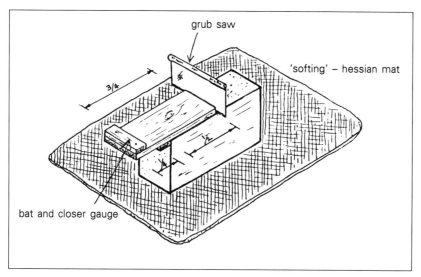

Figure 6.19 Bat and closer gauge on a cutting mat.

Cutting mats

Also known as a 'softing', this is a square of thick hessian sacking or offcut of carpet, or even just a layer of sand, upon which the bricklayer cuts and trims his bricks. This helps to take the 'jarring' action of the hammer blows, thus preventing the brick being damaged on a soft face or arris. It should be kept clean to prevent the brick resting on 'chips' of bricks which could mark it.

SAWS

Masonry saw

A modern tungsten-tipped hand saw will cut some standard hand- and machine-made bricks as well as soft stone. Although used for light-weight concrete blocks, it is ideal for cutting out lime and some cement mortar joints to form toothings on existing work. (See figure 6.20)

Grub saw

Also known as the 'tin saw', this was common in the cutting shops where it was used for scoring a shallow line to profile before cutting with the axe, scutch or wire bow saw. It was traditionally made of tin with a serrated edge, about 150mm × 75mm high, and fitted with a wooden handle.

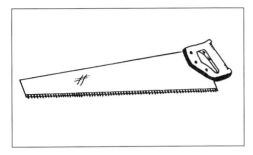

Figure 6.20 Masonry saw.

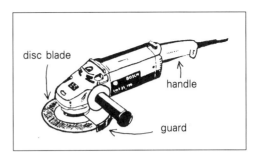

Figure 6.21 Hand-held mechanical disc cutter.

Mechanical disc cutter

These have become very popular on modern sites in the last twenty years. Used with care and skill, and with proper observance of the manufacturer's instructions and correct safety practices, they are of great assistance in obtaining otherwise very difficult precise cuts, especially on very hard bricks. Disc cutters come in two basic forms: hand-held and bench-mounted.

Hand-held

These are powered by petrol or by 110v electrical power. It is essential that the bricks to be cut are secured before cutting, and not held by hands or foot: many avoidable accidents occur this way. Many brick-layers use them not only to cut bricks but to cut out walling, chases and joints, especially on extension work. Although most modern machines are equipped with a clutch drive, if forced or not kept true the blade will 'snatch' which can be very dangerous. Used horizontally the blade can 'gyroscope' making the machine awkward to handle. In either instance one should stop the machine immediately. (See figure 6.21)

Ensure that the blade being used is the correct type and grade for the material being cut, and never inferior. A weaker blade could shatter, with calamitous results. Disc cutting produces large quantities of dust and should be carried out in a well-ventilated area. The operative must always wear protective goggles and face mask.

Bench-mounted type

These are to be preferred to the hand-held disc cutter for accurate brick cutting. The bricks are carefully placed and secured on a movable platform and fed into the blade. There are two cutting methods:

1. Dry cutting uses carborundum discs which are brought down into contact with the brick by either handle or foot pedal, so the brick is cut in a series of 'passes'. The brick moves backwards and forwards as the pressure is increased, allowing the blade gradually to cut through. Again, the correct type of blade must be selected and the operator must wear full protective clothing.

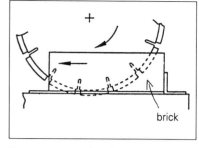

Figure 6.22 With a diamond-tipped blade, the brick is cut in one pass.

2. Wet cutting is always to be preferred, as by the delivery of water to the cutting point all potential dust hazards are eliminated. Water is filled into the tray top of the cutting bench and recycled by a small pump to the cutting head and back again. To prevent blockages, the tray is periodically cleaned of the sludge which invariably builds up. Clean water is replenished periodically, when the levels drop due to absorption by the masonry and to spray loss. If a diamond-tipped blade is used instead of carborundum, it must always be in the fixed head position, the blade adjusted to the depth required and locked, and the brick fed into the blade in a one-cut pass. (See figure 6.22)

The operative must wear full protective clothing, including face mask. Contemporary safety legislation demands that only an operative with an abrasive wheels qualification should change a cutting blade.

LEVELLING AND MEASURING TOOLS

The plumb rule has its origins in antiquity, and is mentioned as a 'plommette' rule at Westminster in 1387. There it was a regulation that it must not be allowed to lie about when not in use, but had to be hung up by the hole provided. Traditionally used for obtaining the correct vertical position of a wall, it was made of a well-seasoned length of yellow pine about 1.2m in length, 125mm in width and 15mm in thickness, planed on both faces and edges. A centre line was gouged, extending from the top of the egg-shaped 'bob' hole to the top of rule. At the top were three saw cuts for holding the plumb line. (See figure 6.24)

About 150mm up from the bottom was a hole cut large enough to allow the plumb bob to swing freely. Central to the centre line, 50mm above this hole, was a leather or wire guard to help to retain the line.

The plumb bob derives its name from the Latin *plumbum* (lead), this being the most common material used. Old craftsmen inform me that the lead 'bob' was cast in the shell of a 'blown' goose egg. Lead was

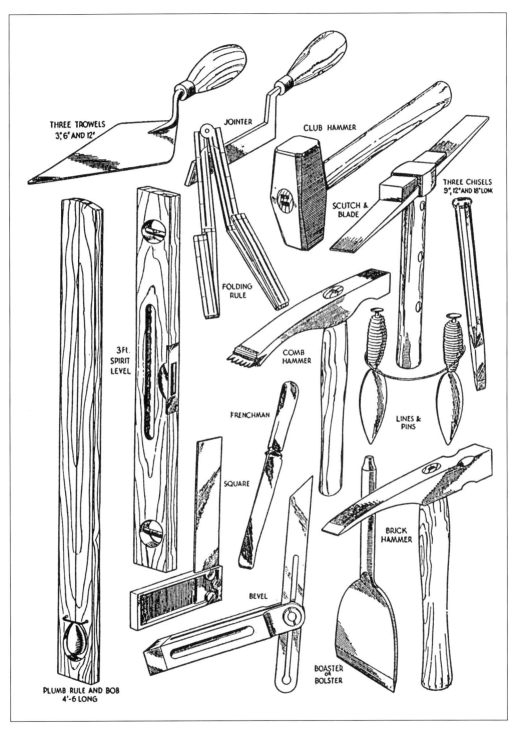

Figure 6.23 A plate depicting tools for an early twentieth-century bricklayer which clearly shows how at this stage a link remained with the tools of the previous century. From *Modern Building Construction* (1945) by Richard Greenhalgh.

gradually superseded by brass in a variety of styles. Some had hollow interiors and were filled with mercury: the greater weight helped the bob to rest quickly, but the cost of mercury meant that this style was very rare. Some 'bobs' had stainless steel points to improve accuracy in establishing the perpendicular. (See figure 6.25)

The plumb bob, which weighed about 3lb (1.36kg), was attached to a length of stiff whipcord. This was stronger than ordinary line. The line was passed through a 3mm hole drilled through the lead bob and also through a brass washer, and was then tied in a knot, or secured at the top of the brass bob on the screw head.

When required for checking plumb, the bob was held in the hole and the line fed under the guard, up the centre line and through the top: any excess line was wrapped a few times round the saw cuts to take up the weight.

If the wall was vertical, when the edge of the rule was placed squarely against the wall face, the swing of the plumb bob would be exactly at right angles to the gauge in the centre of the rule. If the bob swung to the outside the wall was 'overhanging', and if it swung to the inside it was 'battering'. If a 'battered' inclined face was desired, as in a retaining wall, then a length of board tapered to the required 'batter' was secured to the edge.

The plumb rule did not disappear until the early 1960s. It was often used by foreman bricklayers to check quoins, as this tool is always accurate and not affected by external influences. Its use declined because it was time-consuming to use; because of the danger of a bob falling from a height when used on high-rise buildings; because of improvements in the accuracy of spirit levels; and because semi-skilled bricklayers were not trained in its correct use. The use of the plumb rule meant that skilled bricklayers developed an excellent eye for a truly level and plumb quoin, which the plumb rule merely confirmed. The plumb rule was also used as a straight-edge for testing and setting straight surfaces and lines.

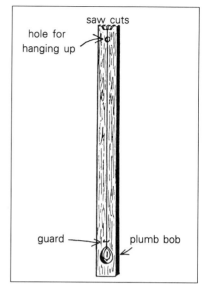

Figure 6.24 Plumb rule.

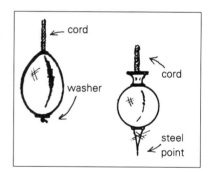

Figure 6.25 Plumb bobs.

The level

The 'greate leavells' as mentioned at Sheene in 1444 also used the plumb bob, to check the horizontal direction of a wall. This device was

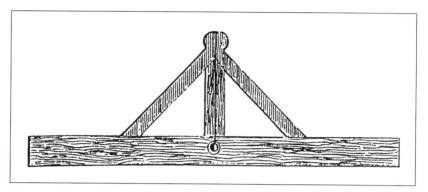

Figure 6.26 Level, *c.*1866 (by kind permission of Richard Filmer).

described by Joseph Moxon as 'being about 10 or 12 feet long, to set out their foundations level, or parallel to the horizon, and also to tell whether the walls of building or jambs of chimneys, be carried level, as they raise the work, that so they may bring up all the brickwork to an exact horizontal height, at the laying on of every floor of carpentry.'

Although it varied in size, design and sophistication, it consisted in essence of an 'A-frame'. When a plumb line was suspended from the vertex, the surface was horizontal if the plumb bob bisected the cross bar by sitting over a central mark or notch. (See figure 6.26) It had fallen out use by the latter part of the nineteenth century. The introduction of accurate machine-made bricks had made the use of the spirit level possible. Until then work was levelled from a quoin brick to a brick some way along the wall, the bricks being laid to the straightedge by eye on each course for the full height of the quoin, stopped-end or pier. In this process, too, the craftsman developed an accurate sense of what was level.

The spirit level

The spirit level, or 'bubble level', is a sealed glass tube containing frost-proof alcohol and an air bubble. It was first developed in the 1660s on surveying instruments, but did not become a builder's tool until the introduction of the factory-made product in the mid-nineteenth century. At first it was mainly a carpenter's tool, but once precise machine-made bricks were available it became standard for bricklayers too. At first they checked level only. Later models for checking vertical planes sometimes had a facility for a plumb bob as well.

Traditionally they were made of hardwood, with brass fittings and adjustable bubble phials. Today the majority are non-adjustable, shock-proof, sealed and made of aluminium alloy. They have top and bottom levels for vertical alignment and a central level for horizontal positioning, and are available in various lengths from 900mm to 1.2m, the latter being the length most preferred. (See figure 6.27)

Care of the level

When awaiting use during building work, the level should be kept out of harm's way. At the end of a day, and when not in use, it should always hang freely in a plumb position. The level should never be hit, as this can affect the accuracy. If the spirit level is adjustable it requires checking. The following procedures should be adopted:

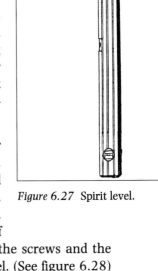

Figure 6.27 Spirit level.

♦ *Check for level.* Place two screws into a board or bench as far apart as the length of the level. Position level and turn one of the screws until the bubble is between the two lines on the tube. Reverse the spirit level and replace on the screws. If the reading is the same the level is accurate. If not, then correct half of it by adjusting one of the screws and the other half by adjusting the spirit tube in the level. (See figure 6.28) The spirit tube is easily adjusted by loosening the screws on the retaining plate and moving the 'phial' by hand, then re-tightening. The level is then re-checked as before.

♦ *Check for plumb.* Fix two screws in a door post or upright length of timber, as far apart as the length of the level. Check for plumb by using the plumb bob and line, resting on the top screw. (See figure 6.29) Adjust the lower screw accordingly. Rest the spirit level against the screws, noting the reading. Turn through 180°, replace it against the screws and note the new reading. If it differs between any of the bubbles, they must be adjusted. The screws are not touched. Sometimes bubble tubes or the enclosed glass phial are 'set' into position to prevent slippage. This is done using wet plaster or, traditionally, red lead putty. After checking and hardening, it is tightened into place using the metal checking plate.

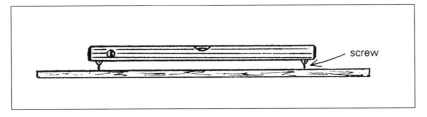

Figure 6.28 Checking for level.

Boat level

So called because of its shape, this is a pocket-sized level about 225mm long, and is useful for plumbing or levelling individual bricks, or in situations where a full-sized level is impracticable. It is made from wood, aluminium alloy or steel, although plastic is becoming popular. (See figure 6.30)

Line level

Not commonly seen today, the line level is made of metal or plastic about 120mm in length, containing a spirit tube with bubble. The case has a hook at either end, which fits over the bricklayer's line. As they are so light they tend to be blown about by the wind. (See figure 6.31)

MEASURING AND MARKING TOOLS

There is only the scantiest evidence from the Middle Ages concerning graduated rules, but it is known that plain straight-edges were the most usual form. Long measuring rods called 'metroddes' were mentioned in York in 1485, and even earlier, also at York, there is a

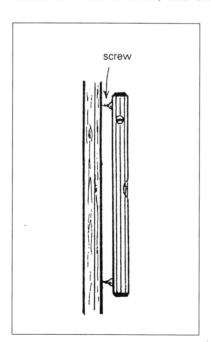

Figure 6.29 Checking for plumb.

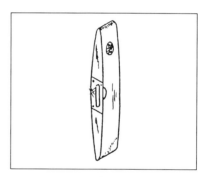

Figure 6.30 Boat level.

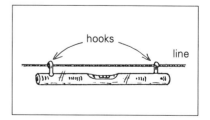

Figure 6.31 Line level.

mention of 'string' (*philo*) bought for measuring fireplaces in 1327. By 1683 an English writer speaks of foot rules having ⅛″ subdivisions. Certainly at that time standard to a bricklayer's kit were the 12″ ruler, two-foot rule and five-foot rod to take and lay down lengths, breadths and heights.

Folding rules

Mass production of boxwood rules with brass tips and hinges began around 1840. This rule has remained popular, and it is now also available in plastic. Although imperial rules are made, they are generally available in metric up to 1 metre in length. They fold down to fit in a leg pocket of a working overall. (See figure 6.32)

Double-fold steel rule

These come in a 600mm length, folding in the middle. Because of their flexibility they are most useful in setting out arches and measuring circular work. (See figure 6.33)

Steel tape

The retractable tape is very popular, being versatile for all types of use including measuring curved surfaces, and suitable for insertion into openings and positions inaccessible to a rigid rule. The 2m to 5m lengths are most popular although retractable rules are made in much larger sizes. They are fitted with a clip to the back so that they fasten on to a belt or top of trousers when not in use. (See figure 6.34)

Builder's square

The use of squares was well known in the medieval period. Squares were made of wood, although at Westminster in 1387 '2 irons made in the shape of sqwirs' are recorded. Factory-made metal squares appeared around 1835. The steel square today is 600mm × 450mm, and is used for setting out and

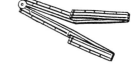

Figure 6.32 Folding rule.

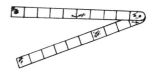

Figure 6.33 Double-fold steel rule.

locking button

Figure 6.34 Steel tape.

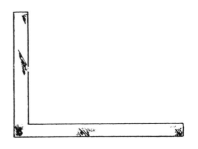

Figure 6.35 Steel square.

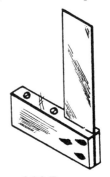

Figure 6.36 Try square.

checking quoins. To avoid distortion, it should always be hung up while not in use. (See figure 6.35)

Try square

Measures 225mm × 150mm, consists of a wooden or plastic handle into which a metal blade is fixed at 90°. It is used for squaring bricks before cutting, drawing voussoir positions across a timber centre, marking gauge rods, and similar tasks. (See figure 6.36)

The sliding bevel

This has its origins in the seventeenth century. It consists of a stock 150mm × 25mm (traditionally made of hardwood, although plastic is used) into which is fitted a moveable blade 150mm × 50mm in width. In the early days the thin metal blade moved stiffly, being riveted into a slot in the thick blade. Later models from the nineteenth century were provided with a wingnut or thumbscrew to loosen or tighten as required. The bevel is used for obtaining soffit bevels for voussoirs, skewbacks for arches and any other angles required. (See figure 6.37)

Dividers

Dividers, usually described in the plural (a 'pair of dividers'), consist of two straight legs sharpened to a point, pivoted at the top and fitted with a wing divider. Such a design was sketched in 1245. The dividers of the medieval master mason were large – often half as tall as a man – for full-scale setting-out. In 1399 at Minster Lodge in York they were described as 'an iron compass' for use on the 'tracyngborde' or drawing-table. They are used principally to scribe circles or to mark out divisions on arches for voussoirs. Because of the point marking these positions the term 'pricking out' an arch arose. Today, dividers are rarely over 400mm long, and are fitted with a thumbscrew clamp and screw for fine adjustment. (See figure 6.38)

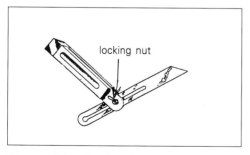

Figure 6.37 Sliding bevel.

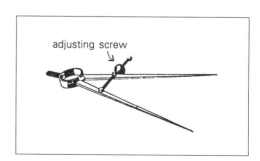

Figure 6.38 Dividers.

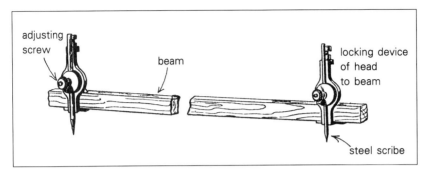

Figure 6.39 Trammel heads.

Trammel heads

The name is derived from the old French *tramail*, meaning an instrument for describing ellipses, and they are so called because the motion of the beam carrying the pencil is 'trammelled', or confined by the restriction of the pins.

Today they consist of two steel clamps with a threaded lock screw fixed horizontally. A hole drilled in the head can carry a steel pin or a pencil as required. The trammel heads are fixed to a length of timber battening, set at the required radius, and then clamped securely. They are used for setting out large arcs for arches, domes and oriels. (See figure 6.39)

JOINTING AND POINTING TOOLS AND ACCESSORIES

Pointing trowels

These are similar in shape to the laying trowel but smaller and with no cutting edge. They vary in size from 50mm to 150mm. The smaller trowel is known as a dotter, for filling-in the 'dots' or cross-joints. The larger is for the bed joints, and is used to place mortar into joints and finish and make compact the joint.

Rectangular finger or margin trowels, measuring from 150mm to 200mm in length to 25mm in width with a rounded end, are ideal for pointing around frames, narrow recesses, or other situations where a pointing trowel would prove awkward. (See figure 6.40)

Traditional jointers

They have been used since the seventeenth century, although the

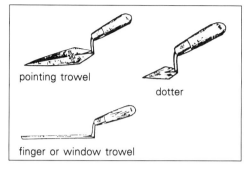

Figure 6.40 Pointing trowels.

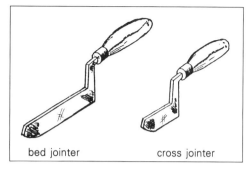

Figure 6.41 Traditional jointers.

styles have changed over the years. They were always sold in pairs and consist of a bed and cross jointer. Blade widths vary from 2mm to 8mm and is fixed by a tang into a rounded wooden handle. The cross jointer is always smaller and thinner than the bed jointer. The 'tuck' jointer has a flat steel blade, while others are profiled to give, for example, 'V' joints, beaded joints or arrowhead styles. (See figure 6.41)

Modern jointing tools

These may be hand-made by the bricklayer himself – from a variety of items such as a cranked handle from a galvanized pail, an electrician's 12mm conduit, a piece of rubber hose, or a plain steel rod – to form the now ubiquitous keyed or 'bucket handle' profile. (See figure 6.42)

Frenchman

The origin of this term is lost to time, but these have certainly been part of the bricklayer's kit for two centuries. They are used in conjunction with the feather-edge to cut and pull clear the surplus mortar 'stopping', leaving a straight, clean joint. They are normally made by the craftsman himself from a table knife. The blade is heated until red hot, cut back about 25mm on each side of the end with the hammer

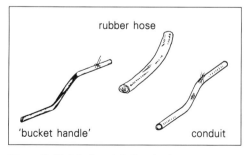

Figure 6.42 Modern jointing tools.

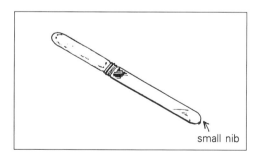

Figure 6.43 Frenchman.

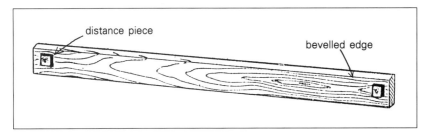

Figure 6.44 Feather-edge.

and chisel, and then sharpened. It is further heated and a little nib is then turned down at 90° to the blade at the end. If the manufacture was attempted cold, the blade would snap. (See figure 6.43)

Feather-edge

The feather-edge, or 'pointing-rule' (also known as the cutting-off-rule) is made from well-seasoned wood, traditionally deal or yellow pine. It is commonly 25mm thick, 75mm in width and 1.2m in length. The top is bevelled on one side with wood, cork or rubber 'distance pieces' fixed about 75mm in from either end: this keeps the feather-edge clear of the wall by about 5mm, allowing trimmed mortar to fall clear of the rule and wall as the frenchman runs along the bevelled edge. (See figure 6.44)

Hand hawk

Traditionally of yellow pine, these are about 200mm square and 20mm thick with a handle underneath, positioned centrally and about 100mm long. Its purpose is to hold a small quantity of 'stopping' mortar for pointing. Traditionally the handle is on a splayed strip of wood which dovetails into a groove on the square board, so that as the board wears it can be replaced. 'Hawkes' for masons to put their lime on are referred to at Kirby Muxloe in 1481. (See figure 6.45)

Spray bottles

These are used in two sizes: small hand-held dispensers ideal for pointing small areas, or larger pump-pressured sprays holding 2 litres of water. Their use prevents 'patch' saturation, giving a wide, even and controllable dampening to a wall prior to applying the pointing mortar.

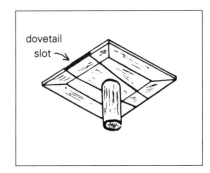

Figure 6.45 Hand hawk.

Brush

Three types of brushes are commonly used in pointing: first, a painter's dusting brush for brushing the joints before pointing to remove particles of grit or dust; second, a painter's stock brush about 200mm wide for wetting the wall; and third, a medium-bristle broom head to brush over the work after applying the finish to the joints, to complete the pointing.

RAKING OUT TOOLS

When a mortar joint has to be recessed to receive a pointed finish, the tool employed is called a raking-out tool. They have always been made to do this job, to suit either fresh or hardened mortar:

1. *For fresh mortar.* A traditional raking tool consists of a block of hardwood, 100mm × 50mm × 50mm. About 30mm in from either end a halving is cut out to a depth of 25mm. Into this is positioned a screw, centrally placed, and adjusted to the depth of recess required. The raking out tool is run along the joints with two ends resting on the bricks. As the screw forces out the stiffened mortar, the halving collects the mortar. To prevent smearing, it must be emptied frequently. (See figure 6.46)

   Today bricklayers use a 'chariot raker'. Manufactured from lightweight metal or plastic, it consists of a shaped handle 225mm long, with wheels on either side, near the end. An adjustable masonry nail or pick is positioned between the wheels. Running

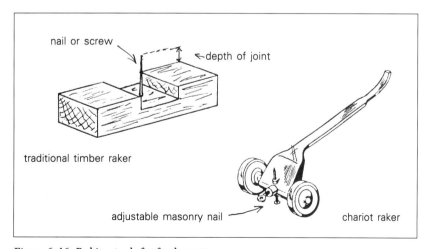

Figure 6.46 Raking tools for fresh mortar.

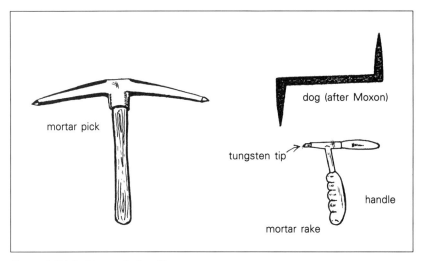

Figure 6.47 Raking tools for old mortar.

the wheels along the wall face allows the nail to gouge out the mortar as it moves along the joint.

2. *Raking out old mortar.* The tool used since the eighteenth century was known as a 'dog', and was a shaped piece of iron about 300mm long, 30mm wide and 3mm thick, formed as a straight centre-piece with the spiked ends turned in opposite directions. (See figure 6.47)

    It was used by being driven into the lime mortar joint and dragged along to the depth required, by pulling on the end with one hand and guiding the centre of the dog with the other.

Mortar pick

Also known as the 'raking-out pick', this had superseded the dog by the turn of the twentieth century. It was shaped like a miniature pick, a double-spiked iron or steel head fixed to an ash handle. Care and skill were required to do a neat and speedy job, if it was not to chip bricks.

Mortar rake

This is a combination of the 'dog' and the pick, shaped like a hammer except that the head has a tungsten cutting point for hard cement mortars. The other end is a rubber handle. Instead of chopping the joints like the pick, it is drawn along the joint after cutting in, by pulling the handles. If the joints prove difficult the point can be punched through the joint at intervals along its length and then pulled.

COMPLEMENTARY TOOLS AND ACCESSORIES

Chalk line

'Snapping a line' was as familiar in ancient Egypt as it is to modern building construction. The principle is that a chalk-covered line, if stretched between two points and 'twanged' or 'snapped', will deposit a trace of that line in chalk on the surface as a guide to set out and build to. The only change in 5,000 years is that the Egyptians used red or yellow ochre in a wet state, whereas modern craftsman, like the ancient Greek masons, use dry white or red chalks.

A modern chalk line consists of a hollow, egg-shaped case containing a spindle upon which a line is wound, and to which a handle for winding up the line is fixed. At the narrow end of the case is a threaded cap, through the centre of which feeds the line. The line has a metal tag at the end to prevent the line being wound right into the case, and to 'hook on' to a nail for setting out lines single-handed. By unscrewing the cap, chalk can be dispensed into the case from a container: this should be done in stages as the line is unwound and, at each filling stage, wound in a little, ensuring that chalk is fully distributed along the length of line.

Hod

Tools described as 'hoddis' were recorded at Westminster in 1532. Made of wickerwork until the eighteenth century, they later became three-sided wooden boxes of various sizes, fixed to a central wooden pole and used for carrying bricks. If larger in capacity (0.014m³) they would be used to carry mortar to the bricklayer. Today they can be made from a lightweight alloy or toughened plastic. (See figure 6.48)

Larry

Today's methods of mixing mortar mean that this is a rarely seen tool. It consists of a metal head fixed at 90° to a long wooden handle, similar to a 'drag-hoe', and is used in slaking lime for mixing lime mortar and spreading a mortar bed for infill brickwork in the interior of thick walling. (See figure 6.49)

Sieve or screen

Until recent times it was always necessary for sand and lime to be

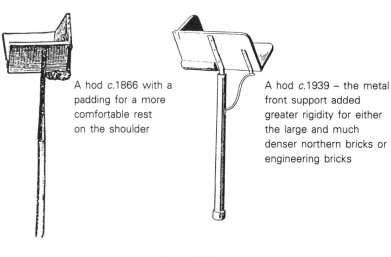

A hod c.1866 with a padding for a more comfortable rest on the shoulder

A hod c.1939 – the metal front support added greater rigidity for either the large and much denser northern bricks or engineering bricks

Figure 6.48 The hod – an Edwardian labourer with his hod of bricks (photograph and prints reproduced by kind permission of Richard Filmer).

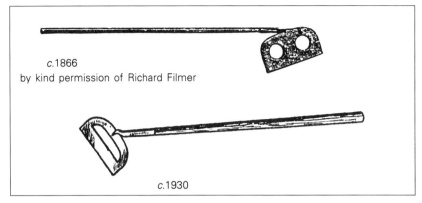

Figure 6.49 A larry or mortar rake.

sifted with sieves or screens to remove over-size particles before making mortar. In 1376 'two ridles and a ceve for cleansing sand' were bought at Corfe for sixpence. Large sieves or screens, often as large as 1.5m by 900mm, were inclined – resting on a timber plank – away from the operative, who would then shovel, 'dash' or 'punch' the material through, leaving large particles behind. Sieves or screens should still be employed when preparing traditional lime mortar mixes for restoration work. (See figure 6.50)

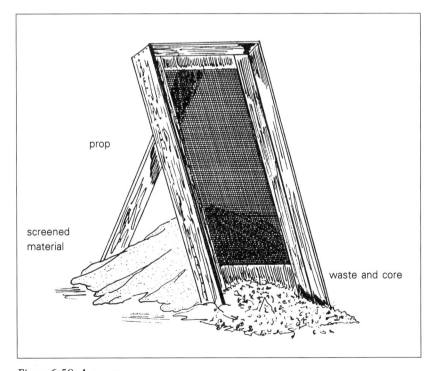

Figure 6.50 A screen.

7

Elementary Practical Skills and Considerations

The high degree of skill and ease with which a bricklayer executes his work is not always apparent to the uninitiated onlooker, especially when the work is done by one who has mastered his craft through many years of careful study and practical experience. Such qualities make his work a pleasure, and a point of personal satisfaction to give a job well done. He cherishes the name he has acquired for his craftsmanship, and is at pains always to maintain his standards. What are the essential ingredients that define a craftsman? He has, from his apprenticeship days, cultivated the habits and tool skills which are essential if his work is to save him excessive time and manual effort, yet gain maximum results.

The habits of being neat in appearance and clean in work are the first priority. Also essential are to be punctual, hard-working and independent, with the ability to think in advance and consider his efforts before making them. He will have pride in his work, derived from a constant striving for elusive perfection, and he will be steeped in his craft and its traditions.

These, then, are the traits of a craftsman who believes that it is the quality of the finished product that matters, and not the time it takes. The aspiring craftsman should aim to acquire these habits on his journey into adulthood and in his quest to master his craft.

There are bricklayers, and there are men who lay bricks. The first have been described above: the second are men who have exchanged the hod for a trowel, and know but little of the essential rules and traditions of the craft. They are motivated by monetary aspirations and little else. Their work has, in the main, only helped to bring discredit to a noble craft.

A few examples will clarify these points. A craftsman will spread a carefully gauged mortar bed and, with a slight pressure of the hand, set his brick. The layer of bricks will hammer his brick into position with his trowel, often damaging the brick. When raising a quoin the thoughtful craftsman will study his brick stacks and carefully select the square, good-faced brick for the corner, while his counterpart will pick up a dozen at random and discard them until selecting one that suits him, thus wasting time and effort. The skilled craftsman sets his bricks to the quoin with an eye to plumb; his level is used only to confirm his skill. The other operative abuses his spirit level by frequently hitting it to obtain plumb as it rests against his quoin.

It is by the care and use of his tools that the craftsman is initially assessed by his workmates and foreman, who can quickly judge his character from the appearance of the tool kit. His skill in the manipulation of his tools make for neat, clean and effortless work, in very marked contrast to the slovenly, laboured effort of the indifferent bricklayer.

In studying a craft and the techniques therein, it is important to emphasize that some books imply that there is one orthodox way of executing a task, and that there is a standard nomenclature for tools and processes. That is not so. With any craft, techniques will vary considerably throughout the country, and even from one worker to another. This is not only because of the differing bricks and mortars, which affect method, but also because of local practices and the ingenuity of individuals in finding their own way of tackling a job or improving their methods. This variety is part of the rich heritage of all old crafts.

Positioning materials

Ordinary or standard brickwork, traditionally referred to as common work, is a classification covering most everyday bricklaying. Although special classes of brickwork require different techniques and treatment, the procedure is basically identical in all types of brickwork for ordinary structures.

The priority should be to place the mortar on spot boards in the most practical positions and to load correctly all materials needed for the erection of the walling. (See figure 7.1) The mortar board should be placed at a sensible distance from the wall face – 600mm is considered ideal – as on a standard five-board-width putlog scaffold this would represent the actual working space. The clean mortar board should be positioned off the ground or scaffold by being rested on bricks-on-edge placed at the corners (blocks will increase this height even further). This is done for three main reasons: it reduces excessive bending by the bricklayer, prevents over-loading with mortar and allows the area around the board to be kept neat and tidy.

The bricks to be laid should always be stacked next to the spot board, although not right against it in case any mortar should accidentally spill from the board during loading and spoil the bricks. For that reason, if either blocks or commons for inner-leaf or back-up work are being laid, they should be positioned next to the mortar board to shield the facing bricks. It is also considered good craft practice to stack the bricks on edge rather than flat on their beds. This is because on edge they allow the bricklayer to observe at a glance both the stretcher and header face before handling. When they are

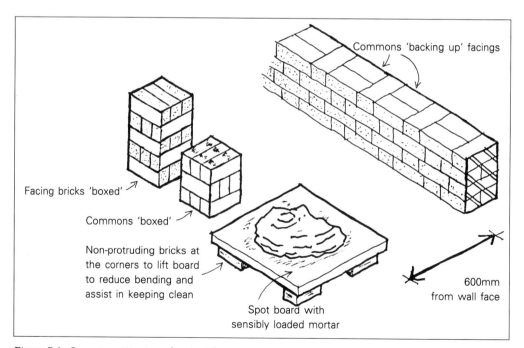

Figure 7.1 Correct positioning of materials.

stacked flat, only the header face is visible. Also, if bricks are stacked flat in wet weather the frogs fill and hold water. This would not only stop bricklaying because of the impossibility of good-quality work with saturated bricks, but if the water should freeze it might produce many problems for the facework.

Wetting bricks

There are two main reasons for wetting bricks:

1. To ensure that sufficient moisture is retained in the mortar to allow the process of setting and hardening to take place.
2. To help the brick to adhere more satisfactorily to the mortar by removing dust and loose particles.

It is, however, necessary to observe that this dampening of bricks should only take place if the bricks are of a porous type, and likely to dry out the joint, and if the season is not winter. Undoubtedly it will be vital during hot summer days, but during the frosty winter months it is liable to do more harm than good. Therefore, sound judgement is needed. Calcium silicate and concrete bricks should not be wetted. Instead, the moisture content of the mortar must be adjusted to achieve the desired workability and allow for some water to be absorbed into the bricks.

With spot board positioned and bricks loaded out, the mortar board must be dampened prior to receiving the mortar. This prevents a dry board absorbing the moisture from the mortar and reducing its workability. The mortar should be of the correct consistency for good work, neither too sloppy nor too stiff. If the mortar is sloppy because of excessive water, clean work will prove difficult as the mortar will tend to be sticky on the trowel and unable to support the brickwork. If the bricks are damp, as they should be for good bonding, then the mortar will probably leak out of joints and run down the facework, while the bricks may possibly slide forward and overhang, as the pressure on the earlier work increases with height. With mortar that is too stiff, either because of insufficient water or lack of plasticizer, using the trowel in preparing beds and joints will become a source of fatigue for the bricklayer, who will have to work very hard to overcome the shortcomings of his mortar.

It is vital that only sufficient mortar is placed on the board. It must be kept replenished to enable the bricklayer to continue his work. A well-loaded spot board leaves sufficient space to the front, next to the bricklayer, so he can select and prepare his mortar bed with his trowel prior to placing it on the wall.

Before he begins laying, the bricklayer will always position himself correctly to his work, something that will have been drilled into him since the days of his apprenticeship. If he is right-handed he will stand with his left side to the wall face and generally operate along the wall from left to right. The opposite would apply for a left-handed brick-layer.

Laying the bed joints

Clean work is essential on all classes of facework and the bricklayer will succeed in maintaining this if he lifts his mortar correctly from the spot board and lays and spreads just sufficient mortar to bed the bricks properly. If this is done with care, and skill in the use of the trowel, he can remove the mortar squeezed out of the bed joint and so keep the facework neat and clean. The waste mortar can then either be returned to the board or used to provide a cross-joint for the next brick.

'It's all in the bed' is an old saying in the craft, meaning that if one can perfect the preparation of the bed joint then the laying of bricks in a neat, clean and accurate way will inevitably follow. Therefore the spreading of this mortar bed is one of the first points the aspiring craftsman must master. Of course, this entails correct use of his laying trowel. The trowel should be held so that the thumb rests on the ferrule and the fingers around the handle. (See figure 7.2) This grasp should never be too tight, as mobility of the wrist is important for skilled work. The trowel should be the right size for the bricklayer: if it is too big and unwieldy it will put excessive strain on the wrist, so reducing flexibility. A 225mm trowel is ideal for the young apprentice whose strength is still developing.

The craftsman selects by eye the amount of mortar he requires from the front of his heap. The trowel is then guided so that it cuts out, in a downward stroke to the board, the required mortar. The mortar is then drawn to the front of the board in a sliding backward and forward motion of the trowel. This 'rolling', as it is termed, consoli-dates the previously loose heaped mortar into a trowel-sized shape. The trowel is then brought in from the back and side of the rolled mortar in a long sweeping action to collect or 'lift' the mortar as the blade passes sharply under it, and in this one continuous action it is moved into position on the concrete foundation or wall. (See figure 7.3)

The laying of the bed is executed by positioning the trowel correctly to the centre of the bricks and, as the trowel is drawn towards the bricklayer, to tilt the point of the blade down while gradually turning the trowel sideways. This spreads the previously consolidated mortar along the centre of the wall for the length of several bricks. This having been done, the point of the trowel is then placed at the

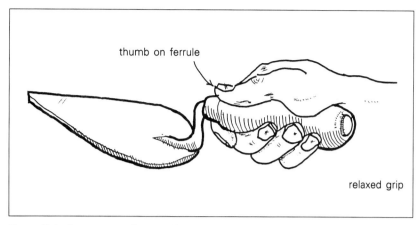

thumb on ferrule

relaxed grip

Figure 7.2 Correct grip of a trowel.

beginning of the mortar roll and with a zig-zag or undulating action, guided by the action of the wrist or forearm, the trowel is drawn towards the bricklayer down the centre of the mortar. This furrows the mortar, leaving a raised edge to either side. The excess mortar, slightly overhanging the bed, is then cut off by setting the trowel at an angle facing away from the wall and pushing it along the wall. The surplus mortar is returned to the board, or used it to prepare a cross-joint. It is, however, important that this furrow is not too deep: evidence shows that if this is the case not only does it bed the bricks on the edges but it allows wind-driven rain to penetrate the walling, which must never be allowed to happen. For structural work care should be taken to ensure that furrowing does not lead to a hollow centre to the bedding, as this will reduce the compressive strength of the wall. A slight furrowing is intended to help the brick to settle more easily to its gauge. It allows the mortar, as the bricks sink into the bed, to spread inwards towards the centre, as well as to the outer faces, and so to consolidate the joint. Like all aspects of any craft only constant practice will hone this skill. (See figure 7.4)

The finishing height before scaffolding is required is usually 22–26 courses, but working at this height – and, in particular, preparing a mortar bed – can present problems for an inexperienced bricklayer. The problem is that the mortar has to be lifted on the trowel above head height and then spread cleanly, so as to be of the right gauge. It must be positioned centrally and be continuous, and must not fall down the front or the back of the wall, which would cause staining of the face or filling of the cavity.

Again, this is a matter of a practised technique, and involves creating momentum, from picking up the rolled mortar on the trowel off the board, raising it horizontally until it passes over the top of the line to the centre of the brick, and pointing the trowel blade down, drawing the trowel blade sideways to release the mortar centrally to the bed. The slight furrowing of the bed can be made with the trowel held with the handle in a downwards position, the excess mortar being cut from the face and back of the wall with the trowel held so as to collect it and prevent it falling.

Figure 7.3 Cutting, rolling and lifting the mortar.

It is a common practice for bricklayers to run out very long mortar beds and then to progress along the wall laying bricks, concentrating only on applying the mortar cross-joints. Although this may achieve speed, it is a bad craft practice. Only sufficient mortar should be spread to allow the brick to be laid. If the mortar has dried it will not bond properly with the brick, no matter how hard it may be tapped down. This defect will reduce the strength of the wall.

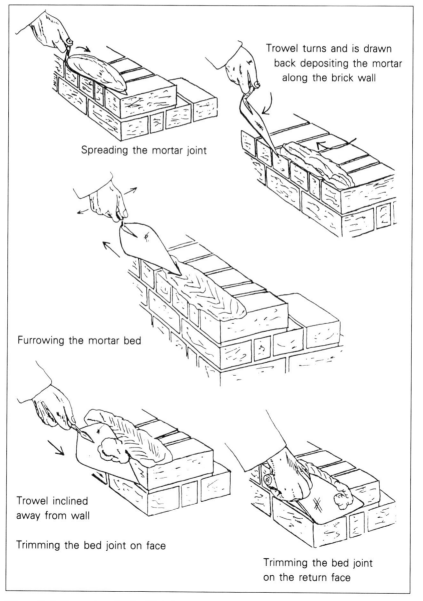

Figure 7.4 Preparing the bed joint.

Laying the bricks

Laying the stretcher brick in its correct position also requires considerable care and practice. The dampened bricks should be laid immediately the mortar bed is prepared: a delay results in a stiffening of the
mortar. The brick to be laid is grasped in the other hand from the

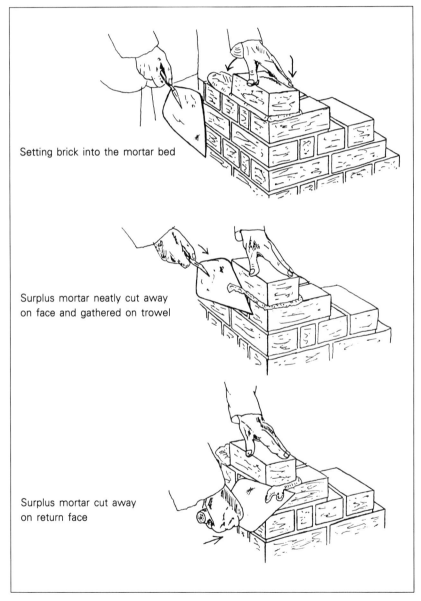

Setting brick into the mortar bed

Surplus mortar neatly cut away
on face and gathered on trowel

Surplus mortar cut away
on return face

Figure 7.5 Bedding the brick.

trowel so that the thumb is to the face, the palm to the middle and the fingers to the back. If the bricks have been loaded out properly this will happen automatically. If the bricklayer notes that his thumb is not to the brick face, the brick must be turned. This is achieved in a simple though skilful way. The hand is turned so that the brick sits in the palm of the hand, the thumb is dropped down level and the fingers swivel or rotate the brick horizontally with a quick flick. As the brick turns, the fingers lie flat until the face of the brick comes into the correct position, and then the hand clasps it again.

The brick is now brought to the wall, placed on to the mortar and glided into position. (See figure 7.5) A slight pressure to the back edge is applied by the fingers. The lower front arris is judged by eye to be directly above the upper arris of the lower brick. Then, especially if laying to a line, the thumb is raised from the stretcher face and placed onto the margin of the brick and by a dexterous pressure of the thumb the front face is brought over to the line. It thus sits upright and flush to the wall face. The bricklayer all this time should stand sideways and close to the wall with his head positioned vertically over the brick which is being laid, so that he can 'eye' his work in, especially if not laying to line, or when rearing a stopped-end or quoin. (See figure 7.6)

Common problems experienced by apprentices and, unfortunately, seen frequently on the brickwork of an unskilled bricklayer, are what are known in the craft as 'hatching' and 'grinning'. 'Hatching', or 'hacking', is when the lower arris of the brick sits in from the upper arris of the previous course. 'Grinning' is when the lower arris of the brick lips, or overhangs, the previously laid course. (See figure 7.7)

Both these problems can be avoided by correctly eyeing in the lowest bed arris to set over the previous course and bringing the upper arris over to the level or line. When the brick is misshapen the bricklayer is required to 'humour' the brick, which means that by a slight alteration in the bedding of the brick, the face may be altered from battering, or overhanging, to perpendicular. All this is achieved by care and practice and – most valuable of all – experience.

The frog is a recess on the top surface of a brick, and there is much debate as to whether it should be laid uppermost or down. It is without doubt best if a brick is laid frog up, thus ensuring that it is completely filled with mortar to give full structural soundness and damp-prevention capabilities. Some machine-made bricks are provided with two frogs, a deep one on the upper surface and shallow one on bed. In this instance the lower frog must be first 'flushed-up' with mortar before laying, to ensure solidity. Such matters are dealt with in BS5628, Parts 1 and 3, as well as SP56: 1988.

It is also important to note, when laying certain textured or rustic bricks, that care must be exercised to ensure that they are laid on their

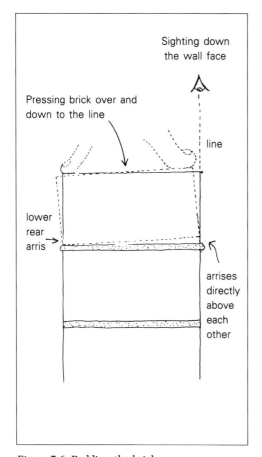

Sighting down
the wall face

Pressing brick over and
down to the line

line

lower
rear
arris

arrises
directly
above
each
other

Figure 7.6 Bedding the brick.

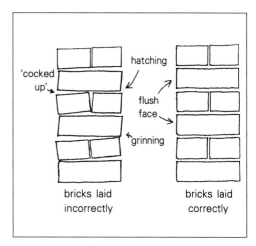

'cocked
up'

hatching

flush
face

grinning

bricks laid
incorrectly

bricks laid
correctly

Figure 7.7 Hatching and grinning.

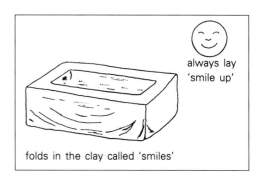

always lay
'smile up'

folds in the clay called 'smiles'

Figure 7.8 Textured faces.

correct bedding faces. (See figure 7.8) If mistakenly laid upside down their face patterns may absorb rainwater instead of shedding it, with calamitous results in frosty weather. The brick manufacturer's advice should be sought on this matter.

Sometimes mis-shapen bricks have to be laid on facework. These may be rather poor-quality machine-made bricks or 'character' hand-mades. (See figure 7.9) In either case the bricklayer must learn to assess the brick quickly, in a similar way to a mason studying random rubble, to decide which way he will lay it for best results. The main problem occurs with what are termed 'banana' bricks. These may need to be laid hollow bed down, with any 'round' (convex) face outwards. This advice also applies to headers. If this is not practised, the wall always appears unsatisfactory in appearance. Do not allow the brick to sit or 'cock-up' at the back edge, as it will throw the wall out of level on width and make it difficult to keep the next course level.

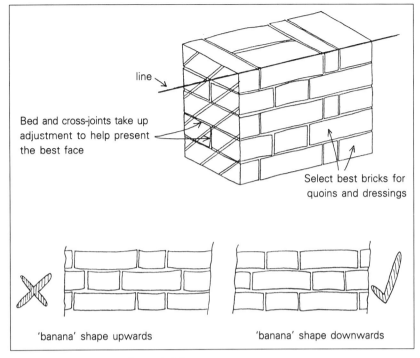

Figure 7.9 Laying mis-shapen bricks.

Applying cross-joints

There are several methods for applying the cross-joints and these depend on whether the craftsman likes to 'push' or 'pull' along a wall and if he prefers to 'butter' the laid brick or the brick in his hand which is to be laid.

'Pushing' or 'pulling' are craft terms referring to bricklaying styles. To push (for a right-handed man) is when the bricklayer builds his wall from right to left, thereby walking backwards along the line and placing the bricks in a pushing action into position. Pulling is the opposite to this, and generally the more popular method. In this instance the bricklayer walks forward along the wall from left to right and, in placing the brick, pulls it backwards to locate it.

Some inferior methods of applying the joints to the bricks are practised on sites by bricklayers. In the shoving method, as a brick is laid and the excess mortar is squeezed out of the joint the trowel blade collects it cleanly, in a swinging action, and then places the mortar upon the cross-joint face of the previously laid brick on front and back arris. (See figure 7.10) In many instances where this method is adopted only the outer arris is buttered, especially if it is 'tight joint

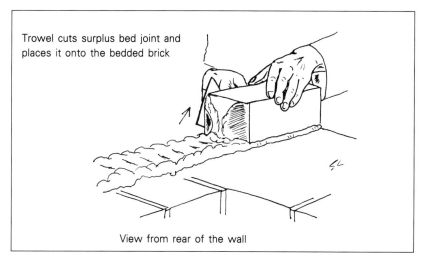

Trowel cuts surplus bed joint and
places it onto the bedded brick

View from rear of the wall

Figure 7.10 A traditional method of applying a cross-joint not suited to modern
half-brick construction.

work'. Thus one has, constructionally, a weak joint and also another
point of entry for wind-driven rain. This method was traditionally used
on thick walling, which was grouted upon completion of each course
and so ensured good solid walling. It has no place on modern cavity
construction and slender walling techniques.

A second, and again inferior, method is where the bricklayer places
rather more mortar in the bed than is usual and allows it to remain
thick even after furrowing with the trowel. The brick is then slid into
position by slightly inclining the end to be 'buttered', so that it scoops
up a mortar joint as the two bricks are pushed or pulled together. Not
only is this wasteful of mortar but, when practised by the majority of
bricklayers, it is messy, not consistent in joint size, or sure in the filling
of the cross-joint.

The correct method of applying a vertical or cross-joint is to place it
on the brick which is to be laid, prior to bringing it to the wall to be
bedded. As the brick to be laid is picked up it is held over the mortar
heap, the trowel is dipped into the mortar by the tip to a depth of about
50mm, the trowel is then tilted back and raised to lift a small 'pat' of
mortar. A small trowel skill is then employed to position the mortar
on the blade prior to placing it on the brick. The blade is flicked lightly
by a small dropping action of the wrist. This causes the mortar to roll
back to the centre of the trowel blade and spread. This serves three
purposes. First, it gives a wider spread of mortar to place onto the
brick. Second, it causes the mortar to hold to the trowel, so that it does
not fall off as the joint is being applied. Third, when perfected it aids
in achieving a cross-joint of uniform thickness. (See figure 7.11)

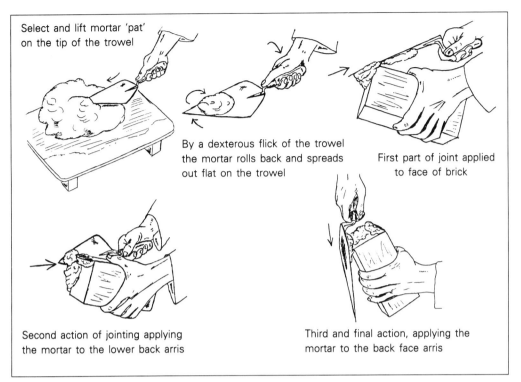

Select and lift mortar 'pat' on the tip of the trowel

By a dexterous flick of the trowel the mortar rolls back and spreads out flat on the trowel

First part of joint applied to face of brick

Second action of jointing applying the mortar to the lower back arris

Third and final action, applying the mortar to the back face arris

Figure 7.11 Applying a cross-joint when 'pushing' a wall.

If one is laying stretchers by the pushing method the brick is dropped on the back header face, so that the front header face presents itself for jointing. The joint can then be applied by holding the trowel at an angle of 45° to the vertical end of the brick, so that all the mortar begins to rest on the header. As the bricklayer draws the trowel towards himself, the joint is made uniform in thickness by using the inside of the blade of the trowel. This style gives a full and flush joint every time a brick is laid and is the method recommended on all load-bearing work, manholes and engineering brickwork. An alternative way of applying a joint on a brick is to divide the mortar on the blade by eye into three equal parts. The first part is applied to the brick by a downward stroke of the trowel blade held horizontally. The second portion is delivered in a similar action to the lower bed arris, and the remaining mortar is then placed on to the back face arris of the header as the trowel descends vertically. With practice this gives a good even gauge and a full joint and is much favoured by the craftsman.

If one is laying by the pulling method then both these styles of applying the joints are recommended and applied in the same way, except that the way of holding the brick prior to jointing is different. In this instance the bricklayer, after picking up his brick in his free

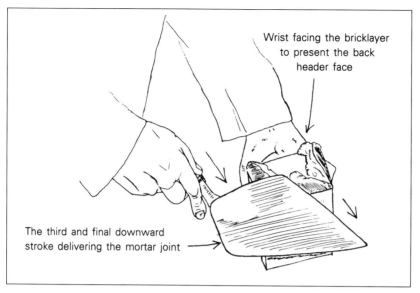

Wrist facing the bricklayer
to present the back
header face

The third and final downward
stroke delivering the mortar joint

Figure 7.12 Applying a cross-joint when 'pulling' a wall.

hand, has to turn the brick over so that it presents the rear header face. This is achieved by turning the hand as if one was trying to read a wrist watch with its face to the inside of the wrist. By so doing the brick automatically presents the header face horizontally so that the joints can be applied. (See figure 7.12)

With the joints firmly placed on the brick by the trowel, it can then be lifted to the wall without fear of the mortar falling off, and driven home against the previously laid brick. In so doing not only will mortar squeeze out on the bed, but also on the perpend. In a half-brick wall to the front and rear, this is lifted clear back and front with the trowel blade and thus the sequence starts again.

If a bricklayer is constructing a one-brick wall, techniques will have to be practised to prepare the bed and lay and joint the bricks. Even if the brick to be laid is a header, the mortar is always spread along the wall, never across it. In the case of headers, two long spreads of mortar on the front and rear of the wall are laid as previously described.

To joint a header, the brick is picked up as normal, but then tipped so that the stretcher face held by the thumb is facing the bricklayer. The trowel picks up slightly more mortar than if one was bedding a stretcher, then the wrist is dropped to ensure that the mortar spreads and sticks. Because of the length of the header the mortar has to be applied in three distinct trowel strokes. The first two downward horizontal passes place mortar on the front and back arrises. The third and final action is a sliding movement along the lower arris of the stretcher face, so that the mortar is spread from front to back. The brick is then laid into position – if pulling, by placing the header down on the finger side first. This allows the thumb to come clear and lets the header join the previously laid brick by an even pressure of the hand across the brick, giving a full mortar cross-joint. As the brick is laid, it is essential to check that the header face is vertical on the face line as well as horizontally level and to the line.

Sometimes it may be necessary to tap a brick down to the line. If so, it should be done with the handle and always to the centre of a brick. If hit at either end or on the sides the brick will tilt and disturb the bond between brick and mortar bed. An experienced bricklayer seldom taps a brick as time is wasted on this action during which he is not setting bricks. Good pressure from either the palm of the hand or the knuckles (depending on style) is sufficient.

To ensure intended strength and impermeability to damp on this walling, it is vital to ensure that correct collar (the long joint between two stretchers on the same course) jointing is achieved. This means that the bricklayer must lay his bricks with ample mortar to bed and cross-joints, so that all the inside faces of the bricks are assured a solid joint. It is common practice to try to do this afterwards by dashing mortar off the trowel in the hope that the joint will be filled. Unless a grout is used, or on every joint the edge of the trowel is used to chop the mortar in, the exercise is a waste of time and fruitless in results.

NOTE
Traditionally on buildings where the walls were very thick, and on heavy engineering works, the facing bricks were laid in the usual manner. Mortar would then be shovelled into the interior of the course and then spread out with a wooden instrument formed like a rake, but without teeth, known as a 'larry'. Water would be added at the same time to thin out the mortar. The infill bricks could then be squeezed into position causing the mortar to rise and fill the vertical joints completely and thus forming an excellent bond. This operation was termed 'larrying'.

Erecting a quoin

The building of a truly level, plumb and gauge corner or quoin (Old French from the Latin *coigne/coygne*, a wall meeting at an angle) is of the utmost importance for upon it depends the accuracy of the whole wall. Therefore it is vital that the process of erecting, or 'rearing' as it is properly termed, a quoin is carefully explained.

Having set out an angle of 90° using the builder's square, the bricks are dry bonded carefully to assess the length of the wall. It is considered good craft practice to use a line if building a wall over 1.125m in length. Therefore an ideal quoin length is four bricks (900mm) × 3½″ bricks (777mm) on the return. This will enable a height of seven courses (675mm) to be achieved. Once the quoin is dry bonded the end positions are carefully marked.

NOTE
By adding the total number of bricks on plan on the first course of the quoin one can determine the height in courses of the quoin, i.e. in this instance 4 bricks + 3 bricks = 7 courses high.

One always begins from the quoin stretcher or header, which then controls the level and gauge of the overall course. Therefore this is the first brick, laid with the apprentice positioned so that he is close in to the wall to sight down the brick onto the building line. (See figure 7.13)

It is a bad habit for the apprentice to straddle the wall, with his feet either side as it cultivates a stance which is no longer practical once work reaches a height of 750mm. Therefore, it is best to learn the best working positions from the start.

The next brick to be laid is the end or fourth brick, which is carefully positioned, after measuring, to the setting-out position and levelled back to quoin stretcher. When this is correct, the centre bricks can be laid and adjusted for level and straightness by placing the level between the end bricks on top and face. This is an old craft technique, from the days when bricks were awkwardly shaped hand-mades. They

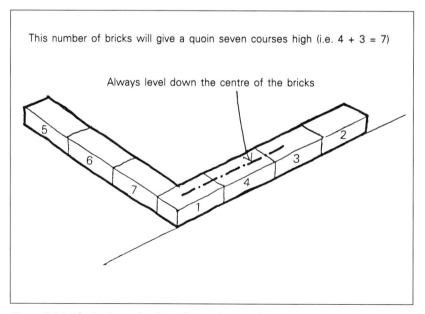

Figure 7.13 The laying order from the quoin stretcher.

were checked using the plumb rule level, where it was virtually impossible precisely to level in each brick as it is today when we have machine-made regular bricks. The craftsmen would 'eye-in' the remaining bricks using a straight-edge for face planing. However, this method is still superior to running work out from the quoin in both directions, as it is always best to work between two fixed points for level and line.

The end brick is laid on the return and levelled back to the quoin stretcher. Again the centre bricks are laid and adjusted to level and line by placing the spirit level on and against the end bricks. (See figure 7.14) It is important not knock the end bricks out of position when placing the final 'infill' brick. This is achieved quite easily if mortar is placed onto the ends of the last laid brick, and the other joint needed is applied to the other end of the brick to be laid. as it is lowered into position the trowel rests lightly against the end brick to absorb any pressure.

To complete the first course, checks for accuracy are made with the builder's square. (See figure 7.15) If one is using a traditional braced square, this is placed on top of the wall and positioned so that one leg is flush with the front of the bricks. If a steel square is being used, then it can be positioned to the outer face of the quoin. The return is then carefully adjusted flush with the other leg of the square, if necessary. The building line is never adjusted – only the return. The building square should never be placed behind the bricks to make the bricks fit around it, as bricks vary in width (especially hand-made ones) and this would throw out the front face to line. This is only practised on internal quoins.

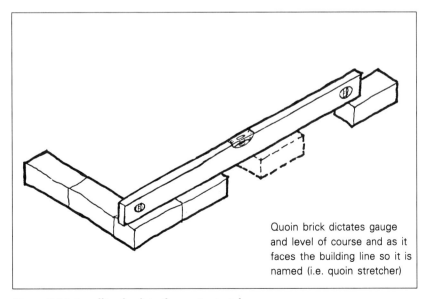

Quoin brick dictates gauge and level of course and as it faces the building line so it is named (i.e. quoin stretcher)

Figure 7.14 Levelling back to the quoin stretcher.

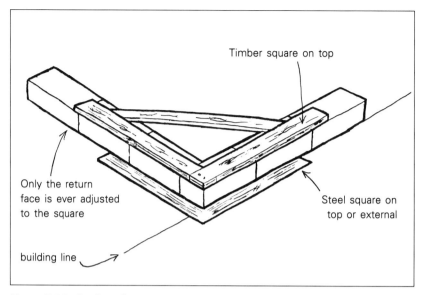

Timber square on top

Only the return
face is ever adjusted
to the square

Steel square on
top or external

building line

Figure 7.15 Checking for square.

The second course is now commenced with the quoin brick again –
this time a quoin header. Once the quoin brick is laid to gauge, 'level
by eye' and sighted down the angle for plumb, the spirit level is
brought to the brick to check the level along the brick and across its
width. It is checked for plumb on both front face and return, by
standing the level upright about 25mm in from the external angle.
(See figure 7.16) The level is controlled by one hand held near the top,
while a foot placed against the outer edge keeps it tight to the wall at
the bottom. If the bubble is in the centre of the tube then the wall is
vertical. If not, then the quoin brick is adjusted by using the handle of
the trowel or, better still, a brick hammer. If the bubble is off centre
towards the quoin, or 'hard', then the quoin brick needs to come
forward: if the bubble is off centre away from the wall, the brick needs
to go back.

Another important point when plumbing a brick is to ensure that
the brick is 'full' to the level. Sometimes it is found that, although the
brick reads plumb, it is not touching either at the top or the bottom.
In such a situation, the level is held in position while the brick is
carefully adjusted to bring all the face into contact with the edge of
the spirit level. If not touching at the top it is tapped down on the
front edge: this brings the front arris over to the level. If it is away
at the bottom arris the brick is tapped at the back edge, to bring the
bottom into contact with the level. Always ensure that the brick is
tapped in the middle of its length, so as not to hit it out of level. (See
figure 7.17)

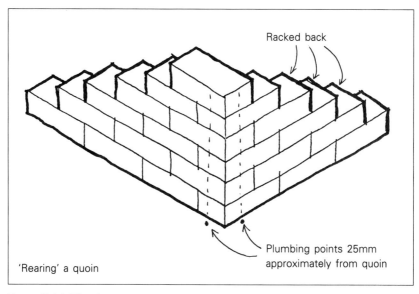

Figure 7.16 Plumbing a quoin.

Gauge rod

As has been already stated, the quoin brick dictates not only the level of all the bricks in that course but also their gauge. It is obvious that there should be some way of ensuring that this is achieved and maintained for regular joint thickness throughout the walls height. Such an aid is the 'gauge rod'. This is a 1-metre length of 50mm × 20mm timber batten marked off accurately with saw-cuts every 75mm from the bottom to the top. The marks are carefully set out with the use of a try-square before sawing, to ensure absolute accuracy. The gauge rod is now brought to the quoin, where it is positioned vertically: the course as constructed should correspond to the division on the rod. Gauge is only checked on the quoin bricks. (See figure 7.18)

The end brick on the front face is now carefully laid to level and gauge by eye, and checked with the spirit level back to the quoin header. It is also plumbed as previously described. The centre bricks can then be laid and once again checked for level and line between the end bricks. The same procedure is completed on the return.

The quoin is now raised to its full height with the apprentice always sighting down the wall face, especially the quoin brick. He repeats the sequences described on each consecutive course, always remembering to start with the quoin brick levelled and gauged. The ends of the wall gradually come closer to the quoin brick by a series of steps, in a practice known as 'racking back': this allows for future bonding of the infill brickwork, but the perpends must be retained absolutely plumb and not allowed to wander, or else either large joints or cut bricks will

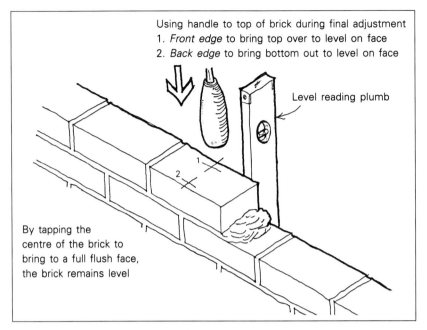

Using handle to top of brick during final adjustment
1. *Front edge* to bring top over to level on face
2. *Back edge* to bring bottom out to level on face

Level reading plumb

By tapping the
centre of the brick to
bring to a full flush face,
the brick remains level

Figure 7.17 Tapping down the brick correctly.

appear in the work. As the wall racks back so the end plumbing points move closer to the quoin with each course.

Face planing

One final procedure is always carried out on a good quoin: check for 'face plane'. When four or five courses have been completed the level is used as a straight-edge, to range from the last brick on the bottom course diagonally across to the top quoin brick. (See figure 7.19) If the face plane is good every brick in between will touch the level. It will need adjusting if the centre is either hollow or proud to the level, by gentle tapping with the brick hammer. The procedure is repeated on the return.

An experienced craftsman erecting a quoin would not check either plumb or gauge until it was at least five courses high, his expert eye being his guide in the judging of plumb and gauge. The level would be used only to confirm his skill. Furthermore, when the quoin is small, initially, the plumbing can only be approximate because of the lack of bricks against which to rest the level. It has been long said that if one gets the first four courses right there is no real reason for the plumb to be lost. It is to be regretted that many people laying bricks on sites today abuse the level. It is laid on to the new brickwork and struck to force the walling level, a use for which it was never designed or intended.

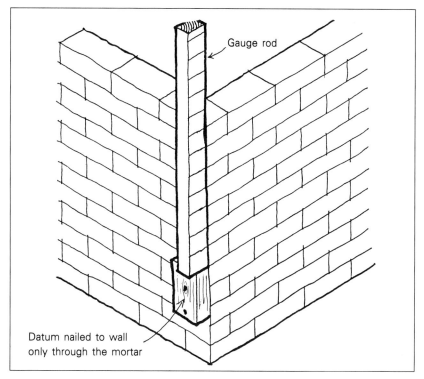

Figure 7.18 Use of the gauge rod.

It is always important when erecting or 'rearing' a quoin to keep the plumbing points at the quoin in the same position on each course. This prevents small irregularities in the bricks causing inaccuracies.

Effects of workmanship on brickwork strength

It is necessary when advising on good craft practices to point out the effects of executing the work in a cavalier manner. Although various tests have been carried out on panels built to high and low standards, it is not yet a problem which can be precisely defined. Much has been done to elucidate the various workmanship factors which influence the structural, thermal and weathering abilities of a wall.

1. *Failure to fill bed joints.* Not only will this allow moisture and sound to gain access to the inside of the wall, but tests have shown that it can weaken a wall by up to 33%. Poorly filled cross-joints are not so critical in compressive strength loss, but have effects on the passage of moisture and sound.
2. *Excessive thickness of bed joints.* This has been the subject of numerous tests which have shown beyond doubt that excessively thick joints (16–19mm) can reduce the strength of a wall by up to 30%

compared with the nominal 10mm joint as standard. It is particularly important to realise this, as it has often been the case that in trying to keep a metric brick to gauge with an imperial brick, bricklayers have opted for thick joints.

3. *Disturbing bricks after laying.* If a brick is hit to adjust a position subsequent to its actual laying the bond between the brick and the mortar will be broken. Although there is no quantitative data available on the lasting effect of this disturbance, its effects are felt to be significant where bond tension and strengths are critical.

4. *Walling not 'plumb and true' to line and level.* The effects of building a wall that is not truly vertical have been measured. *Bricks, Their Property and Use* (1974, p. 179) states that 'two-storey height walls were tested in which the applied load was ¾″ (19mm) eccentric with respect to the axis of the wall and three walls were built ¾″ (19mm), off plumb. Comparing the strength of the walls with eccentrically applied loads with corresponding axially loaded walls indicates a reduction in strength of the order of 12%. The reduction for those built off-plumb is about 20%. In a similar test walls built with a 12mm bow resulted in a 13% loss of overall strength compared with a truly plumb and face planed wall.

The Building Research Station suggests the following permissible deviations in load-bearing brickwork:

(a) Wall plumb over a storey height: 15mm.
(b) Vertical alignment between top and bottom of walls of successive storeys: 20mm. (One should refer to BS800 and BDA: BN1, *Brickwork: Good Site Practice* (1991) for more comprehensive guidance.)

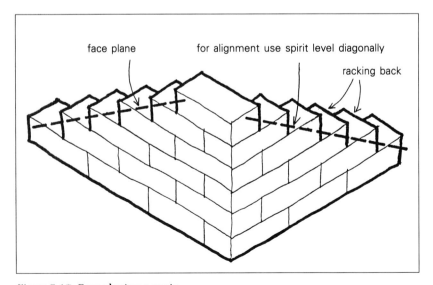

Figure 7.19 Face planing a quoin.

5. *Neglecting to protect newly built brickwork.* At certain times of the year newly completed brickwork may need to be covered to protect it from unfavourable weather conditions. All classes of mortars require protection regardless of materials and additives. Problems are:

(a) *Frost.* If new brickwork is not covered for at least a week after building, it may suffer frost damage. If mortar freezes before the cement has set and hardened, bonding will not occur. In severe instances this will cause unstable brickwork. With a traditional lime mortar the period of time when there is a danger of frost damage is much longer – several months – due to the slower rate of hardening.

(b) *Heat.* During excessively hot conditions 78–100°F (25.6–37.8°C), if the new brickwork is not sheeted to give it shade, the moisture is driven out of the mortar before the chemical set of the cement can complete its cycle. In such instances tests have indicated a loss of strength of up to 10%. Again, a lime mortar will need care and may even require spraying to prevent the loss of vital moisture.

(c) *Rain.* When it is expected that heavy rainfall is imminent, fresh brickwork must be sheeted to protect it from surface damage. On cement mortars this risk is minimal after 48 hours, although traditional lime : sand mortars would be vulnerable for a much longer period due to the lack of an initial set.

     At the very least the damage will destroy the surface texture and the joint finish, and if this is not repaired it usually dries out lighter in shade than the unaffected mortar. In the worst instances – a very heavy shower only hours after construction – the joints may be washed out to a considerable depth and run down the wall face with damaging results. It may be possible to clean the bricks by brushing and washing and carefully to clean out the joints back to a hard square seating and repoint in the same gauge face work mortar. If damage is very bad and has resulted in a weak bond the brickwork must be taken down and completely rebuilt, possibly using new bricks if the original ones are spoilt.

It can therefore be seen that much depends on the standard of workmanship: the effects of poor work are so serious that it could result in a wall being built of only half its intended design strength. Good materials, quality craftsmanship and close supervision to ensure compliance with specifications should lead to brickwork of the highest standard and desired strength.

8

Bonding of Brickwork

To bond brickwork is to unite or bind together two or more adjacent bricks in one course with two or more bricks in the course below. The term is a medieval phonetic variation of 'band', used in connection with 'bind' or 'bound', and links with the German *Bund – binden*, 'to bind'. The arrangement of bricks in a wall to a pre-determined pattern is of great importance, as upon it depend the strength and appearance of the whole wall. The bonding of a wall must follow certain rules and principles which the craftsman readily understands and executes with care to achieve the requisite strength with minimum outlay.

The word 'bond' is sometimes referred to in a structural context rather than the more common aesthetic form (for example, chase bond, block bond, hoop-iron bond), which will be dealt with in later volumes. This chapter is confined to the reasons and rules of the traditional principle of bonding patterns.

The bonding of early medieval brickwork followed no true ruling and was so haphazard as to defy any real classification. By the end of the thirteenth century Little Wenham Hall in Suffolk was built in an early version of English bond, with alternate courses of headers and stretchers. This bond seems to have originated in France, and is followed quite faithfully at Tattershall Castle (*c.*1431–49).

Regular bond patterns had an aesthetic appeal, and their decorative potential was soon exploited. English cross-bond developed during the fifteenth century as a variation of English bond, and by its use some wonderful diaper work was made possible. Diapers are patterns formed by bricks of contrasting colours and/or textures to make diamonds, squares or lozenge shapes.

Dutch bond was introduced into lower Germany over a thousand years ago. Although in use in fifteenth-century France it never really had a great following in England. It is similar to English cross-bond where, by different treatment of the quoins, the stretcher courses could be made to break joint. This made it possible to introduce patterns of small crosses and diapers into the wall, features which are characteristic of much Tudor and Elizabethan brickwork.

Header bond also enjoyed a period of popularity during the eighteenth century, mainly due to the influence of the Bastard brothers. They were architects (after whom the bond was sometimes referred to as Bastard bond) who rebuilt the Forum, Dorset, after the fire of 1734 using header bond exclusively.

In Britain the use of English bond remained in standard use throughout the fifteenth, sixteenth and early seventeenth centuries, when it was to a large degree supplanted by Flemish bond, the style of laying bricks by alternating headers and stretchers in each course. Kew Palace (c.1631) one of the earliest true examples of this bond in England. It was introduced, like so many other brick and bricklaying ideas, from Flanders and the Low Countries, although it is not common there. It is thought likely to have had its source in Poland, where it has a long history. The Germans in fact refer to Flemish bond as *Polinischer Verband*, or 'Polish bond'. Its use almost certainly spread because of the trade links with the Baltic ports. By the eighteenth century Flemish bond was *de-rigueur* for all brickwork other than for civil engineering and industrial buildings.

During the 1800s the use of garden wall bonds became popular, in both the English and Flemish styles. As the name suggests, mainly for use in garden walling, this method gave a fair face on both sides by minimizing the number of through-headers. Flemish garden wall was the more popular of the two types and was also employed quite frequently on houses, especially for flank walls in relation to Flemish bond on the front wall. Flemish garden wall bond, in which there are three stretchers between the headers, is also known as Sussex bond.

A variation of Flemish bond which was introduced during the 1800s was rat-trap bond. This involved turning the bricks on edge so that a larger area of brick was utilized on the face of the wall and thus a great saving in bricks per metre. By laying the bricks in this bond a cavity of 85–90mm between stretchers was introduced. It was considered by designers at that time that this made for a more weatherproof and warmer wall, and was therefore desirable for the modest dwellings of working people.

Although numerous other bonds were available, those described above remained the ones most frequently employed until the rapid increase of the cavity wall in the 1950s. Early cavity walls still used the bonds traditionally associated with thick walling: in those instances the bricklayers cut the headers into bats (half bricks), so that quite a number of walls built at the turn of the century are not solid, but of cavity construction. During the last half-century the main bond used in all types of brick walling is stretcher bond. It is a source of great regret to lovers of brick, and to skilled craftsmen, that in the majority of modern brickwork we now have endlessly repetitive stretcher-bonded walls and little else.

Reasons for bonding

Brickwork is bonded into various arrangements in walling, according to regular patterns, so that it is able to distribute imposed loads throughout the length and thickness of the wall. Bonding thus ensures not only lateral and vertical stability, but also that the work complies with other requirements of the Building Regulations and Codes of Practice. There are three mains reasons for bonding brickwork:

Strength

By systematically arranging the bricks, laid in good mortar and bedded horizontally level and square to the face of the wall, the loading will be spread evenly throughout the whole wall. It is not localized to certain portions of the wall, which could cause uneven settlement and cracking. (See figure 8.1)

However, the effect of bond is less important than is often thought. Provided that quoins, attached piers, junction and separating walls are well tied in to a plumb and level wall, the common bonds in use should prove more than satisfactory. Should high loading be anticipated then a structural engineer's advice should be sought.

The use of decorative patterns which might result in an unbonded outer half-brick wall must be avoided for load-bearing work, and even if employed as a cladding such work will require bonding to the backing wall using proprietary wall ties. Reinforced brickwork may require special bonds to allow for vertical reinforcement.

Appearance

The appearance of brickwork is very much influenced by the joint pattern and therein the choice of bond. A certain bond may be used because it allows for patterns to be introduced in specified positions to

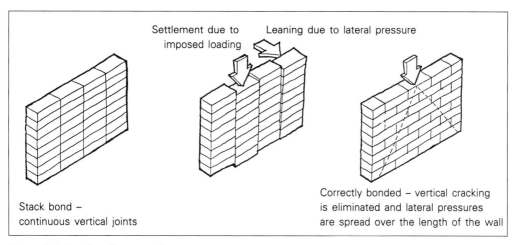

Figure 8.1 Bonding for strength.

give a decorative effect. It is important that if a bond which gives large scale patterns is chosen, the wall area must be both large and uninterrupted, otherwise the effect may be lost.

Economy

The choice of bond pattern will have an important effect upon cost, as the number of facing bricks per square metre will vary according to the bond used: (See figure 8.2)

Table 8.1 Numbers of bricks * † for 1-brick thick walls (215mm) in various bonds.

	Nominal yd² i.e. 900 × 900mm			Equivalent number per m² ‡		
Bond pattern	Facings	Commons (backings)	Total	Facings	Commons (backings)	Total
Stretcher bond ¶	48	48	96	60	60	120
Header bond	96	—	96	120	—	120
English and Dutch bonds	72	24	96	90	30	120
English garden wall bond	60	36	96	75	45	120
Flemish bond	63	33	96	79	41	120
Flemish garden wall bond	57	39	96	72	48	120

* Assumes standard format bricks of co-ordinating size 225 × 112.5 × 75mm.
† No allowance is made for wastage is included in these figures – allow 5%.
‡ Although it is generally not possible to build in whole square metres these figures can be used for estimating purposes.
¶ Half-brick thick leaves in stretcher bond require no backing bricks.

The number of headers per metre is decisive in this calculation. The

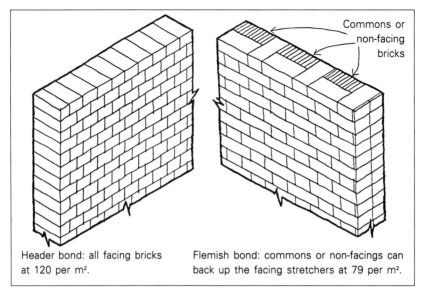

Header bond: all facing bricks at 120 per m². Flemish bond: commons or non-facings can back up the facing stretchers at 79 per m².

Figure 8.2 Economy in choice of bonding arrangement.

choice thus depends on the relative cost of the bricks and the labour involved in the construction of the wall.

A significant cost in bonding can be incurred when an intricate pattern is specified, calling for extra skill and care in workmanship. This may entail much setting of vertical joints and may require particular care if the bricks are not regular in shape, size or appearance. However, even with machine-made, regular-sized bricks, problems may still be experienced in obtaining high-quality facework, because the joint pattern makes any irregularities all the more noticeable.

It is important that bonding should be carefully studied for the external and internal arrangements of walling. However, before turning to study the various types of bonds, the following terms used in brickwork must be understood.

General terms

♦ *Arris.* An edge of a brick. (See figure 8.3)
♦ *Bat.* Common name for a cut half-brick. (See figure 8.4)
♦ *Bed.* The lower or under surface of a brick.
♦ *Bed joint.* The horizontal mortar joint formed between the courses of bricks. (See figure 8.5)
♦ *Bevelled bat (large).* Three-quarter cut on one stretcher face splaying to a half bat on the adjacent face.
♦ *Bevelled bat (small).* A half-bat cut on one stretcher face splaying to a closer on the adjacent face.

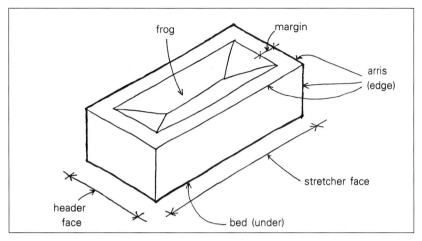

Figure 8.3 Parts of a brick.

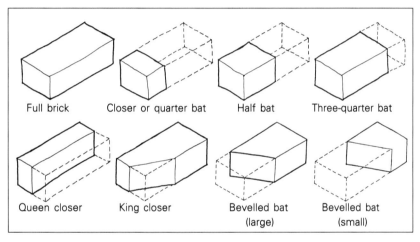

Figure 8.4 Standard brick cuts.

♦ *Bevelled closer.* Cut from a closer on one header face to a full opposite header.
♦ *Closer.* A quarter bat.
♦ *Collar joint.* A continuous mortar joint that runs throughout the height of the wall parallel to its surface. It occurs on walls of one brick or more in thickness in stretcher bond tied with metal ties or reinforcement.
♦ *Continuous vertical joints.* Also known as straight joints. They occur when mortar joints come immediately over each other in two or more consecutive layers. Internally they are sometimes unavoidable, as in Flemish bond, but they must never be allowed to appear on the face. (See figure 8.6)
♦ *Course.* A continuous layer of bricks between bed joints.

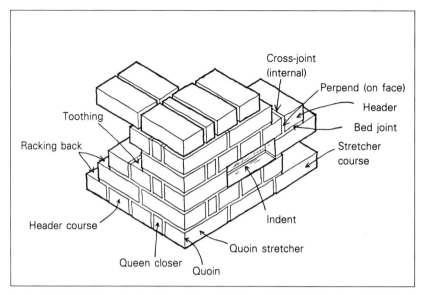

Figure 8.5 Bonding terminology.

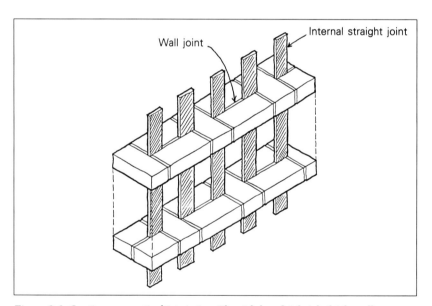

Figure 8.6 Continuous vertical joints in a Flemish bond 1-brick thick wall.

♦ *Cross-joints.* A vertical mortar joint at right angles to the wall face which separates two bricks in the same course.
♦ *Face.* A surface of a brick such as the stretcher or header. The exposed surface of the wall is also known as its face.
♦ *Frog.* Also known as a 'kick' in parts of the country, the frog is a shallow depression formed on one or both bed surfaces of a brick.

◆ *Indents.* 'Sinkings' or hollows formed or left in each alternate course of a wall to allow a later wall to be adequately bonded. The width of indents is equal to the thickness of the new wall and a minimum of a quarter brick in depth, and kept strictly plumb. Indents can also be formed every three courses with a similar number of courses between. In such cases they are known as 'block indents'.

◆ *King closer.* Has one stretcher face splayed (bevelled) from the half bat to the closer position on the header end.

◆ *Lap.* The horizontal distance one brick projects over the vertical joints in the course immediately above or below it, normally quarter- or half-lap.

◆ *Perpends.* The short vertical joints in the face of the wall which fall vertically over one another in alternating courses. The visible part of a cross-joint.

◆ *Purpose-made bricks ('specials').* Standard specials are made to BS4729, 1990, which specifies over 300 standard specials of 63 basic shapes. These are bricks that have been specially manufactured to suit special circumstances. Some 'standard specials' are kept by most brick manufacturers for normal brick detailing and ornamentation. With the increased use of brickwork for artistic as well as utilitarian work, it is vital that the designer as well as the bricklayer understands the application of these products. (See figure 8.7)

The use of specials in facing work not only results in time saving (as otherwise the bricklayer has to cut the shapes) but also improves the aesthetic quality of the finished brickwork. On occasions the brickmakers may be asked to produce a specially designed brick to overcome a bonding difficulty or to gain aesthetic effect. In such a case this is known as a non-standard special and is more costly, as separate moulds have to be made to the required shape. Plenty of time is needed to advise the brick company of these requirements to prevent delay in receiving the specials.

◆ *Queen closer.* A quarter brick cut from half a header throughout the length of the brick. It is always positioned next to a first header in a quoin or stopped-end to form quarter-bond over a stretcher in the previous course.

◆ *Quoin.* A corner or external angle of a wall. If less than 90° it is known as an acute-angled quoin; if more than 90° an obtuse-angled quoin.

◆ *Racking back.* The stepped arrangement, following bond, formed when erecting one portion of a wall higher than the rest.

◆ *Stopped-end.* The squared termination of a wall. Also known as a closed end.

◆ *Toothings.* Bricks projecting like teeth in bond and in alternate courses in order to bond with other brickwork at a later date.

♦ *Transverse joint.* The vertical mortar joint which passes from the front face to the back of the wall. It occurs in walls which are at least 1½ bricks in thickness and provides for 'sectional bonding', and is an arrangement which minimizes 'continuous vertical joints' in the work.

♦ *Wall joint.* A discontinuous vertical mortar joint parallel with the face of the wall. It occurs in walls of one brick or more in thickness.

Standard specials

♦ *Bullnose.* Designed for use in such positions where a sharp arris is not desirable, such as quoins, piers, door or window openings. If the

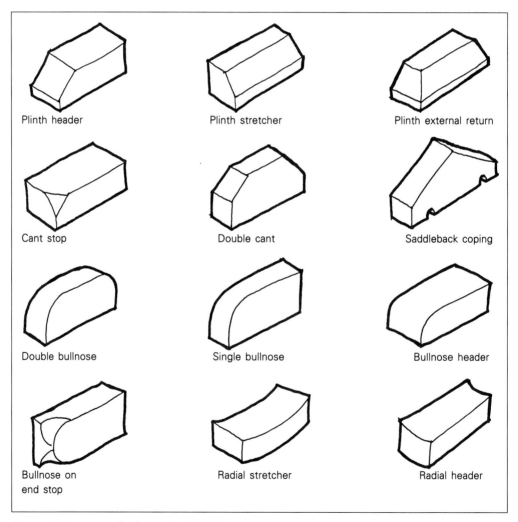

Figure 8.7 Some standard specials (BS4729).

brick has only one rounded header it is termed a single bullnose. A double bullnose has both ends rounded, and if made from a dense brick may be used as a coping.

The radius of the curve is either 25 or 51mm. Because of the difficulty of cutting a mitre at the intersection of 'two bullnoses', special internal or external 'returns' are also manufactured. Where a bullnose edge meets and is continued by a standard brick the transitional special is called a 'stop' for a single brick pier, and a 'double stop' is also provided.

♦ *Cownose.* This is a variation of the bullnose and consists of header formed as a complete semi-circle to a 51mm radius. Used for the ends of a half-brick or a brick-on-edge coping.

♦ *Cant bricks.* Designed to have a splayed end as a single or double cant, and are used for the same purposes as the bullnose, with similar configurations for meeting square-ended bricks at reveals and elsewhere.

♦ *Coping bricks.* These come in saddlebrick or half-round shapes with an overhanging projection with moulded drip. Capping bricks are similar but have no overhang and finish flush.

♦ *Dog-leg (or angle bricks).* Intended to ensure a good bond at quoins that are not right-angles. Their use prevents unsatisfactory mitres and straight joints. The angles on the dog-legs are made to suit 30°, 45° and 60° quoins.

♦ *Plinth bricks.* Shaped to have a 45° splay moulding which is either 42mm or 56mm depending on the vertical upstand on the stretcher face. The splayed bricks are used on plinths to reduce the thickness of wall and piers above ground level. The shape is produced as headers, stretchers, 'handed' returns (external and internal) as well as oblique angles.

♦ *Soldier return (formerly known as 'Pistol bricks').* For use on the quoin position or internal angles when otherwise difficulties would be experienced in trying to present faced surfaces, by cutting standard bricks, around the corner of soldier courses.

♦ *Squint bricks.* These are moulded to three standard angles of 30°, 45° and 60°, and are intended for use on the quoins of oblique angles. The stretcher face is a three-quarter and the header face a quarter brick.

RULES FOR BONDING

1. Bricks of uniform size are manufactured so that the length is equal to twice the width plus one joint. Good bond is impossible otherwise, as the lap would not be uniform.

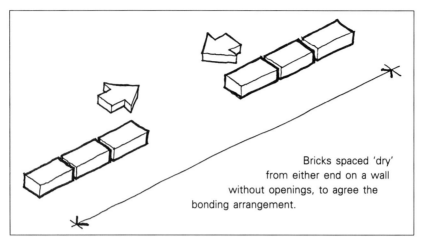

Figure 8.8 Dry-bonding wall to establish bond and 'perp' size.

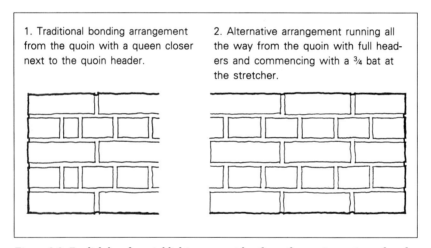

1. Traditional bonding arrangement from the quoin with a queen closer next to the quoin header.

2. Alternative arrangement running all the way from the quoin with full headers and commencing with a ¾ bat at the stretcher.

Figure 8.9 English bond – establishing correct lap from the quoin or stopped-end.

2. The bond should be set out by working in from each end of the wall to the centre, with the end bricks symmetrical. (See figure 8.8)

3. The correct quarter-lap should be established and maintained by having:
   (a) a closer next to the quoin or stopped-end header;
   (b) a three-quarter bat to start the stretcher course. (See figure 8.9)

4. If it is found that the bonding pattern cannot be maintained, or it does not 'work bricks', then this is known as broken bond. This will result in cuts which will be placed in the centre of the wall. However, certain rules apply to sizes of cuts in broken bond:

(a) No cut less than a half-bat should appear on the wall face. (See figure 8.10)

(b) Closers should never be built in the wall face except next to quoin or stopped-end header.

(c) To bond out a quarter brick gap a three-quarter and header bat should be used.

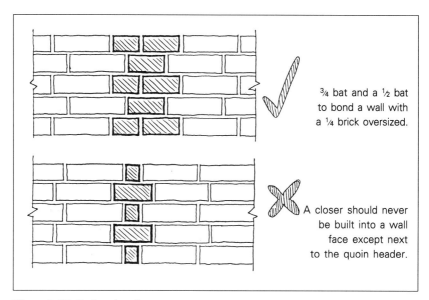

¾ bat and a ½ bat to bond a wall with a ¼ brick oversized.

A closer should never be built into a wall face except next to the quoin header.

Figure 8.10 Broken bond.

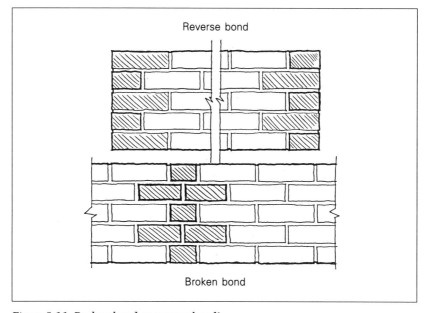

Reverse bond

Broken bond

Figure 8.11 Broken bond or reverse bond?

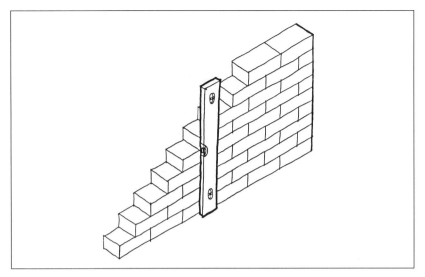

Figure 8.12 Maintaining vertical perpends.

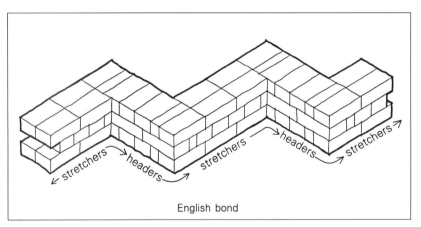

Figure 8.13 When the wall changes direction so the bond changes, i.e. stretchers to headers.

5. If broken bond is undesirable then an exception to the rule is the introduction of 'reverse bond'. This where the bricks at each end of a course are not symmetrical. It should only be used on less important work or by agreement with the supervisor. (See figure 8.11)

6. The vertical joints in the alternate courses should fall in a plumb (vertical) line from the top of the wall to its base, whether on face or back of wall. (See figure 8.12)

7. Where a wall changes direction, the face bond in the same course changes. (See figure 8.13)

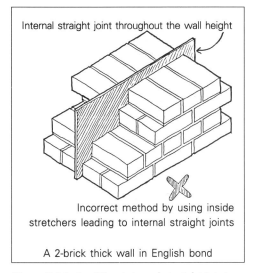

Internal straight joint throughout the wall height

Incorrect method by using inside stretchers leading to internal straight joints

A 2-brick thick wall in English bond

Headers on the inside of the wall at half-bond

Correct method by laying internal bricks as headers

Figure 8.14 Avoiding internal straight joints.

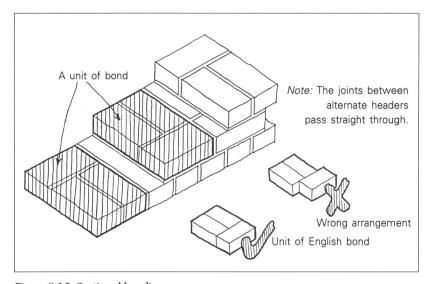

A unit of bond

Note: The joints between alternate headers pass straight through.

Wrong arrangement

Unit of English bond

Figure 8.15 Sectional bonding.

8. There must be no straight vertical joints within a wall, although the overlap of wall joints in some bonds is unavoidable. Should straight joints prove to be unavoidable, they should be kept to an absolute minimum. (See figure 8.14)

9. Sectional bond should be maintained across the width of a wall. That means that the bond on the back will be in line with the bond on the face side. This ensures that there are no straight joints on the back of the wall and minimizes the likelihood of a continuous straight joint within. (See figure 8.15)

10. At junctions or quoins the walls should be bonded by the use of 'tie-bricks' to secure the walls together. (See figure 8.16)
11. All bricks in the interior of a thick wall should be laid header-wise as far as possible.
12. To ensure maximum strength on thick walling all the joints in the interior of a wall should be grouted full and flushed into bed with a mortar slurry, on completion of each course. (See figure 8.17)

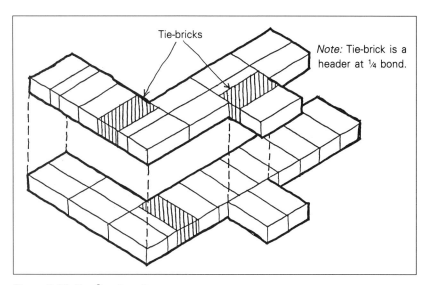

Tie-bricks

Note: Tie-brick is a header at ¼ bond.

Figure 8.16 Bonding junctions.

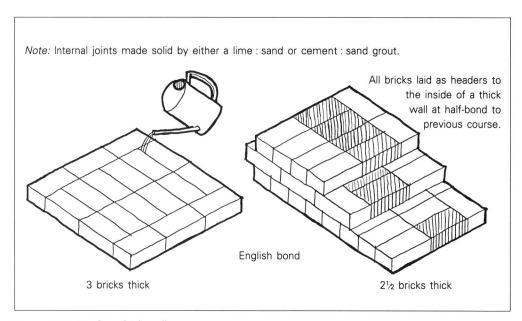

Note: Internal joints made solid by either a lime : sand or cement : sand grout.

All bricks laid as headers to the inside of a thick wall at half-bond to previous course.

English bond

3 bricks thick

2½ bricks thick

Figure 8.17 Bonding thick walls.

TYPES OF BOND

There are numerous types of bond. The three principal ones are stretcher, English and Flemish. If the principles of these three bonds are thoroughly understood, the other bonds, which are but variations, will present few problems.

Although a number of bonds will be shown and explained, and some may present the aspiring craftsman with a little difficulty, in the author's experience it is a futile exercise to try to memorize the many bonding arrangements. Providing he is equipped with the rules and principles, the young artisan should be able to overcome any bonding difficulties he may experience in the course of his work.

Stretcher bond

Formerly known as 'stretching bond', this is used mainly on walls of half-brick thickness. It consists of stretchers for the whole of each course, except that at every other course at the quoin or stopped-end there is a header or half-bat inserted, so that half-bond is maintained. To maintain bond at junctions, attached piers or pilasters, three-quarter bats are used. It can also be used with third lap. When each brick overlaps the one below by a quarter brick it is known as raking stretcher bond, and is sometimes employed with metric modular bricks with a stretcher length of 300mm. During the early 1970s some

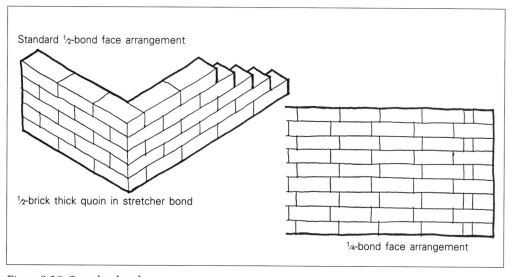

Standard ½-bond face arrangement

½-brick thick quoin in stretcher bond

¼-bond face arrangement

Figure 8.18 Stretcher bond.

designers wished to design buildings to co-ordinated metric dimensions by using modular bricks instead of standard bricks. These looked rather large and coarse, however, and were unpopular. (See figure 8.18)

The over-use of stretcher bond in modern brickwork gave rise to the following doggerel:

> Stretchers to the right, stretchers to the left
> The plainest pattern is warp and weft,
> Of stretchers in the course above and stretchers down below,
> Alack! for houses – it's the only bond that they know.

English bond

This traditional bond is used in walls of one brick or more in thickness, although in early cavity walling it was sometimes used by snapping the headers. It consists of one course of headers and one course of stretchers placed alternately. The bond is formed in a one-brick wall by beginning with a header with a queen closer laid next to it. This ensures that the following header sits centrally to the first perpend of the stretcher course, and thus gives a quarter-brick lap of 56mm.

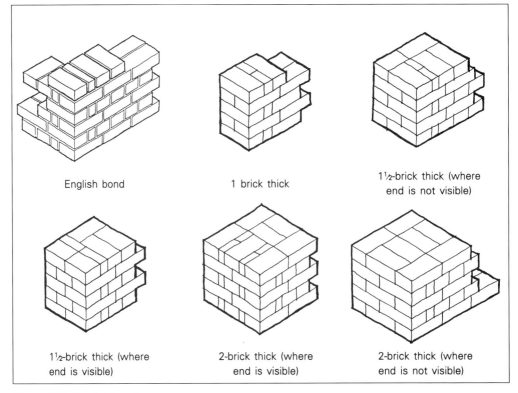

Figure 8.19 English bond.

English bond is generally reserved for walling where high strength is critical, as it possesses no internal straight joints. It has, however, the disadvantage of a monotonous, unattractive, and sometimes stripy face pattern. The bond is easily remembered in the lines:

> English bond is easy to know,
> As all the stretchers are laid in one row,
> And the little closer gap,
> Makes the quarter lap,
> In the headers up above and the headers down below.

This bond pattern was used in brickwork over 6,000 years ago and only became known as English bond with the coming of Flemish bond. (See figure 8.19)

Flemish bond

Although intended for walling of one brick or more in thickness, Flemish bond was also used in early cavity walling by snapping the tie headers. The quoin or stopped-end arrangement is similar to that of English bond, with header and queen closer placed directly over the stretcher to ensure a quarter-bonding. From there the bond consists of

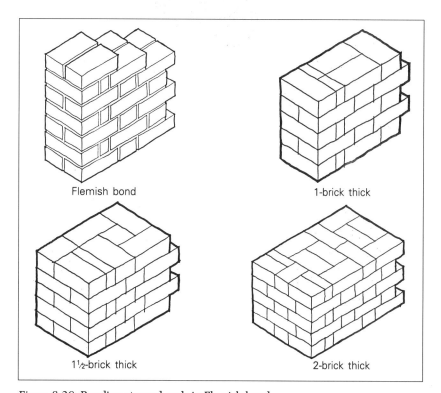

Flemish bond   1-brick thick

1½-brick thick   2-brick thick

Figure 8.20 Bonding stopped-ends in Flemish bond.

alternating stretchers and headers repeated continuously on each course. By using 'flared' or vitrified headers, or headers of another colour, the bricklayers often patterned the wall in what is known as chequered brickwork. (See figure 8.20)

Unlike English bond, Flemish bond is not practicable in walls which are more than 1½ bricks in thickness. If laid sectionally on a 1½-brick wall, the bond involves a half bat placed on one side of the header. In a non-sectional bond, a closer is placed on either side of the header. Terms sometimes used are single Flemish and double Flemish. In the former the appearance of Flemish bond is seen on the outer face only. In the latter, the bond pattern is visible on both faces. However, double Flemish is a term that should be discouraged, as the work is either executed according to the rules of the bond or it is not. (See figure 8.21)

During the periods when Flemish bond was popular in house building, many careless bricklayers resorted to snapping the headers when the inside work ran out of gauge with external work. This was common when the fashion was for front walls to be built of gauged or rubbed bricks. The outer work was laid with a lime putty point and this often meant that the outer and inner work of the same courses

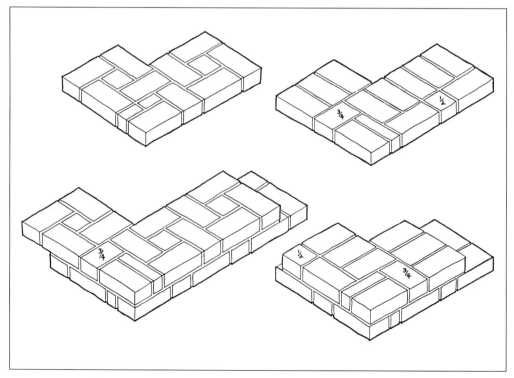

Figure 8.21 Double Flemish bond and single Flemish bond quoin.

did not correspond in height. They were therefore unable to be bonded together, except where occasionally the courses fell even, and a header was used properly to tie the front to the inside. This careless workmanship was often the cause of walls splitting in two along their thickness.

Although this bond does have some internal straight vertical joints, it is an attractive bond often enhanced by the use of coloured bricks for the headers or stretchers to give a basket-like effect. The bonding is remembered in the rhyme:

> The stretchers have a header at each side,
> As tho' each father stretcher has a header for his bride;
> At each external angle, Mother header guards the wall,
> And lying close beside her is a little closer small.

Header bond

This is for walls of one brick in thickness. In Georgian times it was popular for house fronts, especially in grey bricks with red-brick dressings at quoins, reveals and window arches. Its popularity declined as it was too costly when gauged brick fronts became popular. The work is entirely in headers, giving a quarter-brick or 56mm lap. The bond is formed from the quoin or stopped-end by the introduction of a three-quarter bat. (See figure 8.22)

Header bond is generally used for walling (curved or plain) or corbelling and oversailing work. It was commonly employed in the footing courses of brick walls.

Garden wall bonds

Where a fair face is desired on both sides of a boundary wall it is best to use what are known as garden wall bonds. In these patterns the number of headers is reduced and the number of stretchers increased, thereby partially eliminating transverse bond. Both leaves can be tied in by incorporating either mesh reinforcing or wall ties.

With these bonds the bricklayers can line both faces accurately. However, it is also advantageous because fewer headers are required, and the sizes of bricks need not be strictly gauged. This means a saving in the cost of bricks.

English garden wall bond

This is also known as common bond. The true bonding pattern consists of three courses of stretchers to one course of headers, with

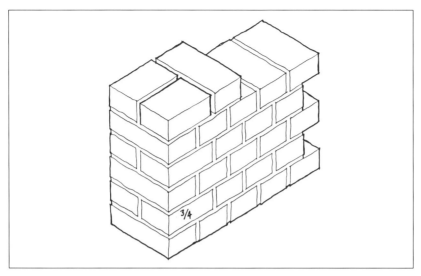

Figure 8.22 Header bond.

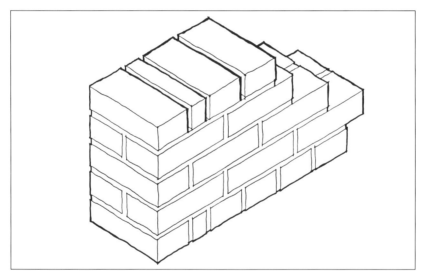

Figure 8.23 English garden wall bond.

the middle stretcher course at half-bond to the other two. This pattern repeats itself throughout the height of the wall. (See figure 8.23) Variations are four or five courses of stretchers to one course of headers. In America six stretcher courses to one header course are usual. This is known as 'American' or 'Liverpool' bond.

English garden wall bond has many of the advantages of English bond but is much cheaper when using expensive facings. It is a popular bond, especially in the Midlands and the North of England.

Because it gives a quick lateral spread of load it is usually adopted for the construction of tall chimneys. When English garden wall bond is employed on a 1½-brick wall, sectional bond cannot be maintained on each course.

Flemish garden wall bond

Also known as 'flying bond' or 'Sussex bond', due to its former popularity on boundary walling in that county, Flemish garden wall bond consists of three stretchers and a header alternately along each course. The header always sits central to the middle stretcher. To bond from the quoin or stopper end, the header, with closer, is followed by three stretchers and the header. In the second course two stretchers followed by the header and the three stretchers is the rule. By working two stretchers in from the end of the wall, the header can be placed central to the middle of three stretchers on the course below. (See figure 8.24)

Flemish garden wall bond was frequently employed on the flanks and backs of houses which had Flemish bond fronts.

Flemish stretcher bond

This is an unusual bond, sometimes called 'American Flemish' in America. It consists of alternate headers and stretchers separated by three to six courses of stretchers at quarter-bond to each other. (See figure 8.25) Mixed garden wall bond is a less common variation of Flemish stretcher bond. It consists of three courses (or less commonly

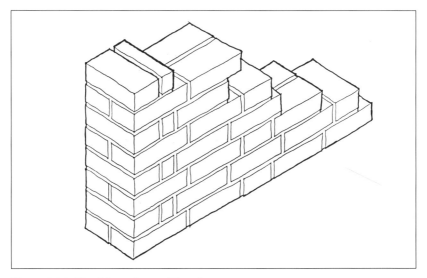

Figure 8.24 Flemish garden wall bond.

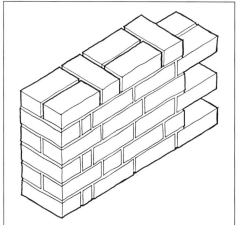

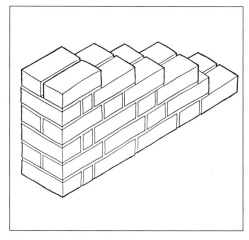

Figure 8.25 Mixed garden wall bond, or
Flemish stretcher bond.

Figure 8.26 Flying bond.

of six courses) of stretchers built in half-bond, with one course of
Flemish bond. The three stretcher courses begin as normal with a
header on the second course to give the half-bond (although in some
variations the stretchers can be quarter-bonded). The fourth Flemish
bond course needs careful attention, so that each header on the course
fits central to a stretcher. It begins with a header, followed by a
three-quarter bat and then a header, followed by stretcher header as
in normal Flemish bonding. This bond is maintained throughout the
height of the wall.

Flying bond

This is a bond similar to a garden wall bond except that the headers
are arranged in a haphazard manner, with no real plan. The number
of headers used is less than in standard bond patterns. The bond is also
known as 'knobbling' or 'Yorkshire bond'. (See figure 8.26)

Irregular bond

This is not an accepted aesthetic pattern with rules, but instead is a
haphazard arrangement of bricks on 1-brick thick walls. It gains
stability through the irregular positioning of headers and broken
vertical joints.

Dearne's bond

So-called because it was developed by the architect of that name in about 1830, Dearne's bond consists of alternate rows of headers laid flat on bed, and stretchers laid as brick-on-edge, giving an economical gain in height, with a continuous cavity of 75mm between them. The headers act as ties or bonders, and by using a three-quarter bat on the header course the quarter-bond is maintained. This bond was some-times used for humble dwellings, garden and boundary walls. Dearne proposed that his 'cavity wall' could even be heated, which was (he said) useful for dwellings, conservatories and vineries. (See figure 8.27)

Rat-trap bond

This was also called 'Silverlock's bond', 'Chinese bond', or 'Rowlock bond'. It is used on 1-brick thick walls as a variation of the Flemish bond. It consists of the stretchers laid as brick-on-edge, with a 75mm cavity between them. The two leaves are tied together with a header (bonder) also laid on edge, and it effected a saving of one brick in three compared with an ordinary, solid 1-brick thick wall. As it had the advantage of connected 'hollows' or cavities it could be heated, mak-ing it ideal for garden walls against which fruit trees were grown. The cavity could also be used as a flue, through which heated air could pass to a chimney. (See figure 8.28)

The bonding at stopped-ends and quoins meant that the wall was solid, but apart from that the bond is not very strong and less weather-resistant than other bonds. This bond was much employed on working men's cottages and almshouses.

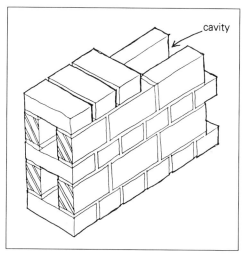

Figure 8.27 Dearne's bond.

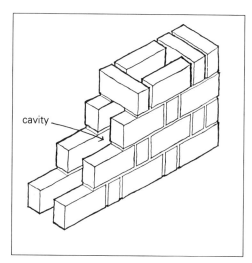

Figure 8.28 Rat-trap bond.

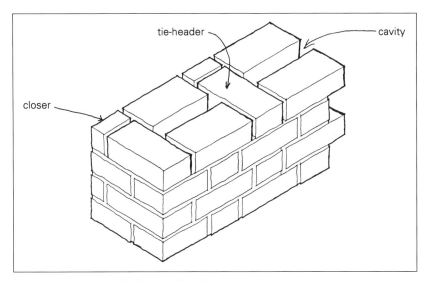

Figure 8.29 Loudon's hollow wall bond.

Loudon's hollow wall

This was named after the architect J. C. Loudon (1783–1843). Like Dearne's bond and Silverlock's bond, it was an arrangement of brickwork to gain a cavity. It was bonded like Flemish bond but with the two stretchers separated by a 2″ (51mm) cavity. The header bonding the two leaves together was laid flush to the outside facework, maintaining the regular bond. On the inner face a 2″ (51mm) closer was laid to the back of the header to bring it flush to the inner leaf. If preferred these closers could be cut smaller and laid set back ½″ (10mm), allowing a better key for the plaster. (See figure 8.29)

STRUCTURAL BONDS

Sometimes bonding arrangements are specified on plan because they impart extra strength or allow for reinforcing to be positioned in the brickwork.

Quetta bond

This is a bond used on walling of 1½ bricks in thickness; its face pattern is similar to Flemish bond. It was first used by British military engineers at Quetta, India, in the 1920s, to increase resistance to seismic pressures. On the first course the first header after the quoin

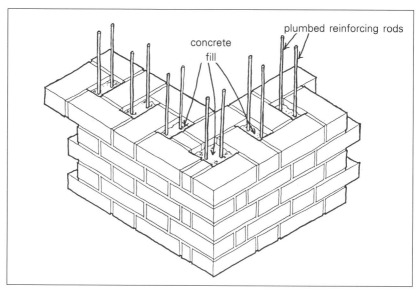

Figure 8.30 Quetta bond.

stretcher is a whole brick and not a three-quarter bat, as it would be in true Flemish. On the second course the brick next to the quoin header is a closer and not a full queen closer as in true Flemish. By bonding this way a series of vertical cavities 100mm × 56mm is introduced. These cavities are used to secure plumbed steel reinforcing rods cast *in situ* into the concrete foundation. The cavities can then be filled with a fine aggregate concrete. Horizontal reinforcement can also be incorporated into the bed joints every third or fourth course if desired, thus giving a wall of immense strength. This bond was frequently specified during the Second World War for the building of air-raid shelters. (See figure 8.30)

Raking bond

Sometimes known as 'diagonal bond', this was frequently specified for walls in excess of two bricks in thickness, where the longitudinal bond would be weak if only headers were used. The internal bonding arrangement was changed every fourth or sixth course, normally on a stretcher course, so that the bonding did not show on the face. (See figure 8.31) The bricks were laid at 45° to the main wall face, and made up round the sides with small, cut bricks. The whole course was grouted upon completion. The first course of diagonal bond would be laid left to right, but the second time the diagonal bond was used it would be in the reverse direction. By doing this throughout the height of the wall, a better combination of internal bonding was obtained.

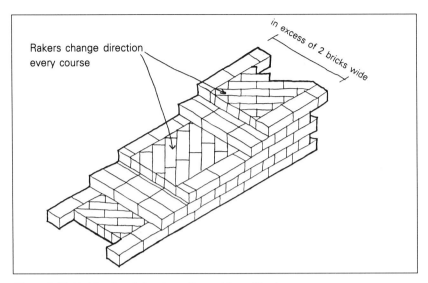

Figure 8.31 Raking bond (to strengthen wide walling).

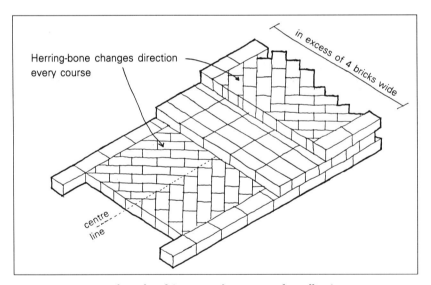

Figure 8.32 Herring-bone bond (to strengthen very wide walling).

Herring-bone bond

This is really a 'double-diagonal' bond and although not as commonly used as raking bond, was sometimes specified for the inside of walls four bricks thick and wider. Half the bricks incline at an angle of 45° from left to right, changing to right to left at the centre line position. The work is usually set out from a centre line, with the first inclined brick touching the line at its top corner. The remaining bond is worked away from that and bricks cut to fit behind the facing bricks. (See figure 8.32)

Traditionally, on all thick engineering walling the internal bricks were 'larryed' into position. Mortar was shovelled into the interior of the course behind the facings, spread out with a larry, and water added at the same time to thin out the mortar. The filling bricks were then squeezed into position, the mortar rising and filling the vertical joints completely, forming an exceedingly strong and solid wall.

Decorative face bonds

Many of the bond patterns which have come down through the centuries were specially designed to provide pleasing decorative effects for the wall face. By the use of contrasting colours and/or subtle projections or recesses, patterns could be arranged to occur in specified positions.

English cross bond

This is considered by some to be the best bond ever designed. It combines an attractive bond pattern with good strength, and was mainly responsible for the beautiful diaper work which distinguishes so many of our fine brick houses (such as Layer Marney in Essex). The bond is similar to English bond, but a header is positioned next to the end stretcher on every alternate stretcher course. This places the stretcher course at half-bond to the previous stretcher course, enabling diapers or diamond patterns to be picked out in contrasting bricks. In the fifteenth century this would have been executed by laying blue 'flared' headers to stand out against the red bricks as 'diapers' – patterns repeated vertically and horizontally over an entire wall face, usually in the shape of diagonal crosses. (See figure 8.33)

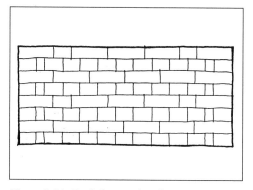

Figure 8.33 English cross bond.

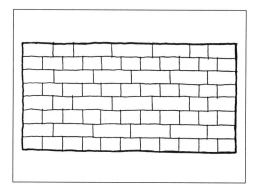

Figure 8.34 Dutch bond.

Dutch bond

This is similar to 'English cross' but is formed by making the quoin brick a three-quarter bat on every course to take the place of a header and closer. A half-bat is introduced next to the quoin three-quarter bat in every alternate stretcher course. (See figure 8.34)

Monk bond

The object of this bonding arrangement is to achieve either a diagonal or zig-zag pattern of contrasting stretchers and/or headers which continues up the full height of the wall face. There are several variations of this bond to help to achieve this patterning. The zig-zag versions are usually referred to as 'monk chevron' bond, and the diagonal as 'monk diagonal' bond. In the most common version each course consists of one header followed by two stretchers, the header being positioned centrally over the perpend between the two stretchers on the lower course. Sometimes when this latter pattern is utilized the perpend separating the two stretchers is deliberately 'blinded' by pointing with a color-matched 'stopping'. In this instance the effect of a long stretcher leads to the name 'flying Flemish' being used. (See figure 8.35)

Chevron bond

This bond is seldom used because to achieve the diagonal and chevron effects it requires complex bond arrangements at the quoin. The effect of this bonding is to make the broadest quoin on one face become the narrowest on the other face. (See figure 8.36)

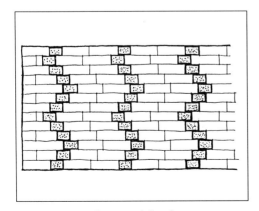

Figure 8.35 Modcrn monk bond.

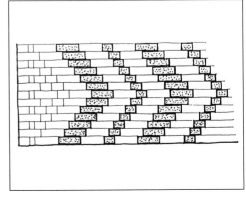

Figure 8.36 Chevron bond.

Modern face bond

This is a quarter-bonding arrangement which gives a vertical pattern of contrasting headers. The header bricks are positioned after every two stretchers on each course. The bond is formed from the quoin or stopped-end by the use of a three-quarter bat upon two headers on alternate courses.

SETTING OUT BONDS

To ensure that bonds are applied correctly it is important that the walling length 'works bricks' in the chosen bond. It would be wise to draw and bond the walling to scale, especially if a balanced decorative effect is desired. In some instances it is prudent for the craftsmen to dry bond the wall to ensure that the chosen bricks work to a good-sized joint in achieving the desired face pattern. This can sometimes be a problem, particularly with hand-made or stock bricks.

Sometimes consistency of bonding proves impossible. On 1- and 2-brick thick walls using bonds such as English or Dutch, the face pattern is identical on both faces, yet in 1½-brick thick walls in the same bond this is not true. On quoins the general ruling is that a change in direction means a change in face bond. Once again, this is not always possible on certain thicknesses of walls, particularly when walls of different thicknesses join.

It is, however, essential to adhere to the basic rule of setting-out and maintaining a tie-brick with adequate lap at the internal angles, to prevent settlement or shrinkage cracks and to give maximum structural integrity to the two walls.

DECORATIVE BONDS FOR PANELS

Stack bond

This is purely decorative, and of low strength, and is therefore not permitted in load-bearing walls except with special reinforcement. It consists of bricks-on-end, or vertical courses of unbonded stretchers, thus giving continuous vertical joints. To be aesthetically effective it is important to use bricks of the same size, and of as regular a shape as possible.

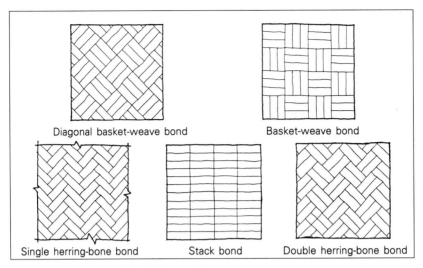

Figure 8.37 Decorative bonds for panels.

Herring-bone bond

Bricks are laid aslant at 45° in opposite directions. This gives an attractive pattern, and a tight interlocking effect is produced by the weight of the bricks. This was a popular arrangement for 'bricknogging' in timber-framed houses. Less commonly, the bricks can be laid singly or in twos (referred to as 'double herring-bone'). It may also be formed by travelling the panel at 45° to the horizontal, as diagonal herring-bone bond, or at 90°, for horizontal herring-bone bond.

Basket-weave bond

This involves laying the bricks in 'blocks' of three, alternating between stretchers and bricks-on-end, for decorative in-fill panels. An alternative to vertical patterning is to lay the panel at 45°, and it is then referred to as 'diagonal basket-weave'. (See figure 8.37)

This catalogue of bonds includes those which a craftsman might encounter in the course of his work. However, miscellaneous bonds can be formed to a designer's individual requirements. The bricks can be made to form patterns, by use of colour, projections and recesses, in many ways. The correct setting-out and building of these decorative bonds will be dealt with in Volume 4, Chapter 5. One thing remains certain. The use of special bonds is stimulating and interesting, and should always be a source of pride for the craftsman who is keen to display his skills and knowledge.

9

Bonding Applications

JUNCTION WALLS

Where two walls meet at an angle the point of union is known as a junction. (See figure 9.1) Depending upon the angle of union, these junctions are categorized either as right-angled or squint.

Right-angled junctions

Right-angled or square junctions are in two forms: tee-junctions and intersecting walls or cross-junctions.

Tee-junction

When bonding this junction the bricks should be arranged so that, if possible, the indent is in the stretching course, and the tie, or projecting toothing of the joining wall, is in the heading course. Although numerous bonds have been dealt with, it will be found that traditionally the main tee-junctions used in construction occur in English, Flemish and stretcher bond. (See figure 9.2) Therefore the rules of bonding are:

♦ *English bond.* If you change direction, change the face bond; therefore, the tie-brick should be a header, bonding half its length, or 56mm.

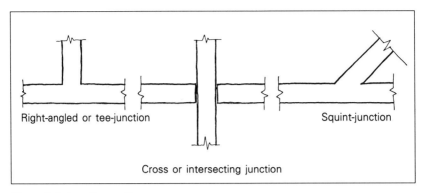

Figure 9.1 Junction walls.

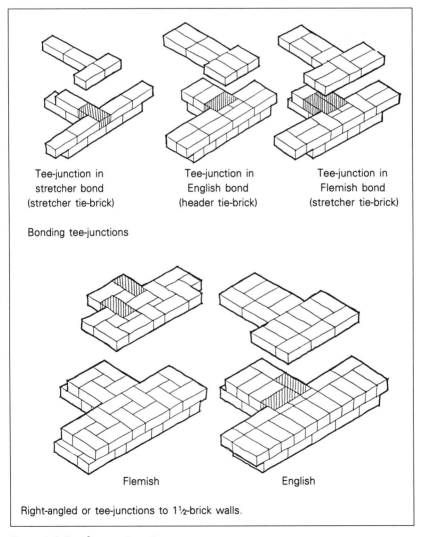

Figure 9.2 Bonding tee-junctions.

♦ *Flemish bond.* The tie-brick is always a stretcher, tying in 56mm, or a quarter of a lap.
♦ *Stretcher bond.* The tie-brick is always a stretcher, tying in a full half brick. To bond the section fully, two three-quarters are placed above the tie-brick, thus maintaining half-bond.

NOTE
To accommodate the tie-bricks in both English and Flemish bonds it is vital to insert queen closers within the straight walling at the position of the junction.

Intersection walls or cross-junctions

Intersection walls or cross-junctions occur where two continuous walls intersect. The arrangement of the bonding will depend largely upon the relative position of the main and cross walls. Variations from the bonding shown may, therefore, be unavoidable. In such instances it is important that continuous vertical joints are avoided, with the minimum number of broken bricks. (See figure 9.3)

As a good rule when bonding 1-brick thick cross-walls, the brick positioned at the centre of the intersection is always a header. Placing it centrally permits the correct bonding arrangements of English and Flemish bonds, as well as allowing for the required quarter-lap or 56mm of tie, to be formed. In walls greater than one brick in thickness this tie or lap can be increased to 168mm.

Squint or oblique junctions

These are relatively uncommon, although on certain restricted sites walling layouts may occur where a junction wall meets the main wall at an acute or obtuse angle. As a rule the angles preferred are 45° or 60°, which allow for a minimum of cutting to avoid continuous straight joints. The bricklayer should therefore obtain good tie-bricks cut to as large a size as possible. In practice the position of the bonding and the size of the angle vary, but for convenience the angle on the illustrated wall has been shown to coincide in detail and give a continuous transverse joint with the main wall. (See figure 9.4)
It should be observed that:

1. The heading course of the oblique wall is tied into the main wall on the stretching course.
2. The stretching course of the oblique wall abuts the heading course of the main wall on the heading course.
3. A three-quarter bevelled bat is the 'lead-off' brick for the stretching

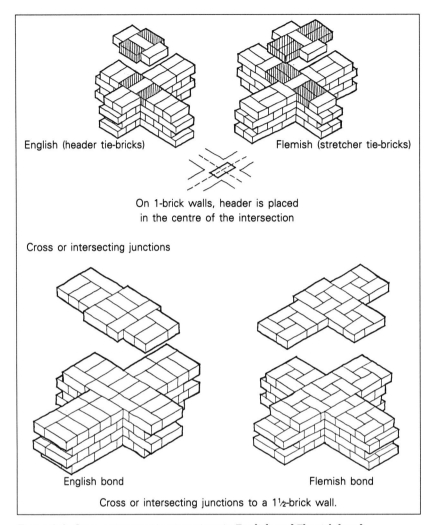

Figure 9.3 Cross or intersecting junctions in English and Flemish bond.

course of the oblique wall, with a suitably-cut back-of-brick to back up.

NOTE
In all these difficult bonding arrangements it is vital that the brick to be cut is 'offered-up' for exact marking to ensure good bonding with nominal joints. Excessive joints with bad cuts can weaken the junction.

Double return angles or 'zed' junctions

These are basically an external quoin with one return stopped by an

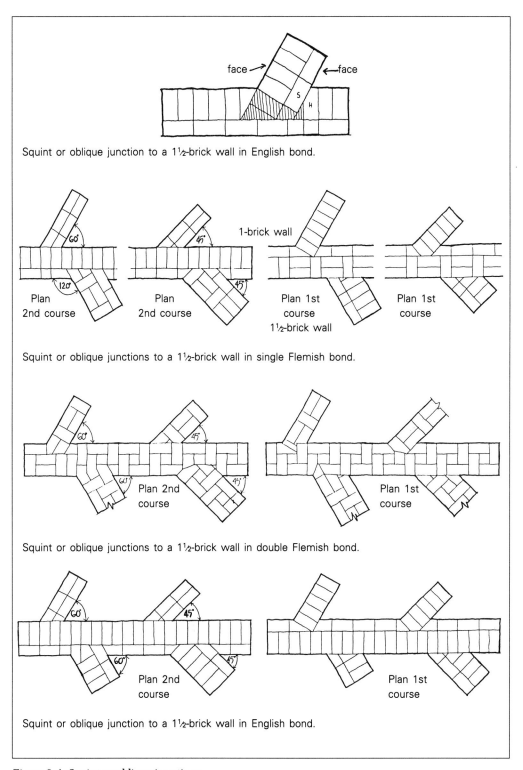

Squint or oblique junction to a 1½-brick wall in English bond.

1-brick wall

Plan
2nd course

Plan
2nd course

Plan 1st
course
1½-brick wall

Plan 1st
course

Squint or oblique junctions to a 1½-brick wall in single Flemish bond.

Plan 2nd
course

Plan 1st
course

Squint or oblique junctions to a 1½-brick wall in double Flemish bond.

Plan 2nd
course

Plan 1st
course

Squint or oblique junction to a 1½-brick wall in English bond.

Figure 9.4 Squint or oblique junctions.

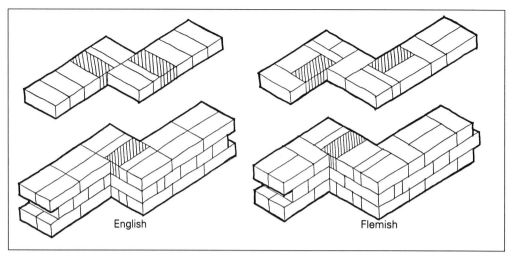

Figure 9.5 Double return or 'zed' junctions.

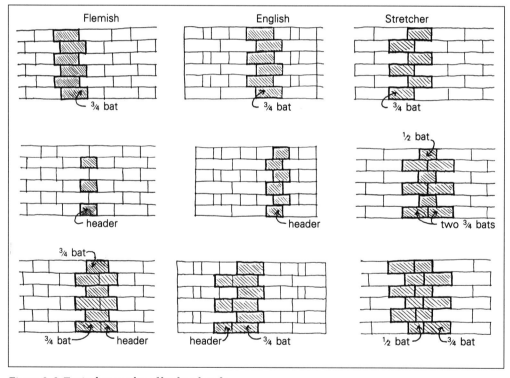

Figure 9.6 Typical examples of broken bonds.

internal quoin. Such an arrangement is termed a 'double return'. The rules on English bond, governing changes of direction, and changes of face bond, apply. The tie-bricks are the headers: with Flemish bond this gives a quarter-lap tie or a stretcher on the alternate course, tying in a quarter lap, or 56mm. (See figure 9.5)

Broken bond

Most designers and all bricklayers are anxious to calculate the dimension of a wall so that it works to a series of brick lengths (or 'works bricks'). However, there are times when this is not possible. Alternatively, the wall may 'work bricks', but not work to 'bond size'. This occurs when the length of the wall is not sufficient for the maintenance of the correct bond. In such instances a cut brick must be placed in the wall: this is referred to as a 'broken bond'. (See figure 9.6) Sometimes by either 'tightening' or 'opening' the perpends, broken bond can be avoided. However, care must be exercised not to open the joints too far, for this creates ugly 'thumb joints' which are more unsightly than the broken bond which one was trying to avoid. (See figure 9.7)

It is not possible to lay down hard and fast rules for the positioning of broken bond, because this varies according to such factors as the bond in use, the position and size of openings and the overall shape of the wall.

The following recommendations are generally accepted craft practices and should be followed when possible:

1. Broken bond should never be placed at a quoin.
2. Broken bond should be placed in the centre of a plain wall without openings.
3. In a wall with openings, broken bond should be positioned to occur below and above the centre of any selected opening.
4. On walls with openings and piers that do not 'work bricks', then

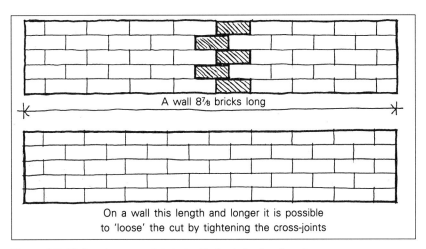

A wall 8⅞ bricks long

On a wall this length and longer it is possible
to 'loose' the cut by tightening the cross-joints

Figure 9.7 Tightening cross-joints to eliminate broken bond.

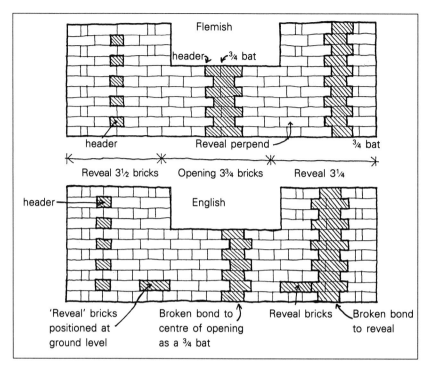

Figure 9.8 Two elevations showing three broken bonds in an English and Flemish bond wall.

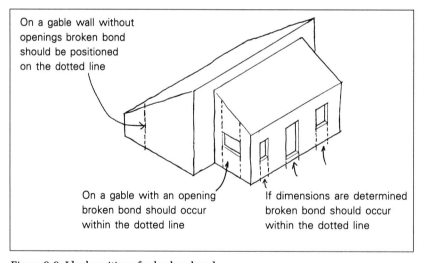

Figure 9.9 Ideal positions for broken bond.

broken bond can be positioned to occur in the piers as well as above and below the centres of the openings. (See figure 9.8)

5. On plain gables with raking cuts it is considered good practice for the broken bond to occur halfway up the angle of rake. It should

never occur in the middle of the gable, as it is maintained for the maximum height of brickwork. (See figure 9.9)

6. On gables with raking cuts which have openings, it is best to place the broken bond to occur centrally below and above the openings.
7. Broken bond should contain no cuts smaller than a half bat.
8. Once the cuts have been decided a cutting gauge should be made so that the bricks can be cut to the same length. (See figure 9.10)
9. Broken bond must not be allowed to travel along the wall, but once positioned must be strictly adhered to and care taken to keep the perpends plumb. (See figure 9.11)

Reverse bond

In some instances, and after consulting the designer, reverse bond could be considered to avoid having to form broken bond. Reverse bond is the deliberate placing of a stretcher at one end of the wall and a header at the other end. However, this could not occur if symmetry

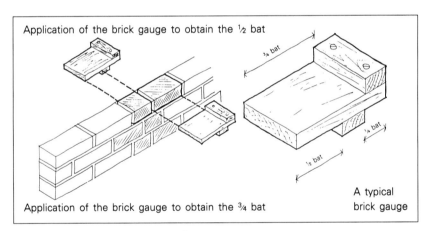

Figure 9.10 Cutting gauge for uniform cuts.

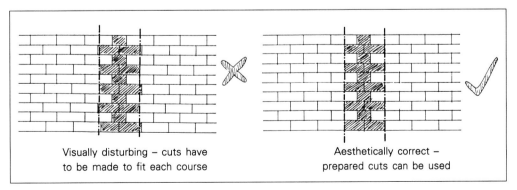

Figure 9.11 Keep broken bond vertically aligned.

was important – for example on block-bonded or stone quoins – or if coloured dressings occur. Reverse bond is generally reserved for walls where symmetry is of secondary importance. (See figure 9.12)

Bonding squint quoins

Where a quoin of a building is formed by two walls meeting at an angle other than a right-angle, then specially shaped bricks such as squints, dog-legs, birdsmouths and elbows are needed and should be used at the angles whenever possible. These purpose-made bricks cover the standard angles such as 60°, 45° or 30°, although different angles are made and manufactured to order. They will vary in shape depending on whether the quoin is obtuse (formed at an angle between 90° and 180°); or acute (angles less than 90°). They will also vary according to whether the quoin is internal or external.

Obtuse quoins

For obtuse quoins the squint brick is preferred, regardless of thickness of wall or bond. These bricks have a stretcher face of 168mm and a header face of 56mm. On walls 1-brick and more thick, lap is obtained by placing a closer next to the header face. (See figure 9.13) On half-brick walls the squint has proved satisfactory, although giving a smaller face, and no cuts are needed to maintain half-bond.

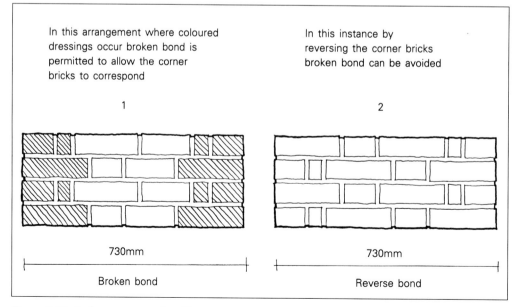

In this arrangement where coloured dressings occur broken bond is permitted to allow the corner bricks to correspond

1

In this instance by reversing the corner bricks broken bond can be avoided

2

730mm

Broken bond

730mm

Reverse bond

Figure 9.12 Broken or reverse bond?

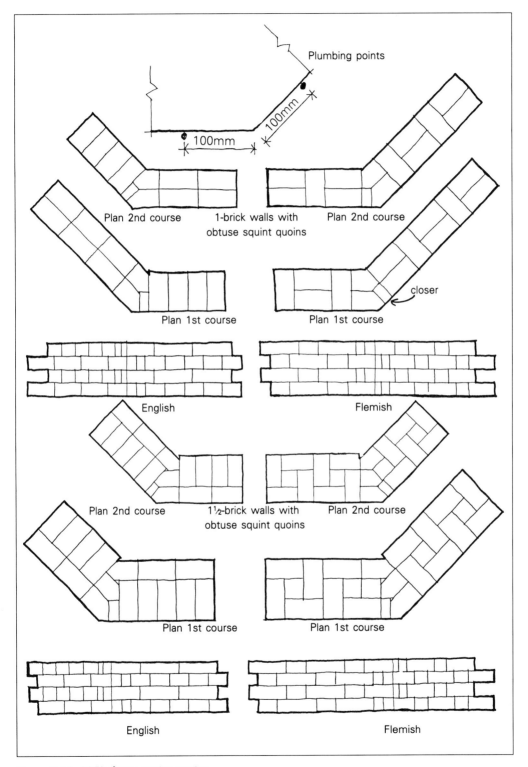

Figure 9.13 135° obtuse squint quoins.

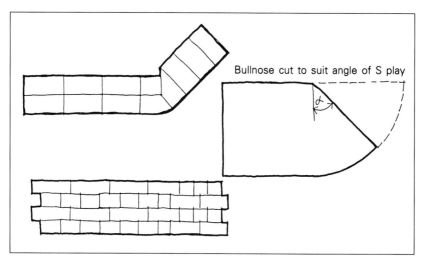

Figure 9.14 Forming an obtuse quoin using a mitred bullnose.

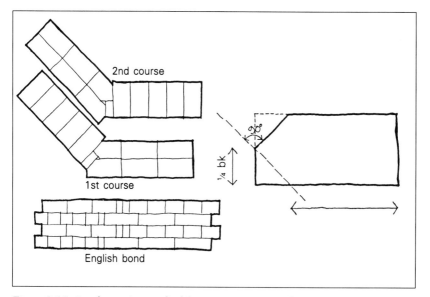

Figure 9.15 An alternative method for constructing an obtuse-angled quoin without using squint bricks.

Some designers prefer a large, purpose-made brick for the quoins, such as a dog-leg brick. These have a longer stretcher length and the header face can also be extended if desired. However, their use can cause constructional problems due to distortion on the faces. It is important that if the bricks are textured one must order left- and right-hand squints, because if they are laid upside down, not only will the appearance be different due to shading, but the brick will weather badly.

A solution sometimes employed was to use a single bullnose brick with a 56mm radius, which could be cut to the required angle. Although the external angle was without an arris the brick could be adjusted equally for either a stretcher or header and provided a less vulnerable angle. (See figure 9.14)

If using a stock or hand-made brick it may prove possible (if the colour of the cut surface is acceptable and the texture is not dramatically different from the face of the brick) to make one's own squints, a task facilitated greatly by the use of a modern bench-mounted disc cutter. First, one needs to determine the angle and then prepare a cutting mould. This is made from pine board or hardboard cut to the shape of the brick on plan. For a standard 135° squint one would cut a board to the exact length and width of a standard brick, i.e. 215mm × 102.5mm, and then mark off from one corner 56mm along the stretcher face and draw a line from that point at 45°. Next, one measures along that line 56mm and squares a line away from that point, thus creating the shape. One can then cut the shape accurately, and by placing it on each squint required, scribe the outline and cut to profile.

Sometimes obtuse quoins are built by overlapping standard bricks at the angle. This saves the cost of specials, but it requires accurate cutting and plumbing if it is not to be both weak and inaccurate. It is an unattractive and, in certain locations, unsafe way to build an obtuse quoin. (See figure 9.15)

Shaped creasing tiles bedded in mortar to the gauge of a brick and

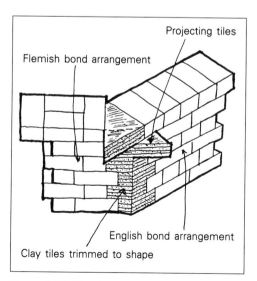

Figure 9.16 Forming a squint quoin using tile blocking.

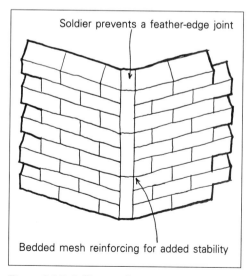

Figure 9.17 Soldier angle to a splayed quoin.

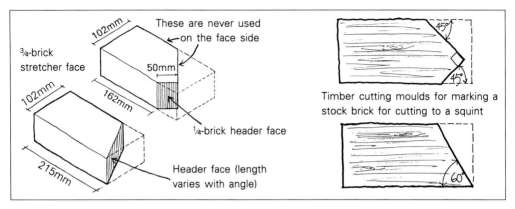

Figure 9.18 Acute and obtuse squint bricks.

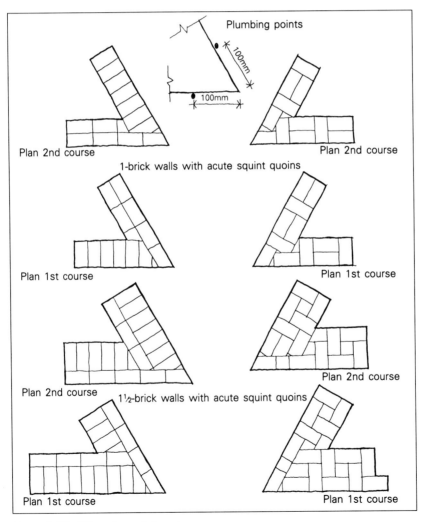

Figure 9.19 60° acute squint quoins.

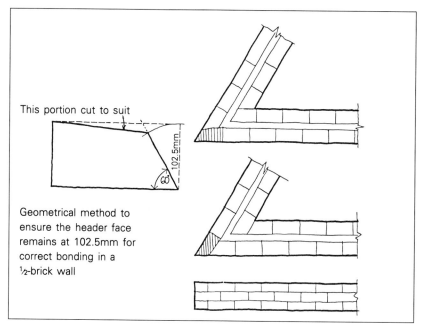

This portion cut to suit

102.5mm

Geometrical method to
ensure the header face
remains at 102.5mm for
correct bonding in a
½-brick wall

Figure 9.20 An acute squint quoin to a brick and brick cavity wall.

bedded at the quoin give a very neat appearance to an angle. (See figure 9.16) An alternative, though seldom used, solution is to place a brick-on-end between opposing faces, which helps to protect an otherwise vulnerable and weak angle. However, it is important to build in mesh reinforcing across the quoin to provide additional lateral stability. (See figure 9.17)

Acute quoin

The standard angles are 60° and 70°, and the special bricks for the quoin can be ordered. However, if the type of brick allows, the shape is simple to determine and cut by mechanical saw. The stretcher face is a standard 215mm, although the header face will lengthen according to the angle required – the more acute the angle, the longer the header face. (See figure 9.18) This presents a problem at the quoin on the header face, as a standard closer will not fit. Therefore, a triangular or slip bat is used to maintain the quarter-brick lap. (See figure 9.19) On half-brick walling half-bond is maintained by normal bonding arrangements. (See figure 9.20)

A very acute angle can be dangerous to the public, and the brick at the angle is vulnerable to damage. In such instances one traditional method was to cut the angle short and thus form two obtuse angles using squints. A further possibility is where a birdsmouth appearance

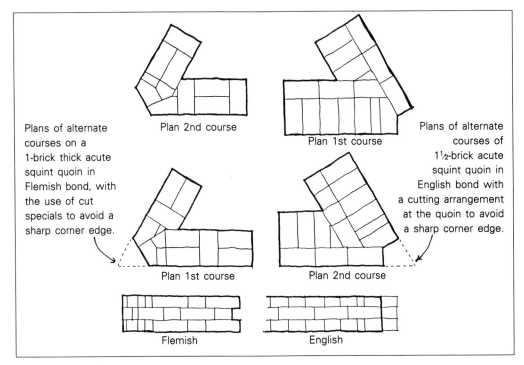

Plans of alternate courses on a 1-brick thick acute squint quoin in Flemish bond, with the use of cut specials to avoid a sharp corner edge.

Plan 2nd course

Plan 1st course

Plans of alternate courses of 1½-brick acute squint quoin in English bond with a cutting arrangement at the quoin to avoid a sharp corner edge.

Plan 1st course

Plan 2nd course

Flemish

English

Figure 9.21 Bonding acute squint quoins.

is obtained by the use of ordinary bricks, which are cut and bonded so that the cut surfaces are not exposed. (See figure 9.21)

When using squint bricks on obtuse and acute quoins, whether internal or external, it is considered good craft practice to place the plumbing points about 100mm in from the quoin arris, instead of 50mm. It is vital, therefore, for the craftsman to use his eye to set his quoin specials to give the quoin an accurate appearance, despite any small variations in the bricks.

CURVED WALLING

Bonding walls curved on plan

Sometimes there is a need for curved walling on such projects as semi-circular and segmental bay windows, free-standing walls, walling around spiral staircases, and cesspools. Depending on the radius of the curve, a decision can be made as to the type of bond most suitable. If the radius of the curve is large enough (in excess of 5,400mm) standard bricks in stretcher bond can be built acceptably. (See figure 9.22) At this radius on 1-brick thick walls in bonding such as English and Flemish there is not a whole number of bricks in the

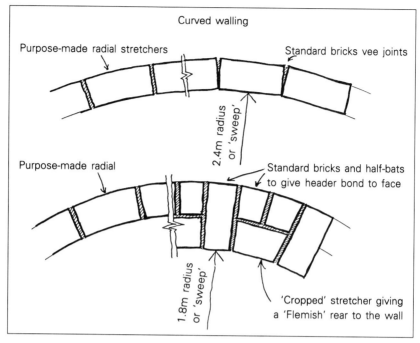

Curved walling

Purpose-made radial stretchers

Standard bricks vee joints

2.4m radius or 'sweep'

Purpose-made radial

Standard bricks and half-bats to give header bond to face

1.8m radius or 'sweep'

'Cropped' stretcher giving a 'Flemish' rear to the wall

Figure 9.22 Bonding on a large curve.

quadrant, and this would require cut bricks to bond with the associated straight walls. If one is using a 'glazed' brick it is necessary for this radius to be greater before standard bonding can be adopted. For curves tighter than this radius (or 'sweep' as it is called within the craft) the use of header bond is normal. (See figure 9.23) Should the wall be in a standard face bond, such as Flemish, on the straight lengths, it would still go into header bond for the curve.

To achieve header bond on a small radius will lead inevitably to some cutting. If only through-headers are used, it involves excessive cutting on the concave or inside face, but even so the external joints may be exceedingly wide and therefore objectionable.

Therefore, to use English or Flemish bond on a sweep of between one and two metres, the bonding would be arranged so that half-bats or 'snap-headers' on the convex face would be backed up with cut stretchers, trimmed or 'cropped' to fit.

For a radius of less than one metre the use of standard bricks on curved walls is unsuitable for both aesthetic and economic reasons, the former because the header face is made up of a series of straight faces or tangents referred to as 'facets', which tend to 'hatch and grin'; and the latter because of the enormous amount of labour spent on cutting and trimming the bricks to achieve what is still an inferior finish. (See figure 9.24) For refined and more precise curved work, it

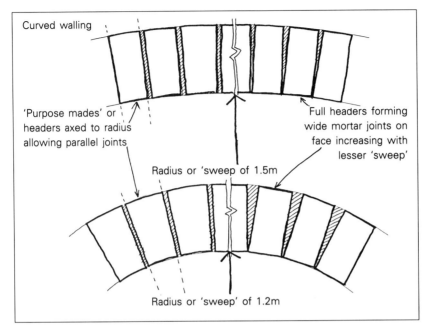

Curved walling

'Purpose mades' or
headers axed to radius
allowing parallel joints

Full headers forming
wide mortar joints on
face increasing with
lesser 'sweep'

Radius or 'sweep of 1.5m

Radius or 'sweep' of 1.2m

Figure 9.23 Effect of different radii on a header bond curved wall.

is therefore better to use special, shaped bricks for radial stretchers or
headers. Because these are shaped to the curves on face, they speed
up laying time and give a quality appearance to the wall. Most major
brickmakers supply radial specials on outer radii from 450mm to
5,400mm and inner radii from 235mm to 5,185mm, as laid down in
BS4729, and these can also be made to any prescribed curvature for
convex or concave faces of the wall by quoting the radius of the
desired curve.

Special radial shapes may be used on bond patterns consisting of all
radial headers, stretchers or a combination of both. Radial special
shapes are not, however, compatible with standard 215mm bricks in
curved work. Radial headers are intended for use in 1-brick thick walls
in header bond or with radial stretchers in Flemish or English bond.
It should be noted that, unless the radius exceeds 3 metres in either
Flemish or English bond, the concave face will not be fair faced, as it
is bonded by using standard bricks 'cropped' to back the radial
stretchers. In English bond this will stop the wall being sectional, and
lead to inconsistency with the bonding of the header courses.

Another consideration which affects bonding is the choice of face
side of a curved wall – is it on the convex or outer face, or the concave
or inner face? It could even be both sides! If the convex side is to be
the facework then this presents little problem, provided it is bonded
out to give equal perpend joints and maintain lap. (See figures 9.25

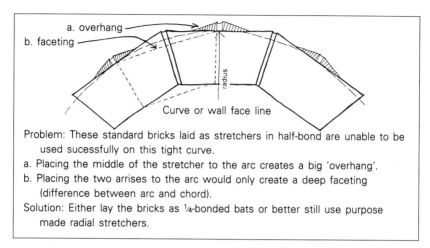

Problem: These standard bricks laid as stretchers in half-bond are unable to be used sucessfully on this tight curve.
a. Placing the middle of the stretcher to the arc creates a big 'overhang'.
b. Placing the two arrises to the arc would only create a deep faceting (difference between arc and chord).
Solution: Either lay the bricks as ¼-bonded bats or better still use purpose made radial stretchers.

Figure 9.24 'Faceting' on a curved wall.

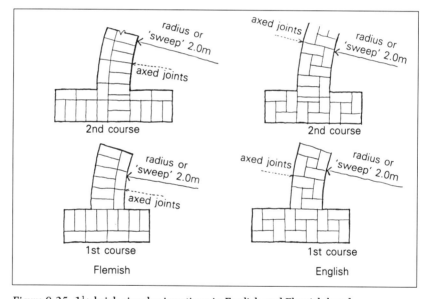

Figure 9.25 1½-brick circular junctions in English and Flemish bond.

and 9.26) If the face is the concave side bonding will be more difficult because of the reduced radius. In such instances careful setting out of the bond is essential to establish cuts. If it is a 1-brick thick wall, the position of through-headers or 'bonders', which unite the inner and outer faces, is also critical. In order to align two acceptable faces when using standard bricks the cutting arrangement allowing through-headers on a 1-brick thick wall often presents header bond on the concave face, and Flemish bond to the rear. If a fair face is required on both sides it is more sensible to specify and to use purpose-made bricks.

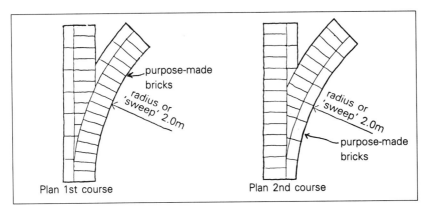

Figure 9.26 1½-brick junction of circular to straight walling in English bond.

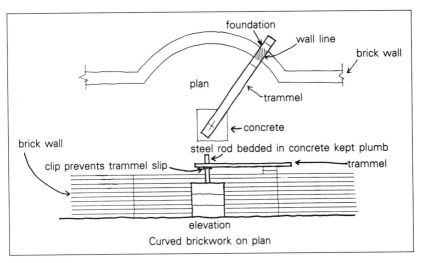

Figure 9.27 Trammel method.

It is worth emphasizing that the correct width of the mortar cross-joints will need careful monitoring, especially on tight sweeps, to prevent too great a departure from the nominal 10mm joint: the joints should be no wider than 16–17mm and no narrower than 6–7mm. A joint profile should be selected which will not draw attention to any differences in joint width. In all aforementioned aspects of curved walling, refer to BDA, DN12 *The Design of Curved Brickwork* (1991).

Construction of curved walling

When the craftsman is selecting the method he will adopt to ensure accuracy in the construction of circular brickwork on plan, several factors and constraints will influence his decision, including:

1. The length of radius or sweep.
2. Whether the radius point is accessible.
3. The height of the wall.
4. The overall shape and size of wall.

When checking for accuracy in construction there are three main methods commonly employed: the trammel method; the bay mould; and the lead brick and solid templates.

Trammel method

When the brickwork is started a thin skim of mortar is spread on the clean and dampened foundations. By following the rotating trammel with the blade of the trowel, against the mark for the wall face, a line can be scribed into the mortar clearly marking the curved wall face. It is then the usual practice to dry-bond the wall to assess bond, size of joints, cuts and plumbing points. (See figure 9.27)

As work on each course is finished it is checked by the trammel, which must be kept in a horizontal position. Traditionally the trammel would be held horizontal by a piece of cord fastened under the bar. Today, this is achieved by fixing two spring clips below the lath. The standard brickwork practice is to choose a series of plumbing points around the curve of the wall from every fourth to sixth brick and maintain those positions throughout the height of the wall. On every course the first bricks laid are at these plumbing points, checked for individual level as well as relationship to each other and to the main

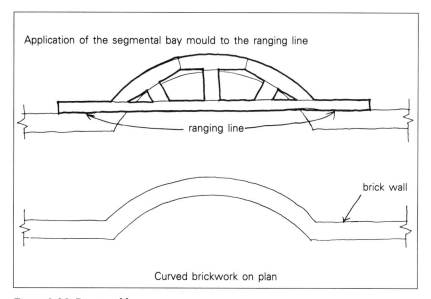

Figure 9.28 Bay mould.

walling. They are then plumbed. Because these are always the first bricks laid they are known as 'lead' bricks. The trammel is then used to check the wall once the 'infill' bricks have been laid and levelled.

Bay mould

To set out the brickwork the bay mould is positioned so that the ends are aligned to the building line or straight walling. The foundations are already cleaned, dampened and a thin skim of mortar has been spread. The trowel blade scribes the wall face into the mortar, resting flat and vertical against the outer edge of the mould. It would be normal to dry-bond the brickwork to assess bonding and plumbing points. (See figure 9.28)

Lead bricks and solid templates

Depending on whether the wall is concave or convex, a solid timber template is cut to the shape required, usually after being marked out by a trammel. The lead bricks are positioned, gauged, levelled and plumbed. The infill bricks are then carefully placed by eye and levelled between the lead bricks. The template is then positioned with the lead bricks to check the walling. It is important to use the template at the same points throughout the height of the wall. (See figure 9.29)

This method particularly suits long walls with slow curves, and walls that were initially set out with a trammel but whose height makes its continuous use impractical – a spiral staircase well is one example.

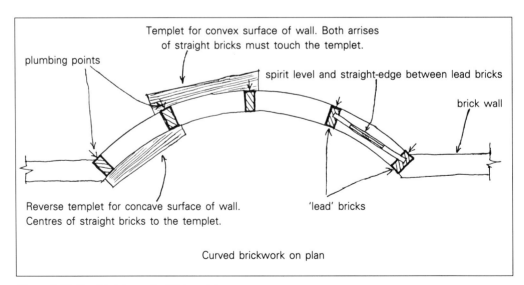

Figure 9.29 Lead bricks and solid templet.

Bibliography

Ashurst, J. and N. (1988) *Practical Building Conservation*, Volume 1, Mortars, Plaster and Renders; Volume 2, Brick, Terracotta and Earth. Gower Technical Press.

Bailey, H. and Hancock, D. *Brickwork and Associated Studies*. London: Macmillan.

Braightwaite, D. (1981) *Building in the Blood*. Godfrey Dove Associates.

Brick Development Association (1993), *Achieving Successful Brickwork*.

British Brick Society, Information Newsletters, nos 30–59.

British Standards Institute (1989) BS8000: Part 3 (Workmanship on Building Sites).

Brunskill, R. (1990) *Brick Building in Britain*. London: Gollancz.

Brunskill, R. and Clifton Taylor, A. (1977) *English Brickwork*. Ward and Lock Ltd.

Campbell, R. (1747) *The London Tradesman*. London: J. Gardner.

Cruikshank, D. and Wylde, P. (1975) *The Art of Georgian Building*. Architectural Press.

Cutter, W. (1981) *Brickwork*, volumes 1–4. London: Cassell.

Dobson, E. (1850) *Treatise on the Manufacture of Bricks and Tiles*. London.

Frank, I. M. and Brownstone, D. M. (1985) *Builders*. Hudson.

Frost, W. (1931) *The Modern Bricklayer*, volumes 1–3. Caxton.

Gaskell, S. M. (1983) *Building Control*. Bedford Square Press.

Greenhalgh, R. (1948) *Modern Building Construction*, volume 1. New Era.

Gwilt, J. (1888) *Encyclopedia of Architecture*. Longmans, Green and Co.

Halfpenny, W. (1725) *The Art of Sound Building*. London.

Hammett, M. (1991) *The Role of Brick in our Environment*. Brick Development Association.

Hammett, M. (1988) *A Basic Guide to Brickwork Mortars*. Brick Development Association.

Hammett, M. and Morton, J. (1991) *The Design of Curved Brickwork*. Brick Development Association.

Hammond, A. (1875) *The Rudiments of Practical Bricklaying*. Lockwood and Co.

Hammond, M. (1981) *Bricks and Brickmaking*. Shire Publications Ltd.

Harding, J. R. and Smith, R. A. (1986) *Brickwork Durability*. Brick Development Association.

Hobhouse, H. and Saunders, A. (1989) *Good and Proper Materials*. The London Topographical Society Publication 40.

Hodge, J. C. (1981) *Brickwork for Apprentices*.

Kerisel, J. (1987) *Down to Earth*. Rotterdam Balkena.

Knight, T. L. (1991) *Brickwork: Good Site Practice*. Brick Development Association.

Langley Batty (1740) *The City and Country Builder's and Workman's Treasury of Designs*. London.

Langley Batty (1936) *Ancient Masonry*, 2 volumes. London.

Lindsay-Braley, E. (1945) *Brickwork*. Pitman.

Lloyd, N. (1925) *A History of English Brickwork*. Montgomery.

Mills, P. and Oliver, J. (volume 1, 1946; volume 2, 1956) *The Survey of Building Sites in the City of London After the Great Fire of 1666*.

Moxon, J. (1703, first published 1684) *Mechanick Excercises or the Doctrine of Handy-Works*. London.

Nash, W. G. (1983) *Brickwork 1–3*. Hutchinson.

Neve, R. (1703) *The City and Country Purchaser . . ..* London.

Nicholson, P. (1819) *Architectural Dictionary*, 2 volumes. London.

Nicholson, P. (1824) *The Builder and Workman's New Dictionary*. London.

Perks, R. H. (1981) *George Bargebrick Esquire*. Meresborough Books.

Phillips, R., Sir (1821) *The Book of English Trade*. London.

Postgate, R. W. (1923) *The Builders History*.

Rolt, L. T. C. (1971) *Making of the Railway*. Hush Evelyn.

Saltzman, L. F. (1952) *Building in England down to 1540*. Clavendon Press.

Searle, A. B. (1936) *Bricks and Tiles*. The Technical Press Ltd.

Thurley, S., *Henry VIII and the Building of Hampton Court*.

Wingate, M. (1985) *Small-Scale Lime Burning*. Intermediate Technology Publications.

Woodforde, J. (1976) *Bricks to Build a House*. Routledge and Kegan Paul.

Yarwood, D. (1985) *Encyclopedia of Architecture*. Batsford.

Index